ℓc

D1060287

The Poetry of Stephen Crane

The Poetry of

STEPHEN CRANE

By *DANIEL G. HOFFMAN*

New York 1957

COLUMBIA UNIVERSITY PRESS

© Copyright 1956 Columbia University Press
First published in book form 1957
Library of Congress Catalog Card Number: 57-11017
Published in
Great Britain, Canada,
India, and Pakistan
by the Oxford University Press
London, Toronto,
Bombay, and Karachi
Manufactured in the United States of America

To my father and mother

ᔢ *PREFACE*

The week after Stephen Crane died in June, 1900, at the age
of twenty-eight, Cora Crane, with whom he had lived for the
last three years of his life, jotted into a notebook her hope of
writing his biography. Unsuccessful in her attempts in England to support herself as a writer, Cora soon returned to
America. In her luggage were hundreds of pages of Crane's
manuscripts, proof sheets, clippings, and literary correspondence, as well as his scrapbooks, editions of his works, and
certain other books from his library. Cora never did write his
life. At her death in 1910 she left the Stephen Crane papers
to a friend in Jacksonville, Florida, and for forty-two years
they remained in private hands, unavailable to either Thomas
Beer or John Berryman, Crane's two biographers, or to any of
his critics.

When in 1952 the Columbia University Libraries purchased
these materials, the first problem was to determine what they
were—many manuscripts were unidentified—and then to see
what they might contribute to our interpretation of Crane's
writings and to our understanding of his intense though narrow sensibility. There is much we do not know about this
strangely powerful writer. Half a century after his death a

definitive biography is still needed, not for want of interest in
Crane's work but for lack of necessary information about his
life. Thus even the diligence and penetration shown in Mr.
Berryman's *Stephen Crane* leave us in doubt as to the influence
upon Crane's art of his family's theology; nor does Mr. Berryman's excellent book trace with exactitude Crane's early reading and its effect upon his development as a writer. Crane's
proper place in American writing cannot be accurately determined until we have a fuller statement of his aesthetic than
the materials available to Mr. Berryman permitted him to
make. As Crane wrote neither critical essays nor analyses of
his own artistic practice, such a statement must be inferentially
concluded from his writings with the support of circumstantial
evidence. And this evidence has heretofore been all too scanty.

Bearing these considerations in mind as I looked over the
papers left by Cora Crane, I found that although the Columbia
collection is rich in reportage and includes stories and sketches
uncollected or never published, some of which are superior
to much of Crane's established work, it lacks the manuscripts
of his most important prose. There are many fragments and
preliminary drafts valuable for the study of his prose style and
methods of composition. Holograph lists of his writings include many titles never before reported, some of which are
still to be traced. These materials and the newly recovered
stories, sketches, and plays, as well as the plethora of correspondence, clippings, reviews, photographs, and memorabilia
should go far toward making possible a complete bibliography
and a definitive life.[1]

[1] For a listing of many of the items in this collection see *Stephen
Crane (1871–1900): An Exhibition,* arranged and described by Joan
H. Baum.

For my purposes, however, it was the manuscripts of Crane's verse which led most readily to a consideration of a unified body of his work and to an evaluation of his sensibility. Of the one hundred and eight poems in his *Collected Poems* [2] the papers at Columbia University include manuscript worksheets for twenty. Crane had written to Edmund Clarence Stedman, the only anthologist to reprint his verse during his lifetime, that "The two little books—'The Black Riders' and 'War is Kind' contain every line which I've written outside of prose form." [3] Yet his two books lack not only five poems Crane had published either in magazines or in his stories but at least twenty other poems which he never published at all. Of these, five have been issued posthumously; three are in *Collected Poems,* the other two in limited private editions. Columbia has manuscripts of fourteen poems unpublished heretofore. A fifteenth has recently been acquired by the Syracuse University Library.

In using these and other new materials from the Columbia collection I have been sensible of trying to fill some of the gaps and to answer the questions raised in the work of earlier writers on Crane. What we have need of is a fuller understanding of Crane's sensibility and of the literary and cultural traditions which lent their rather meager nutriment to its expression in his work. Fortunately, Crane's verse offers a convenient occasion for investigating these matters. Most of the poems were written early in his brief career, and his verse reflects more closely than do his stories the religious and sexual conflicts which are intrinsic to the power of his major work. In his

[2] Ed. by Wilson Follett.
[3] Letter of September 4, 1899. Quoted by permission of The Historical Society of Pennsylvania, owner of the holograph manuscript.

poems, too, he had to evolve a literary strategy unlike that
of his American contemporaries; it is this literary method
which places Crane at the threshhold of modern writing. In
the course of these investigations I have been concerned to
study the qualities and derivations of his poems themselves.
Since none has preceded me in this, I have had to quote or
summarize many poems of little artistic merit in order to do
justice to the emergence of Crane's techniques and to the development of his sensibility. Unschooled in poetics though he
was, I think he nonetheless succeeded in writing perhaps a
score of poems that have a claim upon us for themselves, as
well as for what they portend in the recent history of lyric verse.

Crane seems a rather ungrateful candidate for biographical
study, so little relation do the unlikely events of his short
life appear to have to the singular qualities of his best work.
It is often assumed that his wide-ranging search for subjects
and techniques indicate Crane's affinity with the literary movements of his time, and that once these connections are shown
his qualities have been explained. It is true that Crane is by
turns a reporter of slum life and of war, a western humorist,
an ironist of village hypocrisy, a popular romancer, and an
iconoclastic poet. In technique he is comparably varied, essay-
ing impressionism, naturalism, fantasy, realism, and symbolism
in a way reminiscent of Andreyev, a slightly later writer of
whom he had never heard. In Crane's case neither the search
for subjects, the continual immersion in violent experiences,
nor the virtuosity of his stylistic devices can furnish his reader
the needed keys to his accomplishment. Despite the variety
of his work there is a strong unifying quality throughout the

best of it. And despite his adoption of diverse technical resources, the essential qualities of his sensibility would seem to have been fixed during his formative years, perhaps even before naturalism, realism, and other artistic influences were known to him. These are later accretions, technical means which served him interchangeably. The sources of his intensity lie beneath the surface of his style, behind the diversity of his subjects. John Berryman's biography makes this much plain, and in his provocative reliance upon Freudian interpretation Mr. Berryman suggests one of the important wellsprings of Crane's power. It is not, however, the only source. In my attempts to interpret Crane's work I have been led from his poems to consider his relation to his parents, to the diverse religious views of his family, to his military heritage, to several women whom he loved, and to the works of many authors he had read. This book is not primarily a biography, but I have thought it essential, in trying to validate analysis of Crane's work and of his sensibility, to draw upon biographical information wherever such data was both relevant and accessible. Thanks to the new materials at Columbia University I have been fortunate to have at hand interesting evidence unknown to earlier students of Crane.

Preparing this study has placed me under many obligations pleasant to record. It was my good fortune to have three discerning critics as a first audience for this effort to understand Crane's work, and I am grateful for the stimulating suggestions and encouragement of Professors Lionel Trilling and Richard Chase. To Professor Lewis Leary I owe special thanks, not

only for his generous and friendly guidance of my research
but for the unusual privilege he offered me of first access to
the Columbia Stephen Crane Collection.

In the course of this exercise in tracing ideas and literary
techniques to their sources my less immediate debts to others
became fully clear. What my old friends and teachers in
Columbia College, the late Professors Irwin Edman and Henry
K. Dick, taught me in these disciplines has led, among other
things, to any virtues this study of Crane may possess. Professor F. W. Dupee once held me to his high standards in the
craft of writing, and I owe much to those teachers who helped
me to learn to read in the grammar of poetry, particularly to
Professors Mark Van Doren and William York Tindall. I wish
also to thank my students at Columbia from whose discussions
in English 291–292 I have learned a lot about Crane.

Without the generous cooperation of several libraries and
the help of other scholars I should not have had access to
original materials and to other rare items of information necessary to my study. My first thanks are due to Mr. Roland Baugh-
man, Head, Department of Special Collections, Columbia
University Libraries, and his staff, for their kindness and as-
sistance. Mr. Lester G. Wells, Curator of the Stephen Crane
Collection at the Syracuse University Library, generously
granted me access to the unpublished memoir of Crane by
C. K. Linson, as well as to all other Crane materials in his
charge. I wish also to thank Mrs. Elizabeth D. Meier, Reference
Librarian of the Rose Memorial Library at Drew University,
for her diligent though fruitless search for writings by Stephen
Crane's mother among the files of Methodist publications de-

posited there. Others who extended courtesies far beyond the calls of duty are Miss Miriam V. Studley, Principal Librarian, New Jersey Division, The Public Library of Newark; Mr. John D. Gordan, Curator of the Berg Collection at the New York Public Library; Miss E. Marie Becker, Reference Librarian of the New-York Historical Society; and the libraries of Union Theological Seminary and The Historical Society of Pennsylvania. Mr. Ames W. Williams, Crane's bibliographer, faithfully answered my queries. Professor R. W. Stallman and Miss Lillian Gilkes generously furnished helpful information.

Thanks are due for permission to quote from the writings of Stephen Crane to Alfred A. Knopf, Inc., publishers of *The Work of Stephen Crane* and of *Stephen Crane: An Omnibus*, edited by R. W. Stallman, and holders of the literary rights to Crane's manuscripts and uncollected writings; to William Sloane Associates, Inc., for permission to quote from *Walt Whitman Reconsidered* by Richard Chase; to Citadel Press for the use of passages from *The Collected Writings of Ambrose Bierce*, edited by Clifton Fadiman; and to Lester G. Wells and the Syracuse University Press for quotations from *Stephen Crane's Love Letters to Nellie Crouse*.

I wish also to acknowledge the intermittent encouragement of Elizabeth McFarland Hoffman, who for many months allowed the intransigent ghost of Stephen Crane to inhabit her home; and the cooperation of Kate and Tad, who wrote on very few of my papers.

DANIEL G. HOFFMAN

CONTENTS

The Poetry of Stephen Crane

The abbreviations BR and WK will refer to THE BLACK RIDERS *and* WAR IS KIND *respectively. Unless otherwise specified, the edition used is* THE COLLECTED POEMS OF STEPHEN CRANE, *edited by Wilson Follett (New York, 1930).*

One ∽ REPUDIATIONS

Why should we be interested in Stephen Crane as a poet, or consider his verse apart from his achievements in *Maggie, The Red Badge of Courage,* and "The Open Boat"? Crane's importance in the history of fiction is an acknowledged fact. One must reckon with him as the author of the first naturalistic novel of the slums in America, as writer of a striking psychological study of man facing death, as pioneer in the development of stream of consciousness and symbolism as narrative methods. But what of Crane's poems? Although considered worthy in some quarters, they were not even discussed in either the *Cambridge History of American Literature* (1918) or the *Literary History of the United States* (1948). Nor does Arms and Kuntz's *Poetry Explication: A Checklist of Interpretation Since 1925 of British and American Poems Past and Present* (1950) list the analysis of a single poem by Stephen Crane. The most recent survey of American poetry avows that his two books "must stand at the beginning (although in a rather unformulated relation) of any discussion of modern American poetry." [1] The relation *is* unformulated. Or else it is formulated by a profusion of contradictory critical attitudes.

[1] Louise Bogan, *Achievement in American Poetry*, p. 17.

There is no agreement as to Crane's merit or as to his historical place.

One thing, however, is certain—he is almost the only American poet of the 1890's still read with much interest today. It is
true that the first books of Emily Dickinson and Edwin Arlington Robinson appeared in that decade, but Dickinson's
posthumous work, written in an earlier generation than the
'nineties, would have its effect upon a later one; Robinson's
Children of the Night (1897) was but a foretaste of his more
definitive work after *Captain Craig* (1902) and *The Town
Down the River* (1910). Interest in Crane's verse continues
because he alone, during the interval in this country which
Carl Van Doren aptly called "the poetic twilight," [2] challenged
the conventions of poetic form and diction of late Victorian
verse and its provincial imitators. The permanent breaking-
loose from this poetic gentility was not accomplished until a
generation later, when Pound, Eliot, and Frost emerged just
before the war. But what Crane in his unformulated and an-
ticipatory way was trying to do in the 1890's has been said to
resemble the much more sophisticated attack on formalism
characteristic of the symbolist movement in France. Yet Crane
seems to have had no knowledge either of symbolist verse or
of the aesthetic theories on which it was based. The first of
many anomalies in Crane is already apparent. His place in
literary history is assured by his daring technical experimentation, yet despite his anticipation in verse and prose of symbolist, imagist, stream-of-consciousness, and naturalistic techniques, he seems never to have expressed the slightest interest

[2] "Stephen Crane," *American Mercury*, I (January, 1924), 11.

in defining his literary theories except to state a simple creed of "realism" similar to that of Howells and Garland, whose fiction his own does not much resemble, and to call himself an "impressionist." Apparently without theory, lacking involvement in traditions of aesthetic reflection or poetic craft, his verse seems simply to come into being. But literary history, even in a provincial culture such as Crane's American milieu, is seldom as simple as that.

2

"In style, in method," wrote H. G. Wells, ". . . he is sharply defined, the expression in literary art of certain enormous repudiations."[3] Crane's repudiations in fact go far beyond method and style. They are so large as to seem to deny their maker almost all the relationships and metaphors on which literature itself depends.

First, Crane repudiates most of the involvements of the will with society. If, as Lionel Trilling suggests, the work of the novel is to deal "with reality and illusion in relation to questions of social class,"[4] even in his prose Crane would seem to be outside the tradition in which the preponderant authority of fiction as an art resides. The social order, as his contemporaries Henry James and William Dean Howells conceived of it, is almost wholly absent from Crane's work. One feels the presence of society as a complex interrelationship of persons and classes only in *Maggie* and *The Monster;*

[3] "Stephen Crane from an English Standpoint," reprinted from *North American Review* (August, 1900) in *The Shock of Recognition,* ed. by Edmund Wilson, p. 671.
[4] *The Liberal Imagination,* p. 258.

in both of these works (despite the greater range of characters in the latter) society operates as a primal force, like nature, crushing the individual who would define his integrity by challenging its mores. Elsewhere in his major fiction the world Crane envisages is one in which men seek, or seek to avoid, physical danger. They are menaced not so much by each other's ambitions as by elemental forces. But if man is alone in a hostile universe in Crane's fiction, the conditions of isolation and menace are intensified still further in his verse:

> There were many who went in huddled procession,
> They knew not whither;
> But, at any rate, success or calamity
> Would attend all in equality.

> There was one who sought a new road.
> He went into direful thickets,
> And ultimately he died thus, alone;
> But they said he had courage.   [BR xvii]

In Crane, then, we have an extreme instance of the literary figure as isolato. "*Isolatoes,* too, I call such," wrote Herman Melville, "not acknowledging the common continent of men, but each *Isolato* living on a separate continent of his own." [5] The sources of Crane's sense of isolation, we shall see, were both cultural and personal. To the extent that they were personal, Crane's sensibility is his special burden, limiting our interest in his narrowly motivated writings. But to the extent that social conditions reinforced his isolative sensibility Crane is representative of a tendency in American culture. "It must be acknowledged that equality, which brings great benefits

[5] *Moby-Dick,* ed. by Mansfield and Vincent, p. 118.

into the world, nevertheless suggests to men . . . some dangerous propensities. It tends to isolate them from each other, to concentrate every man's attention upon himself," De Tocqueville observed.[6] But it is not egalitarian feeling alone which separates men from one another. We have also to consider the sense of isolation which their religious heritage imposed upon many Americans in the nineteenth century. Even in a state of grace the New England Protestant stood alone in his unmediated relation to God. The sinner was alone with the knowledge of his unconfessed sin, his undischarged guilt. The anguish of Hilda in Hawthorne's *The Marble Faun,* driven to Catholic confession by the knowledge of an evil act which she herself did not commit, may represent the psychological weight of this burden. We think, too, of Dimmesdale on the scaffold, of Ethan Brand, Hollingsworth, Mr. Hooper, Judge Pyncheon, all isolated from the kinship of human sympathy by their sins of pride and lust. Those among his sinners whom Hawthorne makes capable of redemption must seek by acts of will to renounce their isolative pride and rejoin the communal family. The isolative strain is dramatized again as Ishmael, oppressed by the "damp, drizzly November" in his soul, seeks to renounce the world of society by taking passage on the *Pequod*—only to learn that the world is with him and cannot be escaped. It is dramatized too in Thoreau's conviction that to penetrate to the core of life one must repudiate society's claims upon the soul. Emerson had pronounced such a creed in "Self-Reliance": "Society is everywhere in conspiracy against the manhood of every one of its members. . . .

[6] *Democracy in America,* II, 22.

Whoso would be a man, must be a nonconformist." And in the
same essay he had maintained,

There is a time in every man's education when he arrives at the
conviction that . . . imitation is suicide; that he must take himself
for better for worse as his portion; that though the wide universe is
full of good, no kernel of nourishing corn can come to him but
through his toil bestowed on that plot of ground which is given
to him to till. The power which resides in him is new in nature,
and none but he knows what that is which he can do, nor does he
know until he has tried.[7]

From the mingling of these two tendencies, egalitarian and
religious individualism, the isolative strain in the American
sensibility emerges.

Isolation and nonconformity, its logical outcome in action,
may be achieved either through the activity of the will in conscious opposition to convention, or through the unwilled expression of one's inner nature, a nature that is not in consonance with the assumptions of society. Crane is usually regarded as an activist. His world is filled with violence, and in
his life as in his writings he sought to immerse himself in the
experience of conflict, making himself a witness of lawlessness
on the Bowery, banditry in Mexico, and wars in Greece and
Cuba. Yet Stephen Crane once said "An artist, I think, is nothing but a powerful memory that can move itself at will through
certain experiences sideways and every artist must be in some
things powerless as a dead snake." [8]

This seems a commitment to submission, to passivity. For
Crane it was a necessary requisite to the intensity of his work,

---

[7] *Complete Works,* II, 49, 50, 46.
[8] Quoted in Berryman, *Stephen Crane,* pp. 6, 256.

"an intensity disproportionate to his strength and yet unequal to the fervor of his spirit." [9] We usually are prone to prize energy as a value in itself, yet in order to tap the energies latent within him Crane, like Whitman, must loaf and invite his soul. Crane's passivity, his refusal to recognize most of the involvements society demands or to take advantage in art of what these involvements offer, enriches his writing with a concentration upon the energies his inner tensions bring forth. But Crane's personality, like his style and his repudiations, is extreme. The new materials in the Columbia collection lend support, it seems to me, to the view of Crane's psychology proposed in Mr. Berryman's biography. There we find Crane to have fulfilled exactly the specialized conditions of an unusual variant of the Oedipus complex described in Freud's study, "A Special Choice of Type of Object Made by Men." [10] The special choice involves the repetition by the lover of attempts to "rescue" women sexually promiscuous and already possessed by other men. These conditions, discussed in my fourth chapter, might seem of themselves to guarantee a sensibility so very eccentric as to be of little general interest. Yet this is not the case. Crane's extremity is but the intensification and isolation of certain psychological impulses widely shared. It is responsible for what we prize in his work, as well as for what disturbs us.

Crane's isolativeness, as we shall see, begins in his somewhat unusual psychic orientation, yet corresponds to tendencies in the religious and egalitarian culture around him. Only

[9] Alfred Kazin, *On Native Grounds*, p. 69.
[10] *Collected Papers*, ed. by Ernest Jones, IV, 192–202.

in Poe, in Bierce, and in Hemingway among American writers is the sense of the individual's isolation as overwhelming as it is in Crane. Elsewhere—in Hawthorne, Melville, Dickinson, Whitman, Twain—it is present as a source of tension, opposed by the contrary tendency of willed commitment. Yet there is in Crane too a strong active counter-principle, a passionate need to affirm an involvement in society at the same time that he must repudiate most of the ties that bind. As is true of the other reclusive or isolative sensibilities, the degree of his isolation is an index to the intensity of his need to seek a principle uniting him to life. But Crane was compelled to search for that unifying principle in an extremely narrow compass of possible relationships, a compass narrower than theirs. The willed involvement in reality which is for Crane the necessary principle of existence is sacrificial suffering. Despite his passivity, his crippling introspection, Crane's ultimate commitment is to an heroic ideal.

3

The second of Crane's "enormous repudiations" is his remoteness from most sources of cultural continuity and power. This further limits the range of his literary materials and metaphors. If we compare Crane to his most talented American contemporaries, we realize the disabilities his birth, fortune, and choice put in his path. While Crane was playing baseball instead of going to his classes at Lafayette and Syracuse, the two provincial colleges he briefly attended, Edwin Arlington Robinson, William Vaughn Moody, Trumbull Stickney, and George Cabot Lodge were studying at Harvard. There Santayana adorned a faculty which proudly carried on a tradition of speculative thought going back to the seventeenth century and a commitment to literary culture continuous since the days of Ticknor, Lowell, and Longfellow. Henry Adams, no longer at Harvard, was a close friend of Stickney and of Lodge. The list of advantages Crane lacked, all of which were available to these young poets, reads like the famous tally of America's shortcomings which Henry James introduced into his appraisal of Hawthorne's literary situation.[11] Compared to these Harvard contemporaries, Crane, although not so ill-read as his critics suppose, was an ignorant man. Nowhere does his writing show any acquaintance with world history, with speculative philosophy, with science, with classical literature, with other languages, with myth, with any of the culturally important sources of metaphor—excepting religion—available to these university-trained poets. While Moody and Stickney and Lodge were reading Greek poetry, Crane quit college to write *Maggie* and *The Red Badge of Courage,* to cover the Bowery for New York newspapers, and to write the rebellious poems in *The Black Riders.* Had he lived, Crane could not possibly have responded as did those three poets to Henry Adams's speculations on physics and progress suggested by the Paris exposition of 1900; for Crane had no acquaintance with the cultural influences that led each of the Harvard men to write philosophical verse dramas on the theme of Prometheus. Of Durkheim's sociology, the other important theoretical influence on Stickney's *Prometheus Pyrphoros,* Crane had probably never heard.[12] On the other hand he had none of Robinson's devo-

[11] James, "Hawthorne," in *The Shock of Recognition,* pp. 459–60.

[12] Thomas Riggs, Jr., has traced the influence of Adams's thought upon their plays in "Prometheus 1900," *American Literature,* XXII (January, 1951), 399–423.

tion to medievalism; nor in his verse does Crane share the
Maine poet's objectivity in creating *personae*, for Robinson's
characters are conceived of as part of a society, the society of
Tilbury Town.

Not to have any of these resources is assuredly to forgo
much. There was, however, one important strain of culture
which was Crane's birthright. De Tocqueville, in the passage
quoted above on the tendency of democracy to isolate men
from one another, goes on to say that "the greatest advantage
of religion is to inspire diametrically contrary principles."
Crane's father, maternal grandfather, and all his uncles were
Methodist clergymen, his mother a writer for religious journals.
The Bible and certain of his relatives' tractarian writings provide him with the chief stock of images in his verse aside from
those drawn from the reading of some minor authors and from
his personal experience. Crane's commitment to his heroic
ideal of sacrificial suffering naturally clothes itself in sacramental metaphors.

Although H. G. Wells relates that Crane had shown him "a
shelf of books, for the most part the pious and theological
works of various antecedent Stephen Cranes," none of Crane's
critics or biographers has followed the hint that there might be
an intrinsic connection between his writings and "these alien
products of his kin." [13] When this connection is supplied, however, we can see the unexpected ethical coherence of Crane's
serious work.

Few had thought to seek religious affirmation in Crane be-

[13] "Stephen Crane from an English Standpoint," in *The Shock of Recognition,* p. 671.

cause his characteristic gesture, especially in his verse, is to deny the God of his fathers. This gesture conforms with a general tendency in the age of social Darwinism to deny the divine, to substitute for predestination the determinism of natural selection or of the historical process. Yet Robert E. Spiller, writing on Crane in the *Literary History of the United States,* observes,

The appearance of an original artist, springing without antecedent into life, is always an illusion, but the sources of Crane's philosophy and art are as yet undeciphered. Neither the cold-blooded determinism of his belief nor the sensuous awareness of his writing can be without source, but nowhere in the scant record he has left is there evidence that he, like Garland, read widely in the current books on biological science.[14]

Neither was he, like Jack London, aware of Herbert Spencer. In so far as the scientific bases of the determinism of the times reached him at all, it was probably indirectly, as an attitude he appropriated from his environment, a point of view confirmed by his own experience. Although untouched, apparently, by natural or social science, he nonetheless absorbed the literary doctrine "that environment is a tremendous thing in the world and frequently shapes lives regardless," as his inscription in several copies of *Maggie* makes explicit. But, as the inscriptions go on to say, "If one proves that theory one makes room in Heaven for all sorts of souls. . . ."[15] Even as he inscribes his most naturalistic book Crane writes of Heaven. Yet in *Maggie* there is no God. When we turn to the poems—

[14] Spiller *et al., Literary History of the United States,* p. 1021.
[15] Stallman, *Stephen Crane: An Omnibus,* pp. 594–95 (hereafter cited as *Omnibus*).

The Black Riders, his first book of verse, was written at about
this time—we discover that while Crane is smashing ancestral
idols, he is attempting to reconstitute a more humane image of
divinity than the vengeful one with which society menaces his
individuality, his aloneness. The alternative image, the divine
mercifulness which he feels within himself, may correspond
to Emerson's doctrine of natural goodness, but its immediate
source is more likely Stephen Crane's father, the Reverend
Jonathan Townley Crane. His father's theological views gave
Crane a God of Love with whom to oppose the God of Vengeance who was the heritage of his mother's family, apocalyptic
Methodists from New York State's western frontier. However
he learned of naturalism (perhaps through reading Zola's
L'Assommoir), Crane was drawn toward its world of huge
forces and insignificant men. This generalized his isolative sensibility. But after *Maggie* and *George's Mother* Crane grew
less and less naturalistic. After *The Red Badge of Courage* he
could envisage heroes with the power of self-determined action. In his pessimistic fictional world of blind force, and in
his poems attacking God, Crane does share in the widespread
negation of divinity characteristic of the end of the century. He
bears a general resemblance to authors as different from himself and from each other as Thomas Hardy, Samuel Butler,
James Thomson, Henry Adams, Theodore Dreiser, and Mark
Twain.

4

Since Crane's thought is not original and his cultural resources
are constrained, what claim do his poems have upon our atten-

tion? Surely it is his style—that style which has kept Crane's
verse in the awareness of readers and historians of modern
verse. His two books of verse have been seven times reprinted
in the past thirty years. Crane is still a presence in poetry, but
today his contemporaries Stickney, Moody, and Lodge, for all
the advantages of their training, are practically unread. They
were dedicated to poetry, they involved themselves in the
mainstreams of literary tradition and contemporary thought,
yet their teacher Santayana remarked of them that "All those
friends of mine . . . were visibly killed by lack of air to
breathe. . . . the system was deadly, and they hadn't any alternative tradition (as I had) to fall back upon"; neither had
they "the strength of a great intellectual hero who can stand
alone." [16] A recent critic, commenting on the *Prometheus* of
Stickney, the most talented of the group, observes, "Beneath
the mechanical conventions that govern the language and the
structure, there is the struggle of an intelligence to find ways
of saying things . . . for which there is no convention extant." [17] These writers had committed themselves to the extant
poetic conventions, accepting them as part of the culture to
which it was their ambition to contribute. But Crane had not
given hostages to culture in the sense that they understood the
word. "Culture in it's true sense, I take it," he once wrote, mis-
spelling the pronoun, "is a comprehension of the man at one's
shoulder. It has nothing to do with an adoration for effete jugs
and old kettles. This latter is merely an amusement and we live
for amusement in the east. Damn the east! I fell in love with

[16] Quoted by Edmund Wilson in *The Shock of Recognition*, p. 743.
[17] Riggs, "Prometheus 1900," p. 412.

the straight out-and-out, sometimes hideous, often-braggart westerners because I thought them to be the truer men. . . . When they are born they take one big gulp of wind and then they live." [18] This reminds us of Crane's affinities to Mark Twain and the American frontier, a connection more obvious in "The Bride Comes to Yellow Sky" and "The Blue Hotel" than in his verse. It is present there too, not as subject but—inferrably—as style. Remarking the effects of democracy on literary expression, De Tocqueville had predicted,

Style will frequently be fantastic, incorrect, overburdened, and loose—almost always vehement and bold. Authors will aim at rapidity of execution, more than at perfection of detail. Small productions will be more common than bulky books: there will be more wit than erudition, more imagination than profundity; and literary performances will bear marks of an untutored and rude vigor of thought. . . . The object of authors will be to astonish rather than to please, and to stir the passions more than to charm the taste.[19]

The American poets of the nineteenth century who fulfill this prophecy best are those who owe least allegiance to the aristocratic literary culture of the east: Whitman, Dickinson, and Crane. The nature of Crane's debts to the two earlier poets is discussed in my seventh chapter.

We might expect Crane somewhat to resemble other American poets who had responded to similar cultural conditions; what is more surprising, however, is that to the extent that Crane's verse exemplifies the qualities De Tocqueville predicted for the democratic style, its formal intentions seem to

[18] Quoted in Stallman, *Omnibus,* p. 629.
[19] *Democracy in America,* II, 59.

approximate those of two concentrated poetic movements, symbolism and imagism. At least the first of these, opposing positivism and rationalism, was anti-democratic in spirit. In the Paris of Crane's decade, and dispersed through the English-speaking world of poetry twenty years later, these aesthetic programmes were defined in an atmosphere of group effort, in a climate of criticism as serious as it was volatile. Crane, who did not know a single poet when he wrote *The Black Riders*, appears never to have discussed poetic technique with any of his later literary acquaintances. "The best things come, as a general thing, from the talents that are members of a group," Henry James observed in his "Hawthorne":

Great things of course have been done by solitary workers; but they have usually been done with double the pains they would have cost if they had been produced in more genial circumstances. The solitary worker loses the profit of example and discussion; he is apt to make awkward experiments; he is in the nature of the case more or less of an empiric.[20]

Crane certainly pays the price idiosyncrasy exacts from isolation. Yet in his rebellion against the mechanical conventions of late nineteenth-century poetry he was closer to the main current of verse since his day than were such genteel contemporaries as Cabot Lodge, who, Henry Adams relates, "meant to make himself a literary artist, and in Paris alone he could expect to find the technical practice of the literary arts." But this young poet wrote to his mother from the Paris of Mallarmé and Verlaine, "I usually go to the Bibliotheque in the morning and work on Spanish. . . . It is hard work reading the old

[20] *The Shock of Recognition*, p. 450.

Spanish of the twelfth to fifteenth centuries." [21] Even Robinson, who has an imitative sonnet to Verlaine among the bleak New England portraits in *Children of the Night,* does not come nearly as close as Crane to paralleling the symbolist attack on poetic convention. It remained for T. S. Eliot a decade later to make Lodge's pilgrimage to better purpose, and to recover for poetry in English what Baudelaire, Mallarmé, and Valéry had made of the poetic theories of his fellow-American, Edgar Poe.

Besides his isolative sensibility, his religious heritage, his daemonic negation, his willed commitment to a sacrificial ideal, and his rebellion against literary convention, Stephen Crane had one further resource. This was a metaphoric imagination. If the solitary worker is, as James says, necessarily "an empiric," it is Crane's metaphoric imagination that on occasion endows his empirical successes with their genuine artistic power. If the result of Crane's "enormous repudiations" was severely to limit the range of possibilities he felt open to the human will, the effect of his metaphoric thought was boldly to transform into an imagined world, autonomous and alive, the stark and lonely barricade from which he held at bay the primal forces that besieged him.

5

This, then, is Crane's *donnée.* It excludes much that we value from the possible materials of his art, yet Crane makes miraculously the most of what he has left. Such is the persuasiveness of his intensity that at his best he has the power to make the limitations of his view of life seem the conditions of universal

[21] Henry Adams, *The Life of George Cabot Lodge,* pp. 29, 36.

law. The disproportion between his meager resources and the resolute strength of his results leads critics of his fiction to concentrate upon his style, the techniques by which he achieves his effects. His verse, however, while attracting praise from other poets (Pound, Sandburg, Amy Lowell, Horace Gregory, Berryman), has not been analyzed at all. Despite its anticipations of general tendencies in the verse of a later period, it proves on scrutiny to be in curious ways almost unique.

Although Crane's sensibility is indeed narrow, the range of his technical experimentation proves to be surprisingly wide. His imaginative world of menace, violence, and isolation is the gift of his own nature; for this vision he is in no one's debt. Yet it is not as unique in American writing as the solitary eminence most critics give to Crane would suggest. In his technical experiments even more than in his shared sense of isolation, however, Crane may properly be placed in a tradition. That tradition in America goes back to Emerson and Hawthorne and Whitman, different as their subjects often were from his, and extends after Crane to Hemingway. In his development from allegorist to symbolist Crane proves to be both representative and influential.

Two 𝄢 *A TONGUE OF WOOD*

There was a man with tongue of wood
Who essayed to sing,
And in truth it was lamentable.
But there was one who heard
And in the clip-clapper
Of this tongue
He understood
What the man wished to sing
And with this
The singer was content.

"I suppose I ought to be thankful to 'The Red Badge,'" Crane wrote to an editor of *Leslie's Weekly* in 1895, "but I am much fonder of my little book of poems, 'The Black Riders.' The reason, perhaps, is that it was a more ambitious effort. My aim was to comprehend in it the thoughts I have had about life in general, while 'The Red Badge' is a mere episode in life, an amplification."[1] The poems, therefore, are particularly useful to the critic who wishes to understand Crane's sensibility. In his verse Crane defines or implies his essential convictions about man's relations to God, to nature, to women, and to his fellow-man. These convictions are the assumptions on which his fiction is based.

[1] Reprinted in Stallman, *Omnibus,* p. 628.

From the standpoint of style, however, his verse is paradoxically different from his prose. On the one hand, there is his purposely prosy poetry—he strove to perfect his "tongue of wood" (the poem printed above is typical of that); on the other, a style in prose compounded of the most remarkable images, which accumulate in resonant cluster to form structural units in the development of his narrative themes. From the disorganized profusion of color-words in the early *Sullivan County Sketches* [2] to the taut integration of epithet and imagery into the structure of "The Open Boat" there is an impressive development. Crane grows, from a brilliant youth with an undisciplined gift for literary impressionism to a mature master of symbolism and style. He is more: an innovator, a maker of his own way. The verse, too, is an innovation, but it is so different in language from his prose that it has had a career of its own. It poses certain problems unrelated to those in his fiction, and its influence on later poetry, although generally acknowledged, is most difficult to trace with exactitude.

One way out of the difficulty is to regard him as primarily a poet of his own decade. Yet compared to what the better poets were writing when he wrote, Crane's wry lines are indeed amazing in their deliberate avoidance of all known ways of making what the English-speaking world of letters agreed to recognize as poetry. As will be seen, Amy Lowell, a leader of Imagism, the modern movement most critics take to be most indebted to Crane, considered him to fit into no period at all, lacking antecedants for his verse or influence after it. In the 'nineties he is an anomaly. Where does he belong?

[2] See Melvin Schoberlin's introduction, p. 15.

Stephen Crane was assuredly in advance of his time. Many of his poems are patently the work of a youth—of adolescence, as Miss Lowell not very kindly put it; but the best of his verse can stand on its own merits. His fame as poet rests on a handful of poems: "Black riders came from the sea" (which may have influenced Joyce's "I hear an army charging on the land"); his mordant fables, "I saw a man pursuing the horizon" and "In the desert," the parable of him who ate of his own heart; "Do not weep, maiden, for war is kind," surely, with the exception of half a dozen poems by Melville and Whitman, the most remarkable poem on war in the entire body of American verse. These staples from college anthologies, however, do not by any means suggest the range or quality of Crane's achievement. Because of the inconclusive state of criticism of his verse, most anthologists are content to choose his more sensational poems, to demonstrate his iconoclasm, pessimism, or naturalism. But these selections actually misrepresent his work. While they link Crane to intellectual currents of the 'nineties, they fail to suggest why he continues to be interesting in his own right in the mid-twentieth century.

It is easy to forget, because Crane wrote so young and died so long ago, that Edgar Lee Masters and Edwin Arlington Robinson were older than he, that he was born in the same decade as Robert Frost, Carl Sandburg, Vachel Lindsay, Gertrude Stein, and Wallace Stevens. W. H. Auden has suggested that fundamental changes of style in the arts occur only in those eras which experience great dislocations in man's relation to nature or to society; and he further remarks that the last time such social causes operated to change sensibility was in the generation of artists born between 1870 and 1890.[3] Crane, born in 1871, remains a contemporary of the other poets listed above. Longer-lived than he, they have partly by their personal presence and larger body of work been more strongly felt as influences in the twentieth century. Crane's brief career was over before any of theirs had fairly begun, yet in his best work he portends the assault on traditional poetic form and diction which those authors and their younger contemporaries would make a characteristic of twentieth-century verse.

There have been attempts to trace both the antecedents and consequences of Crane's poetry, but few of the critics who have concerned themselves with Crane can be considered objective. Some who dealt with his verse were content to speak in general terms from an acquaintance with only a portion of his work. Others were themselves deeply committed to poetic movements or critical methods which have perhaps limited their judgments. Thus Crane has been attacked or ignored by critics in the genteel tradition; foes of that tradition valued him chiefly as an idol-smasher; while more recently, proponents of Imagism, literary psychoanalysis, and the "new" criticism have had their say. The bibliography of critical work on Crane's poetry (apart from contemporary reviews) is not long, yet only two essays show any conscientious attempt to deal with the whole of his published verse. Amy Lowell in her posthumous introduction to Volume VI of Crane's *Work* (*The Black Riders,* including also *War is Kind,* 1926), and Everett A. Gillis in an article in *The Prairie Schooner* (1954), at least did Crane

---

[3] "The Anglo-American Difference: Two Views of Poetry," *Anchor Review,* I (1955), 217.

the honor of reading all of his published poems. Miss Lowell's remarks are important, especially as regards the attitude of Imagism's chief public figure toward an alleged forerunner of that movement; Mr. Gillis's is an impressionistic appraisal, suggestive but undeveloped. Crane's stature as a poet remains to be determined.

In his own day Crane's verse was notorious. His talent was recognized at once in the places that counted in the long run— by Hamlin Garland and W. D. Howells, both of whom used their influence in his behalf, and by such intelligent literary journalists and critics as Harry Thurston Peck of the *Bookman* and John D. Barry of the *Forum*. Peck, for instance, hailed Crane as "A bold . . . original, and powerful writer of eccentric verse, skeptical, pessimistic, often cynical; and one who stimulates thought because he himself thinks," and praised *The Black Riders* as "the most notable contribution to literature to which the present years has given birth." [4] But newspapers across the country were less kind: Crane's "lines" were ridiculed in Cincinnati, called "disjointed effusions" in New Orleans and mocked for their "futility and affectation" in the New York *Tribune*.[5] Vance Thompson, editor of the chic *Mlle New York*, wrote in another New York paper that "His verse is merely the word-exercise of the clever sixth-form boy." [6]

[4] "Some Recent Volumes of Verse," *Bookman*, I (May, 1895), 255.

[5] Clippings from Stephen Crane Collection, Columbia University Library: Cincinnati *Commercial Tribune*, October 18, 1896; New Orleans *Times–Democrat*, October 11, 1896; "Literary Notes," New York *Tribune*, Sunday, July 9, 1895, p. 24.

[6] "American Literature Discussed," New York *Commercial Advertiser*, August 7, 1896.

Over a hundred parodies of his poems appeared between 1895 and 1900, some in such bannerets of the Bohemian vanguard as *The Clack Book* and Elbert Hubbard's friendly *Philistine;* others, in the general magazines, were reprinted gleefully by the press. Most of these parodies reveal in their obtuse conventionality the chasm between Crane's sensibility and that of his contemporaries. "When I was the mark for every humorist in the country I went ahead," Crane wrote to a friend in 1898, "and now, when I am the mark for only 50 per cent of the humorists of the country, I go ahead, for I understand that a man is born into this world with his own pair of eyes, and that he is not at all responsible for his vision—he is merely responsible for his quality of personal honesty. To keep close to this personal honesty is my supreme ambition." [7] This is an uncompromising aesthetic creed; the young man who held it was proof against ridicule. Although the parodies and abusive comments must have pained him—he subscribed to a clipping service which supplied him with samples from the nation over, and these were among his effects when he died—he was not in the least deterred from writing as he felt he must. Amy Lowell sentimentalizes Crane, comparing him to Chatterton, "A boy, spiritually killed by neglect." [8] This was not so. Crane had a sense of proportion and knew that Howells and Garland and Peck did not count for nothing, whatever else came in from the ever-watchful Author's Clipping Bureau. "I would already have been a literary corpse, had I ever paid the slightest attention to the reviewers," he wrote in 1896.[9] He probably laughed at

[7] Stallman, *Omnibus,* p. 680.   [8] Introduction to Crane, *Work,* VI, xxix.
[9] *Love Letters,* ed. by Cady and Wells, p. 35.

the inanity of this notice from a far province: "I wonder how many Householders have read Stephen Crane's 'Red Badge of Courage,' or his volume of poems, entitled 'The Black Riders.' . . . Oh, it is something like taking a drink of olden, golden wine in some frozen palace of the wonder-world, attended by radiant forms of angel brightness, just to read him." [10] In this wise gushed Minnie Kidd ("Golden Gossip") of Vincent, Alabama, in the distant *Sunny South.*

Crane's reception thus ran the gamut from discerning praise to ridicule and total incomprehension. Most of these reviews tell us more about bohemian, genteel, and provincial taste in the 'nineties than they tell us of Crane. But two opinions of the time were influential upon later attitudes toward Crane's verse. Some contemporaries saw him as a decadent; some, as a symbolist. These were the views with which later critics had to deal. The two most important theories they in turn proposed are that Crane is an imagist in advance of that movement, and that he is a nonpareil, exempt from the causal chains of literary history.

2

Those who viewed Crane as a decadent may well have taken as their text the opening sentence of Peck's encomium in the *Bookman:* "Mr. Stephen Crane is the Aubrey Beardsley of poetry," an impression fortified by this posthumously published poem:

[10] *Sunny South* (Atlanta), July 18, 1896, clipping in Columbia Stephen Crane Collection.

A naked woman and a dead dwarf;
Poor dwarf!
Reigning with foolish kings
And dying mid bells and wine
Ending with a desperate comic palaver
While before thee and after thee
Endures the eternal clown—
—The eternal clown—
A naked woman.   [*Collected Poems,* p. 132] [11]

"The general impression," Peck wrote, "is of a writer who is bidding for renown wholly on the basis of his eccentricity." It did not matter, for such readers, that Peck went on to insist that "just as Mr. Beardsley with all his absurdities is none the less a master of black and white, so Mr. Crane is a true poet whose verse, long after the eccentricity of form has worn off, fascinates us and forbids us to lay the volume down. . . . Mr. Crane's work has traces of Entartung, but he is by no means a decadent." [12] There was the tag: a decadent, "The Aubrey Beardsley of poetry." Soon there was ample cause for morally upright citizens to use it.

[11] Follett's edition of the *Collected Poems* reprints Amy Lowell's compilation of *The Black Riders* (1895) and *War is Kind* (1899) from Crane's *Work,* Volume VI, with the omission of Miss Lowell's introduction and the addition of the three posthumous poems first published in *Bookman* (Vol. LXIX, April, 1929). Crane's poems are numbered but untitled, except for "Intrigue," a ten-part poem, the parts of which are numbered separately, following the last lyric (xxvii in the present edition) of *War is Kind.* It should be observed that both Lowell and Follett include as the twenty-seventh poem in *War is Kind* "lines" which Crane did not publish in book form (see my discussion of "The Blue Battalions" in Chapter Five).

[12] "Some Recent Volumes of Verse," *Bookman,* I, 255.

Although Crane lived only five more years after *The Black Riders* appeared, those years were crammed with dissolute, libidinous, even criminal incidents: was not the young man whose godless lines had made a stir in 1895 identical with the writer arrested for interfering with the apprehension of a prostitute? Was he not the author of that "explosion in a sewer," that indecent book called *Maggie, A Girl of the Streets*? Did he not marry—indeed, *did* he marry?—the proprietress of a notorious Florida pleasure palace? These are indeed the facts, or some of them; given the self-congratulatory smugness of the upper middle class of the time, one might predict how the Crane legend would develop from such beginnings. Thomas Beer has traced the ugly story. Crane becomes a drunkard, a dope-fiend, a syphilitic, a profligate, a wastrel, a reincarnation of Poe. The Puritan residue in American culture, that distrust of the senses and the arts against which Henry James inveighed in his study of Hawthorne, resulted in fanatically held moral prejudices, an eagerness to attack any form of expression which tried to present a view of life outside the limits of gentility. Pallid though the American decadence of the time now appears beside the purpureal works of Oscar Wilde, Beardsley, and Symons, the dandiacal ironies of Laforgue, or the hallucinatory *dérangement* of Rimbaud, it pursued its own extremes in self-conscious reaction against this repressive and corroded puritanism which was indeed the only ground from which it could spring.

The decadent movement was but an interlude. Soon enough the *Yellow Book* became a jape of literary history, as not only the bourgeois middlebrows whom the Decadents had tried too hard to outrage but men of taste and sensibility as well turned away from the cult of sensation. By 1926 decadence was so passé that Amy Lowell could claim that "Stephen Crane owes the thirty-year neglect of his poetry largely to his various publishers," pinning on them the onus for presenting his "virility and harsh passion" to the world in eccentric type faces on vellum. "No man could be taken seriously who had perpetrated a book which looked like this," she says of *War is Kind,* and she laments that his best work first appeared under the aegis of Fra Elbertus Hubbard, that Crane became "a cranky and unexpected star beaming above the amateur magazines and proud to shed its light upon East Aurora. . . . But a man must not quarrel with his audience. He must pipe to who will listen, and America was not ready for Crane." [13] This, however, is to overlook the fact that Crane's first book was designed by his good friend, that he concurred with the artist in choosing the orchid which trails "absurdly" on its cover. This is to ignore his later friendship in England with several contributors to Harland's *Yellow Book.* And finally it is to ignore some of his verse. The man who wrote a poem about "A naked woman and a dead dwarf" was not wholly alien in temper to the decadent movement in his own time.

Decadence, it must be remembered, was not completely extinguished by the Oscar Wilde scandal in 1896. Its consequences have been stronger and slower to die out in America than in England, perhaps because the continuing strength of the class Mencken dubbed "the Booboisie" continued to make exquisiteness attractive as a means of artistic revolt against

[13] Introduction to Crane, *Work,* VI, x, ix, xxvii, xx, xxvi.

what seemed the mass and the crass. The extent to which Crane not only was influenced by decadent sensibility but contributed in his verse to the continuation of that sensibility in America has been underestimated. Crane's "decadent" poems are less successful than his verse in other modes, however, and what Donald Evans, Wallace Stevens, T. S. Eliot, and Conrad Aiken felt they needed to learn of *dandysme* they found in France, during the years before 1915 when Crane was all but forgotten.

3

Inevitably, it was suggested during Crane's lifetime that he had been influenced by the Symbolists. Had this been true, Crane would be celebrated indeed as anticipator of the Little Renaissance in introducing into American verse Laforguian ironies and the symbolist techniques of suppressing logical links and moving the poem by indirections rather than narrative. As it happens, he knew no French, and once (perhaps in jest) mistook Mallarmé for an Irish author.[14] His early sponsor John D. Barry, writing in 1901, the year after Crane's death, categorically denies any French influence whatsoever. Barry tells the much-repeated anecdote of how Mr. Howells read the newly published work of Emily Dickinson to Crane, and feels that this was the most seminal literary experience in the formation of his style.[15] I shall discuss the Dickinson influence in the seventh chapter; my feeling is that, in the absence of other precise information as to Crane's reading, it has been greatly overestimated. On the other hand ignorance of Mal-

---

[14] Beer, *Stephen Crane*, p. 124; hereafter cited as Beer.
[15] "A Note on Stephen Crane," *Bookman*, XIII (April, 1901), 148.

larmé and innocence of French may not completely eliminate
the possibility of symbolist influence on Crane, however indirect. Both Amy Lowell and Louise Bogan note that the ironies
of his verse parallel those of the French school.[16] Not until
1956 was any of Crane's verse translated into French; in that
year Alain Bosquet introduced three of his poems with the
comment that this "poète concis et rageur, est de ceux qui ont
fait le plus pour dénoncer l'absurdité d'un monde matérialiste;
il n'est pas sans rappeler Corbière et Laforgue." [17]

There is no way to know what Crane was reading before
he wrote his "lines." A list of books owned by Crane in the
last year of his life contains no French verse, even in transla-
tion, nor any of the early English imitators of Symbolism, such
as Symons, Dowson, or Johnson. The list, in Cora Crane's
hand, gives no indication of the editions of the books named
or the dates of their acquisition, so we cannot tell whether
Crane owned in the years before 1895 (when *The Black Riders*
appeared) such books as Rossetti's *Poetical Works,* Swin-
burne's *Poems and Ballads,* or Shelley's *Poems.* Any of these
might have been partly responsible for the lushness of his "Intrigue"; contrarily, their examples may have been what Crane
sought to avoid in the sparse diction, ironic structure, and indirect movement of his better verse. His library at Brede Place
in Sussex contained some surprising volumes. He owned Hen-

[16] Lowell, introduction to Crane, *Work,* VI, xxix; Bogan, *Achievement
in American Poetry,* p. 17.

[17] Bosquet, introduction to *Anthologie de la Poèsie Américaine des Origines à Nos Jours,* p. 22. Bosquet translates the title poem from *War is
Kind;* "In the desert / I saw a creature naked, bestial"; and "Two or
three angels"—the third is mistitled "The Black Riders" ("Les Cavaliers
Noirs"); pp. 115–16.

ley's *Lyra Heroica,* an anthology for boys of poems "on the
glory of battle and adventure . . . the sacred quality of pa-
triotism," as well as Kipling's *Departmental Ditties, Barrack-
Room Ballads and Other Verses, Recessional,* and *Seven Seas.*
Despite his aversion to Stevenson he had *A Child's Garden of
Verses, St. Ives,* and *Ebb Tide.* And Crane owned as well an
incongruous batch of standard authors: Shakespeare, Burns,
Dryden, Gray's *Elegy* (in "fine edition"), Thomas Moore's *Irish
Melodies, Poems of Passion* by Ella Wheeler Willcox, the
poems of Meredith, Longfellow, and Browning, Fitzgerald's
Rubaiyat, Heine's *Works,* Ossian, and Volume One of Leigh
Hunt's *Autobiography.* Redolent of the Celtic Twilight are
Yeats's *The Secret Rose,* Richard Le Gallienne's *The Quest of
the Golden Girl,* and Fiona MacLeod's *The Sin-Eater.*[18]

So rootless a life did Crane live as a penniless free-lance
journalist before he and Cora settled at Brede in 1899 that it is
hardly likely that all these books were in his possession while
he roomed with the "Indians," his bohemian art-student friends
on East 23d Street, in the days when he was writing *The Black
Riders, Maggie,* and *The Red Badge of Courage.* Yet the library list also contains books belonging to Crane's father.[19]

[18] "List of Books, Brede Place," notebook in Cora Crane's hand, in the
Columbia University Library Stephen Crane Collection. The list is alpha-
betical by title, and contains also novels by such authors as Turgenev,
Conrad, James, Ouida, Hardy, Kipling, Twain, Zangwill, Scott, and
Stevenson, Shaw's *The Quintessence of Ibsenism,* Grimm's *Fairy Tales,*
and *Democracy, An American Novel.* The list includes books published
in 1899.

[19] ". . . in mother's will, his interest in the library is larger than the
interest of any of the rest of us." William H. Crane to Cora, April 21,
1900 (letter 120 in Columbia Stephen Crane Collection).

We cannot really tell when Crane himself read any of them, particularly since not one of the books of verse is among those Cora Crane brought back from England. Nor can we tell how many of them were bought and read only by Cora, whose tastes, as her commonplace and manuscript books reveal, were wildly eclectic, not often able to distinguish passion from bathos. At any rate the titles listed above constitute possible influences upon Crane; yet the originality of his own verse is made only the more evident by comparison to these possible models.

As for Symbolist influence, the library list offers little evidence for that. How then can one explain the parallels to the French poets' attitudes and technical resources in Crane's work? Granted his intransigent sensibility and given Crane's exposure to certain American influences pointing toward antiheroic statement, ironic paradox, and a personal style purposely contrary to established models, it seems probable that Crane arrived independently at whatever in his verse may resemble the Symbolist school.[20]

[20] The question of possible French influence upon Crane's fiction has not been resolved either. Lars Ahnebrink adduces detailed parallels in *Maggie* to street scenes, depictions of fights, and the effects of domestic violence upon children in Zola's *L'Assommoir*. He further concludes that the character of Maggie as a young girl reflects Nana, while Maggie as a child is based upon Lalie Bijard (in *L'Assommoir*), and in her last phase Maggie is derived from Gervaise Coupeau. Of the chapter depicting Maggie as a street-walker, Ahnebrink says, "The methods used by Zola and Crane in depicting this episode are almost identical." *The Red Badge* this critic finds to be closely modeled upon Zola's *La Debacle* and Tolstoi's *Sebastopol*. *Beginnings of Naturalism*, pp. 250–63 ff. Ahnebrink seems to verify the impressions of indebtedness voiced by many reviewers at the time *The Red Badge* appeared, and reiterated by Spiller

Despite Crane's literary fame and personal notoriety, when he died suddenly at twenty-eight in the first year of the twentieth century he was quickly forgotten. His English admirers, particularly Conrad and H. G. Wells, kept his fiction from complete oblivion, but so far as his verse was concerned it seemed as though history had justified the irony of the reviewer who commented in the *Nation* on *War is Kind* in 1899. Objecting to what seemed in this second volume a willful perpetuation of the eccentricities in the first, the reviewer thus dismissed Crane's verse: "Mr. Crane has chosen his part, and the world now finds other experimenters more interesting. . . . Mr. Crane has written his own epitaph." [21] Except for a page and a half in Stedman's all-inclusive anthology in 1900, Crane's poems were forgotten for a decade and a half. They were rediscovered by a new generation of literary rebels. Iconoclasts and revolutionaries seeking to change the taste of their time, they found what they needed in Crane: an ancestor.

In 1916 a poem entitled "Letter to Dead Imagists" had this to say to "Stevie Crane":

> War is kind and we never knew the kindness of war till you
>   came;
> Nor the black riders and clashes of spear and shield out of the
>   sea,
> Nor the mumblings and shots that rise from dreams on call.

Carl Sandburg apparently seeks sanction for the formlessness of his own verse in the irregular metrics of Crane. Ezra Pound,

---

in *Literary History of the United States*, p. 1021. Yet many of the parallels cited may well be coincidental results arising inevitably from treatments of similar subjects from similar points of view.

[21] "Recent Poetry," *Nation*, LXIX (November 16, 1899), 378; see also review of *The Black Riders, ibid.*, LXI (October 24, 1895), 296.

too, is reported to have praised Crane as a forerunner of Imagism, although presumably on different grounds.[22] Only two years after Pound's prescriptions for Imagist verse appeared in *Poetry* (March, 1913), Edith Wyatt compared the work of this school to Crane's with respect to direct treatment of subject, which Aldington had proposed as "the Imagists' first tenet." Citing "poems the Imagists themselves regard as their most distinctive work—poems such as 'After Ch'u Youan,' 'Aion (after Joannes Baptista Amaltheus),' and 'To Atthis (after the mss. of Sappho now in Berlin),'" Miss Wyatt observed that although they share "the same brevity, exactitude and simplicity of outline which characterize Stephen Crane's verses," these Imagist poems treat their subjects "by no means in the method of a straightforward, first-hand understanding, but very indirectly and through the media of the spirit and manner of certain remote, approved civilizations and habits of thought. . . . In this peculiar quality of an authentic first-hand vision, Stephen Crane's poems seem to me to evince a far deeper and better conception than the Imagists' of direct expression in poetry."[23]

Crane's sparse economy seemed less attractive to Harriet Monroe, who, after all, had been publicizing the contemporary school, printing their derivative simplicities and chinoiserie directness in *Poetry*. "Of course Crane was something of an

[22] Harriet Monroe, "Stephen Crane," *Poetry*, XIV (June, 1919), 152, discussing Crane's relation to "the new poets," says, "Ezra Pound, indeed, has somewhere spoken of him appreciatively." I have not found the reference; nor has Mr. Pound replied to my letter of inquiry sent in 1955, asking if he could supply it or would care to restate his opinion of Crane's verse at that time, and whether he still considered it interesting.

[23] "Stephen Crane," *New Republic*, IV (September 11, 1915), 150.

innovator in his poetic experiments," she admitted in 1919. "His free verse was different from Whitman's; his use of the short line especially was a presage, and may have influenced some of the poets—the Imagists, for example—who are now trying out its tunes. . . . But if he rebelled against the older verse forms and took up a new instrument, he never became a master at it. He struck a few slight strains, and then passed it on." [24]

Similarly, Amy Lowell, in her rather condescending encomium of Crane's verse, denied that the Imagists had even heard of Crane until after they no longer needed what he might have offered them. She sees his work as adolescent, created "from inner consciousness alone," praises its "sincerity," "virility and harsh passion," and asks "how did Stephen Crane stumble on his form?" She then identifies the form as *Vers Libre,* or Free Verse," admits that "He speaks in symbols, far out-distancing his time," and selects for highest praise four poems most like her own—none of them his best. [25] Mis Lowell concluded her ambiguous tribute with these remarkable statements:

What then is Stephen Crane, in so far as his poetry is concerned? A man without a period. That is at once his plume and his forfeit. He sprang from practically nowhere, and he has left us only the

[24] "Stephen Crane," *Poetry,* XIV, 152. Miss Monroe devoted the 30-page verse section of the issue containing this article on Crane to an extract from *The Domesday Book* by Edgar Lee Masters.

[25] Introduction to Crane, *Work,* VI, x–xxix, *passim.* Miss Lowell characterized as "Crane's high-water mark in poetry" three poems from *War is Kind* first published in Hubbard's *Roycroft Quarterly:* "A slant of sun on dull brown walls"; "Each small gleam was a voice"; and "I have heard the sunset song of birches." She chose as particularly "beautiful and satisfying" the last six lines of "Intrigue," part II.

most isolated of descendants. There were forerunners of his type of verse, but he had never heard of them. . . .

So short a time as twelve years after his death, a type of poetry extremely like his came into being. By all rights he should have been its direct parent, but he was not. . . . A marvellous boy, potentially a genius, historically an important link in the chain of American poetry.[26]

But Amy Lowell had done her best to show that Crane is anything but a link in the chain of American poetry. In making him an anomaly, a poet with neither a period, literary ancestors, nor descendants, she lays the groundwork for another theory lately espoused by John Berryman, whose views will be discussed below.

Although Miss Lowell disavowed Crane as an influence upon her own movement, one of his latest critics, R. W. Stallman, finds that Crane "anticipated the very program she took over from T. E. Hulme and Pound, and it was Crane who fulfilled certain tenets of imagism more truly than the imagists themselves. . . . It is Crane's priority in this historical perspective that places him as important."[27] Which tenets of Imagism Crane fulfills Mr. Stallman does not specify, but Horace Gregory had earlier suggested that Pound's use of the "sublimated epigram" derives from Crane,[28] and Gregory "readily admits that much of [Crane's] verse seems to anticipate the characteristic economy of phrasing, lightness, and verve of style that the Imagists claimed was a particular virtue of their art"[29]—an

[26] Introduction to Crane, *Work*, VI, xxviii–xxix.
[27] Stallman, *Omnibus*, pp. 569, 575.
[28] "Stephen Crane's Poems," *New Republic*, LXIII (June 25, 1930), 159; and again in *A History of American Poetry, 1900–1940*, p. 136.
[29] *A History of American Poetry*, p. 135.

amplification of Edith Wyatt's prior advocacy of Crane's excellence in direct treatment.

While it is true that Crane's lines correspond to the dicta laid down by Pound in "A Few Don'ts" [30]—direct treatment, economy of diction, and organic rhythm—we must also remember that these three rules are insufficient to define the imagist aesthetic. There are other fundamental qualities in Imagism, particularly its attempt to create a moment of stasis which is universalized in terms of the associations the image suggests; [31] these aspects are scarcely to be found in Crane. But I postpone a detailed comparison to my concluding chapter.

4

Crane's latest biographer, John Berryman, like Amy Lowell denies his poems much influence upon later verse, but for different reasons: "There is no evidence in the poetry or outside it that he ever experimented in verse. . . . As for 'anticipation': some of the later people probably learned from him. . . , but his work is quite different from theirs. . . . it differs in intention and mode from the poetry both of his period and of ours. It is primitive, not designedly so, but naturally primitive." [32] Mr. Berryman evolves a theory of Crane the poet as nonpareil, an "unexampled reversion" to the "primeval," the "medicine man," the "bushman." [33] Probably influenced by

[30] *Poetry*, I (March, 1913), 200, reprinted in *Literary Essays*, p. 3.
[31] Pound, *Literary Essays*, p. 4.
[32] Berryman, *Stephen Crane*, p. 274; hereafter cited as Berryman.
[33] *Ibid.*, pp. 273–74.

Hamlin Garland's assertions five, twenty, and thirty-five years after the event that Crane had "drawn off" his poems "precisely as if some alien spirit were delivering these lines through his hand as a medium,[34] Mr. Berryman moves from Garland's inference of automatic writing to his own avowal of artlessness: "There is obviously no attempt to write regular verse, or even, perhaps, verse at all"; and, apropos Crane's striking three-line poem,

> A man feared that he might find an assassin:
> Another that he might find a victim.
> One was more wise than the other.   [BR LVI]

Berryman remarks, "The indifference to craft, to how the thing is said, is lunar." [35]

These, then, are the most important suggestions as to where Crane belongs in the modern poetic tradition. Each has some merit, but all seem to me to evolve from the reading of only some of Crane's poems, or few, and to be based as much on the special vision of each critic as upon an objective examination of the poetry under discussion.

If it seems audacious in me to aspire, after these sixty years, to be the

> one who heard
> The clip-clapper of this tongue of wood
> And knew what the man
> Wished to sing,

[34] *Roadside Meetings*, p. 194; see also "Stephen Crane: A Soldier of Fortune," *Book Lover*, II (Autumn, 1900), 6–7; and "Stephen Crane as I Knew Him," *Yale Review*, III (April, 1914), 494–506.

[35] Berryman, pp. 270, 272.

and even further, to hope that

> . . . with that the singer was content

my diffidence before so challenging an enterprise is somewhat
dispelled by examination of the new materials which have
been so generously placed at my disposal. Until now there has
been no evidence with which to question Garland's assertion
that Crane's poetry "flowed from his head like oil . . . not
only without blot or erasure, but perfectly correct in punctuation." [36] When Garland tells us that "He wrote steadily in
beautifully clear script with perfect alignment and spacing,
precisely as if he were copying something already written and
before his eyes," [37] we may judge for ourselves whether Crane
was creating his poems on the instant or was giving his friend
clean copies of verse already written and held in mind. It is
true that Crane had the remarkable gifts even in his prose of
seeing the entire work whole at the moment of composition
and of finding his inevitable and surprising epithets exactly as
he needed them. Manuscript corrections are few, revisions
minor. But this is not to say that he wrote automatically, or
without craft.

The reader may have noticed some slight discrepancies be-

---

[36] *Roadside Meetings,* p. 194.

[37] *Yale Review,* III, 501. As for Crane's handwriting, his classmate at
Syracuse Frank W. Noxon once remarked on its "exquisite legibility," so
surprising in the script of a professional newspaperman. Crane replied
that "from the outset of his writings he had kept in mind the compositor,
whose earnings depended upon the amount he could set, and this in
turn upon the time it took to read the copy." Quoted in *Love Letters,*
ed. by Cady and Wells, p. 63. This would have been three years before
Crane sat down at Garland's desk on 105th Street to "draw off" his
"lines."

tween the two quotations above in the last few lines from the same poem. The epigraph to this chapter reproduces the earlier manuscript version of poem XVI from *War is Kind*.[38] Here are five rhymed lines and one near-rhyme (wood, wood, understood, satisfied; sing, sing) in a poem only ten lines long. But Crane must have realized that the strong reiteration of sound in *wood, understood* and its echo in the final *satisfied* militated against the wooden clip-clapper effect he had to create were the poem to be what it described. In the final published version there are no proper rhymes. Consequently the repetitions of *wood* and *sing* are not rhymes but identities; their flat unmusicality is just the opposite in the revision of the refrain-like quality the strong rhyme of the earlier version had given them.

On another random sheet in the Columbia Stephen Crane Collection, half covered with doodles, there is a jingle of Crane's, a dig at Longfellow. As a New Jersey schoolboy Crane had probably had to memorize the metrically perfect platitudes of "The Psalm of Life." Here is his revenge:

> Tell me not in joyous numbers
> We can make our lives sublime
> By— well, at least, not by
> Dabbling much in rhyme.

---

[38] From MS in the Columbia Stephen Crane Collection. The poem was written by 1895 and Crane meant to include it in *The Black Riders;* it was one of seven poems omitted at the insistence of Copeland and Day, the publishers. C. K. Linson, "Stephen Crane, A Personal Record," MS in Syracuse University Library; hereafter cited as Linson MS. Linson claims that the poems for *The Black Riders* were completed by February, 1894 (pp. 194; 188, note to p. 64).

This little *jeu d'esprit* may suggest that Crane knew very well what he was about, that his rejection of conventional form, rhyme, and treatment was as much a conscious as a compulsive choice. The trifle may serve to warn us while we smile at it. We are dealing with a consciously original craftsman, not with an inspired but artless prodigy, or a bushman.

If it seems unlikely, then, that Crane's poems were written "from inner consciousness alone" or that he "sprang from practically nowhere," the sources of his ideas and of his techniques still remain to be traced. So, too, do the influences which conditioned that special vision of life which was the gift and the burden of Crane's unusual sensibility. Crane's progress as a writer is neither logical nor orderly, yet by taking up his most recurrent themes we can find patterns of consistency and of development. These themes in his verse are the relations of the individual to God and Nature; love; war; and social injustice. Each of these is the subject of a succeeding chapter. But the influences upon Crane's aesthetic include still other sources than those determining his attitudes toward his subjects, or his choice of those subjects. A later chapter accordingly examines Crane's early models and the authors and artistic movements in whose terms his work may best be considered and judged. My final chapter attempts to estimate what in Crane's verse may be of lasting value, and to find his place in the development of contemporary literature.

Three ⌇ *WAR IN HEAVEN*

What fame Stephen Crane has as a poet largely rests upon half a dozen anthology pieces, and most of these present him in iconoclastic defiance of a wrathful Jehovah. "God fashioned the ship of the world carefully," begins one well-known poem (BR vi), "Then—at fateful time—a wrong called," and God, distracted, allowed the hull to slip away "slyly, / Making cunning noiseless travel down the ways." Thus the world is doomed from its creation: "forever rudderless, it went upon the seas / Going ridiculous voyages." The final couplet places this cosmic irony in its proper relation to the Universal Plan:

> And there were many in heaven
> Who laughed at this thing.

This view could hardly win accolades from a large public in 1895, although a similar mood of ironic despair was being expressed—or soon would be—in the writings of many other authors of the decade. Mark Twain was rapidly moving toward the nihilism of *The Mysterious Stranger* (begun in 1898) and *What is Man?* (1904); five years after *The Black Riders* Dreiser was to complete, and Doubleday to suppress, *Sister Carrie,* which dramatized the irrelevance of faith in such a cosmos as Crane envisaged. Interpreting history and the times

against a more complex background and with a more disciplined intelligence than any of theirs, Henry Adams too was
approaching the "mechanistic catastrophism" [1] which would
characterize his autobiography, first issued in 1907. When
Crane's poems appeared, a columnist in the *Bookman* (probably H. T. Peck) suggested that one of them "might serve
some purpose if pinned to the title page of *Jude the Obscure*,"
since Crane epitomizes "the bitterness of Mr. Hardy's pessimism, his keen remorseless sense of the ironies of life, the
passionate insurgence of his heart against Nature's injustice,
and the revolt of his soul against this mad, sad world. . . ." [2]
The poem concerned a man who ate his own heart and liked
it, because it was bitter. We shall return to this mordant fable
a little later.

To most readers of *The Black Riders* it seemed that when
the heedless God who set the world adrift did turn His attention to mankind, the result is "the cruel injustice of omnipotence torturing weakness." [3] One poem, for instance, carries as
its epigraph this passage from Exodus 20.5: "And the sins of
the fathers shall be visited upon the heads of the children,
even unto the third and fourth generation of them that hate
me."

> Well, then, I hate Thee, unrighteous picture;
> Wicked image, I hate Thee;
> So, strike with Thy vengeance

[1] Newton Arvin's introduction to *The Selected Letters of Henry Adams*,
p. xxv.
[2] "Chronicle and Comment," *Bookman*, III (March, 1896), 1.
[3] Lowell, introduction to Crane, *Work*, VI, xx.

> The heads of those little men
> Who come blindly.
> It will be a brave thing. [BR xii]

The theme seems obsessive. Crane states it again:

> If there is a witness to my little life,
> To my tiny throes and struggles,
> He sees a fool;
> And it is not fine for gods to menace fools. [BR xiii]

And he returns to it again and again (in BR xix, xxv, WK x, and, as will be seen, in many other poems by implication).

In view of these uncompromising, gnomic statements, it is not surprising that some critics should see no other theme in Crane's verse than the smashing of idols. Harriet Monroe, for one, dismissed his work on these grounds. "*The Black Riders* is full of the wisdom of yesteryear. . . . as old-fashioned as Bob Ingersoll's fiery denunciations. Crane's startling utterances . . . somehow cease to startle after twenty years." [4] Amy Lowell, more perceptive, finds Crane haunted by his religious background. "He disbelieved it and he hated it, but he could not free himself from it. . . . Crane's soul was heaped with bitterness and this bitterness he flung back at the theory of life which had betrayed him." And Miss Lowell wisely proposed the Bible as a source for the form of his poems. "Its cadences, its images, its parable structure" must have been "ground into his consciousness." [5] It was of course beyond the scope of her introduction to trace in detail the influence she here suggests.

[4] "Stephen Crane," *Poetry*, XVI (June, 1919), 150.
[5] Introduction to Crane, *Work*, VI, xix.

Since there is general agreement that Crane was in revolt against his religious background, it would seem logical to investigate the exact climate of belief and opinion against which he was rebelling. Most recently, Marcus Cunliffe had this to say (in another connection) of Crane and the religion of his immediate family:

. . . he is anti-clerical though belonging to a clerical heritage. In his early work, I do not think he knows where he stands—whether it is religion or religiosity he disapproves of, whether he is adapting or burlesqueing. He reacts against the familiar elements of his world where these seem to him hypocritical, but they shape his thought.

Quoting the character of Crane's father given by the *Dictionary of American Biography*, Cunliffe adds that his "one serious fault seems to have been his monumental innocence," and mentions that Crane's mother, too, came from "a clerical family."

What Crane was reacting against, therefore, was nothing very rigid or terrible; hence, his adolescent reversal of what he had been taught consisted in condemning *false* religion; in showing that there was "greater viciousness" than Jonathan Townley Crane ever suspected, in smoking and drinking; and in not only reading "trashy novels" but actually writing some.

In fact, Stephen Crane strives to be free not of merely a family but a national atmosphere. Its restrictions are irksome, just because they are on the whole, kindly.[6]

Mr. Cunliffe's view is at variance with the suggestions given in John Berryman's biography of Crane. Berryman remarks

[6] "Stephen Crane and the American Background of *Maggie*," *American Quarterly*, VII (Spring, 1955), 42–43.

that Crane's mother held religious views "evidently much narrower and more insistent than her husband's." [7] The biographer presents his estimate of the Reverend Dr. Crane based upon Stephen's reminiscence, the *DAB*, and the father's book on *Popular Amusements*, a gently earnest warning against sinful pleasures known only vicariously to the author. Berryman concludes that Crane's father led "a saintlike life." [8] Of his mother Mr. Berryman has little to say biographically, although she looms as a stern and forceful figure in the fantasies which, according to the psychoanalytic interpretation this critic proposes, lie at the source of Crane's creativity. With respect to the poetry, Berryman makes this valuable suggestion:

God is the brutal villain of *The Black Riders,* and some pieces that set this Old Testament swaggerer against an interior pitying God (xxix, li, liii) went unnoticed. His mother's had been warring with his father's God in Crane's thought. Neither won; both perhaps disappeared and were replaced by a notion we shall come to— already now when the little book appeared, some of it had ceased to represent his thought, transformed in the Southwest.[9]

Berryman recognizes that Crane's anticlerical verse is not all of a piece, that his treatment of religious themes is marked by a tension between Divine Justice and Divine Mercy, and suggests that his parents had different conceptions of God. But the cryptic unclarity of the last sentence is less than helpful, and the assertion that "Neither won" seems to me unsubstantiated by the verse itself.

. In the following pages I shall try to show that such poems as attack the brutal God represent only the first phase of Crane's

---

[7] Berryman, p. 8.   [8] *Ibid.,* p. 12.   [9] *Ibid.,* p. 114.

war in heaven. It would indeed be surprising were this all there was: as though a youth growing up with a crowd of distinguished clergymen in his own family could defy God a dozen times in verse and be done with the theme. In fact there is in Crane's treatment of God and of religion a progress from the utter denial of "Well, then, I hate Thee" to an affirmation of faith in the "interior pitying God." Crane goes even beyond proposing an alternative deity: in his best and most neglected poem there is an apocalyptic vision of the triumph of this God of love. But between the denial and "When a people reach the top of a hill" (WK xxvii) there are many poems and several stages. As we trace them we shall have to look further into the doctrines and dogmas of both sides of Crane's clerical family.

2

"In doctrine . . . a strict Methodist of the old stamp, filled with the sense of God's redeeming love. . . . In controversy he was gentlemanly, in his judgments charitable. . . . He leaves the impression of an unusually noble mind straightened by dogma and a narrow education." So is Jonathan Townley Crane characterized in the *Dictionary of American Biography;* [10] to his youngest son he was "so simple and good that I often think he didn't know much of anything about humanity." [11] Yet Stephen Crane owed much to the loving, unworldly soul of his father, who may not have known much of human iniquity but felt passionately what he did know of the merciful nature of his God. His biographer in the *DAB,* like the critics and biographers of his son, seems to have depended chiefly

[10] *DAB,* IV, 506.   [11] Stallman, *Omnibus,* p. 693.

upon his books *Popular Amusements* (1869) and *Arts of Intoxication* (1870) for this description, which Berryman uses and Cunliffe quotes: ". . . deeply concerned about such sins as dancing, breaking the sabbath, reading trashy novels, playing cards, billiards, and chess, and enjoying tobacco and wine, and too innocent of the world to do more than suspect the existence of greater viciousness."

But a more useful guide to the influence of Jonathan Crane's thought upon his son's is a theological tract published when Stephen was three years old. We can reasonably assume that the religious sensibility exhibited in *Holiness the Birthright of All God's Children* (1874) represents the man young Stephen knew as his father. Nor is it unlikely that the Reverend Dr. Crane drew upon the ethical attitudes, the researches, and the occasional exempla in this book for his sermons and family devotions in the six years of life that remained to him. In it he undertakes to refute Wesley himself on the doctrine that innate depravity remains in the soul of the regenerate believer. This view the Reverend Crane denies with a fine sense of historical relativity, showing that Wesley held different positions on the question over a period of years, each being the reply or defense of the founder of Methodism against specific arguments of critics and dissidents who threatened his early religious societies by proclaiming their own complete perfection after conversion. The historical arguments need not concern us here, but we should note the view of human nature Crane's father propounds in the course of refuting the "residue theory." Interpreting a passage in Wesley's *Sermon on Sin in Believers,* Dr. Crane remarks, "By the term 'sin' . . . he can-

not mean that there is guilt in a believer, nor any state of mind
or heart which involves condemnation. Consequently, instead
of sin, properly so-called, he means simply temptation." And
"All trial life implies temptation." [12] But is not temptation itself
sinful? Consider the first temptation and the first sin:

Eve was pure in her whole being; with no defect, no taint of depravity of any kind. By the craft of her adversary she was drawn
into discourse. . . . Her eyes and her thoughts were kept upon the
tree until she *saw that it was good for food, and that it was pleasant
to the eyes, and a tree to be desired to make one wise.* Here were
three enticements, each of which appealed to an element of perfect
human nature, and tended to create a desire which in itself was
wholly innocent. . . . The elements of her nature to which appeal
was made were holy.

Sin did not begin until "at last she began to weigh the question
of obedience or disobedience. . . . to ponder that question is
to begin to yield." [13]

This analysis may not be as wise in the psychology of human
frailty as Milton's, but what is noteworthy is its recognition of
the holiness of natural impulses; among these is the "inner
taste, which delights in beautiful forms and colors." [14] Such
convictions Stephen Crane was to share. His father continues:

To be human is to be endowed with appetites and passions, innocent in themselves, but unreasoning, required to be guided by the
intellect and the conscience, and controlled by the will. These appetites and passions may ally themselves to thought, but in themselves
are void of thought, and know only to press onward. Man's duty
and safety demands that they be subjugated, taught to obey. . . .

[12] *Holiness the Birthright,* pp. 89–91, 96.
[13] *Ibid.,* pp. 92–93, 95, 96.   [14] *Ibid.,* p. 93.

There are affections, also, in themselves not only innocent, but essential to a perfect humanity, which at times impel in the direction of sin.[15]

Jonathan Crane, returning in bitter weather from an errand of charity, took sick and died when Stephen was only ten. In the next few years the boy was exposed to another variety of Methodist profession, less tolerant of "affections . . . essential to a perfect humanity, which . . . impel in the direction of sin."

Crane's mother had been before her marriage Mary Helen Peck, daughter of the Reverend George Peck, D.D., a prominent Methodist clergyman. She was a forceful woman who did not fear to risk censure by "taking care of a girl who had an accidental baby. . . . Mother was always more of a Christian than a Methodist," Stephen Crane recalled. In the same reminiscence, transcribed by a young admirer—a circumstance to be remembered in evaluating these remarks—Crane said,

My mother was a very religious woman but I don't think she was as narrow as most of her friends or her family. . . . After my father died, mother lived in and for religion. We had very little money. Mother wrote articles for the Methodist papers and reported for the [New York] *Tribune* and the [Philadelphia] *Press*. Every August she went down to Ocean Grove and reported proceedings at the Methodist holy show there. . . . My brother Will used to try to argue with her on religious subjects such as hell but he always gave it up. Don't understand that mother was bitter or mean but it hurt her that any of us should be slipping from Grace and giving up eternal damnation or salvation or those things. You could as well argue with a wave.[16]

[15] *Ibid.*, pp. 100–101.   [16] Stallman, *Omnibus*, pp. 691–92.

There are several things to remark in this passage. First, that his mother's family and friends seemed narrower in religion than she herself—evidently Crane felt he had to defend her against the reputation of these associates to his young admirer. We may add to this a passage from a letter of Crane's about her family: "In those old times the family did its duty. Upon my mother's side everybody as soon as he could walk became a Methodist clergyman—of the old ambling-nag, saddlebag, exhorting kind." [17] Indeed they did: her father and his four brothers, one of whom, Jesse Truesdell Peck, rose to the eminence of Bishop of Syracuse. Partly because of the weight such an office would have in a family so ecclesiastical, and partly too because Stephen was sent to Syracuse University, which his great-uncle Jesse had helped to found, the views of Bishop Peck will merit further consideration.

A second point is the obvious one that Mrs. Crane supported herself by religious journalism. This, as well as the plethora of preachers in the family circle, suggests that the sermon and evangelical tract, as well as the Bible, may have been influential upon Crane's poetry. Third, when he says it hurt his mother that any of the children should be backsliding, is it not curious that he mentions her concern with their defection from "eternal damnation" before her hope that they be saved? They should not give up damnation! This is most suggestive of the nature of her belief, of the language of her persuasions. And finally, her persuasions: "You could as well argue with a wave."

[17] *Ibid.,* p. 690.

Yet, says Mr. Berryman, "His father's had been warring v his mother's God in Crane's thought." It is time to look at ___ war. We may well begin with a poem which seems to have nothing to do with God. Its subject, in fact, is not immediately apparent. One critic takes it to be "the positive, ethical side" of Crane's verse, as contrasted to the negativism of the "un-righteous picture"; in this poem "he celebrates integrity." [18]

3
In the desert
I saw a creature, naked, bestial,
Who, squatting upon the ground,
Held his heart in his hands,
And ate of it.
I said, "Is it good, friend?"
"It is bitter—bitter," he answered;
"But I like it
Because it is bitter,
And because it is my heart."   [BR III]

"It is not clear that these [lines] were verse," Berryman remarks after quoting them; Stallman examines the structure of this poem and finds it to be syllogistic.[19] But what does the poem mean?

If, as Gillis suggests, the poem celebrates integrity, why are we "in the desert"? And what are we to make of its *persona,* more a brute than a human being, "a creature, naked, bestial, . . . squatting"? Despite the brutishness of the heart-eater

[18] Everett A. Gillis, "A Glance at Stephen Crane's Poetry," *Prairie Schooner,* XXVIII (Spring, 1954), 76.

[19] Berryman, p. 74; Stallman, *Omnibus,* p. 574.

and the bitterness of his feast, the lines somehow lend his stubborn gesture a kind of dignity. Such intransigence suggests that not to eat his own heart might be a still more bitter experience than his present unsavory feast.

By a chain of lucky coincidences we can find the passage which may reveal the elusive significance of this parable of Crane's. Among the fifty-five books from Crane's library (exclusive of his own writings) preserved by Cora Crane there is a much-battered pocket edition of a little manual, its green binding waterstained and gnawed at the edges. This work is "intended to lead the unconverted to a grave consideration of the wrong of sin, and the duty of immediate efforts to secure forgiveness." In the course of analyzing the sinner's present condition the book presents this passage, in a chapter called "The Depraved Heart":

To understand in how deep a sense you are lost, you must know your own heart; but "the heart is deceitful above all things, and desperately wicked, who can know it?" "From within, out of the heart of men, proceed evil thoughts, adulteries, fornications, murders, thefts, covetousness, wickedness, deceit, lasciviousness, an evil eye, blasphemy, pride, foolishness; all these evil things come from within and defile the man." And *you* are the sinner thus depraved. It is *your* "heart" that is thus "deceitful above all things, and desperately wicked." . . . No healthy human figure can illustrate this fallen moral state. A mass of loathsome corruption alone can show how vile is the depravity of man.

It would be rash to assume that just because a book is found among an author's effects that he must have read and been influenced by it—especially when, like Crane, he scarcely annotated a line in any of his volumes. Yet one can make a strong case for the probability that Crane had not only read this book, but for a time had been practically reared on it, steeped in it, and that much of his mother's family's Methodism and her own can be represented by the grim unrelenting didacticism of *What Must I Do to be Saved?* The copy in the Columbia University collection is inscribed on the flyleaf, "Rev. Dr. Crane / With the respects of / the author"; below this is written, in Stephen's clear hand, his autograph and the year 1881. The author who gave this book to Crane's father was Jesse T. Peck, D.D., who by 1881 had been a bishop for nine years.[20] The Reverend Dr. Crane had died the year before. We can reconstruct the scene with fair confidence: "Mother lived in and for religion. . . . it hurt her that any of us should be slipping from Grace and giving up eternal damnation or salvation or those things." We can imagine with what hopes and admonishments Mrs. Crane gave her favorite youngest son this volume, inscribed from her most eminently religious uncle to her lately deceased husband. It made interesting reading for a boy of ten.

Did he read it? At that time, he would have been of a mind to. "I used to like church and prayer meetings when I was a kid," he wrote in the year of his death, "and when I was thirteen or about that, my brother Will told me not to believe in Hell after my uncle had been boring me about the lake of fire and the rest of the sideshows." [21] This was another uncle—they were all clergymen.[22] From them, from his mother, from

[20] The passage above is from *What Must I Do to Be Saved?*, pp. 20–21; hereafter cited as *What Must I Do*.

[21] Stallman, *Omnibus*, p. 692.

[22] Not only his four great-uncles but his uncles too. A religious encyclopedia of the time calls his grandfather, the Reverend George Peck, "literally 'a father of ministers,' having left two sons and two nephews

Great-uncle Jesse's salvation tract, Stephen had by the age of
thirteen learned all about "the sideshows."

This work by Crane's great-uncle is not produced in order
categorically to state that it is the single source of Crane's
poems on religious themes. There are, it is true, several in-
stances—"In the desert" is among them—where parallels in
idea and even in statement are close enough to make fair an
assumption of direct indebtedness. But rather than insist upon
immediate influence it seems more valuable to use Bishop
Peck's book to indicate the climate of religious opinion in
which Crane grew up, particularly in the years after his father's death. It is most valuable—perhaps more so than the
Bible itself—as an index to the attitudes toward God, man,
and the universe of Methodists "of the old ambling-nag,
saddle-bag, exhorting kind," as Crane described them. And
although Great-uncle Jesse was a bishop and founded a university, and Grandfather George Peck "through half a century
of the Church's history . . . had an important part in shaping
its legislation," [23] Crane's evocation of a backwoods revivalist
does them no injustice.

For George Peck had been born in a log cabin in the wilds
of Otsego County, New York, in 1797—only six years after the
death of Wesley. From *The Life and Times of Rev. George
Peck, D.D., Written by Himself* (1874), we get a vivid picture
of the emotional frenzy of frontier Methodism and the arduous

---

in the pastoral work of his own conference, and one daughter, Mrs. Rev.
Dr. Crane [*sic*], of the Newark Conference." McClintock and Strong,
Cyclopaedia of Biblical, Theological, and Ecclesiastical Literature, VII,
862.

[23] *DAB*, XIV, 374.

dangers the circuit-riding preachers faced from forest, beast, and hostile settlers. The fortnightly arrival of the exhorter was the one ray of human fellowship in the isolated cabins along his route. Camp meetings, held on grounds hewn out of virgin forests, were occasions of great communal feeling. Singing mighty hymns together, hearing out the long oratory from the pulpit, kneeling in common prayer—these eagerly shared experiences made the most welcome contrast to the weeks and months of bleakly lonely frontier life. The climax of the camp meeting was the conversion of sinners. Just after George Peck had been licensed to preach, in 1816, he attended such a meeting at which "Father" Timothy Dewey "preached a terrific sermon on the words, 'Prepare to meet thy God' ":

Father Dewey . . . stood before the crowd like a giant among pigmies, and his voice was clear as a trumpet, and terrible as thunder. He came down upon the wicked in such sort that hundreds . . . listened with amazement and terror. . . . There was an unbroken roar of fervent supplication all over the ground, while the awful voice of the preacher resounded above the tempest of prayer, and every word was heard as distinctly as if in the silence of midnight. "O sinner, sinner," thundered the preacher, "are you determined to take hell by storm? Can you dwell with devouring fire? Can you stand eternal burnings? Are your bones iron, and your flesh brass, that you plunge headlong into the lake of fire?" [24]

The effect of such preaching under such conditions was often "the curious experience which has been termed religious ecstasy":

Perhaps while engaged in fervent prayer or joyous song a man would fall prostrate, his eyes fixed, his whole form rigid, and remain thus

[24] *Life and Times,* p. 63.

sometimes for several hours. . . . Unconverted persons, deeply convinced of sin, not infrequently "fell," as the current phrase expressed it, "under the power of God." . . . often while the lips were silent, and the powers of voluntary motion were suspended, the soul passed through a great moral crisis, surrendered to the Divine rule, trusted in Christ; and when the physical effects of the intense mental conflict began to subside, the first words uttered were exultant praise and thanksgiving. However we may reason or doubt in regard to these phenomena, one thing is certain, they occurred in connection with genuine religious emotions, and a truly Divine work.

George Peck, seeing such conversions at the camp-meetings, "leaped to the conclusion that they were indicative of a great grace" and "earnestly desired to share the joy and the benefit." Great was his disappointment that his own conversion at fifteen was unaccompanied by this frenzy.[25]

George and his youngest brother Jesse were the sons of a Half-Covenant Congregationalist[26] who, soon after his removal to the frontier from Connecticut, was converted to Methodism by a terrifying dream. Two dead friends summoned him "to the eternal world. . . . He expected at once to be ushered into the presence of a God whose repeated warnings he had disregarded. . . . The most intense horror seized his soul. He had no hope of mercy." Awaking in terror, "He expected to die before morning, and saw nothing before him

---

[25] *Ibid.*, pp. 49–50.

[26] A Half-Covenant Congregationalist was a person admitted to the Church in childhood as one who "shared in the covenant taken by [his] parents." He himself had not as an adult had the "Christian experience" which, before the last third of the seventeenth century, had been requisite for Church membership. Sweet, *Story of Religion in America*, pp. 86–87. That is, Luther Peck, Stephen Crane's great-grandfather, had been an indifferent Christian before his vision.

but 'the blackness of darkness forever.' . . ." But Luther Peck survived the dawn, joined the Methodist Society, and "his house became the home of preachers, and a true house of God." When the service was held at a neighbor's, the Peck family attended; one sermon, on "the end of the world," delivered "in a voice of thunder," haunted George Peck's imagination "for years." [27]

Such was the apocalyptic religion of the early nineteenth-century frontier to which Stephen Crane's great-grandfather, grandfather, and great-uncle were converted in their adolescence. Moderate as their Methodism seemed to their contemporaries,[28] in theology, forensics, and tractarian fervor they preserved to the end of the century the essential features of frontier evangelism. Crane's mother, reared in such a family, carried on its tradition in her own household in turn. Thus in the 1880's Stephen Crane was brought up on a tract written in 1858 by a forebear whose great religious experience—his own conversion—had occurred under circumstances like those Crane's grandfather describes, in a frontier clearing in 1827. Jesse Peck's book, *What Must I Do to Be Saved?* is, like the above-quoted sermons of half a century earlier, redolent with the fumes of sulphur. The effort is to frighten the sinner out of hell on earth, not to win him by love to heaven. Throughout the 74-page admonition to sinners (later sections, less germane to our inquiry, give counsel to penitents and converts), there

---

[27] *Life and Times,* pp. 25–28.

[28] Jesse Peck is cited in McClintock and Strong's *Cyclopaedia* for his "broad catholic spirit" which "led him to regard Christians of all denominations as brothers in Christ." *Supplement,* II (1887), 766. See also *What Must I Do,* p. 88.

is continual emphasis upon the temerity of the sinful individual, the terrifying jeopardy in which his unrepentent rebellion
against God prolongs his soul. The section preceding "The
Depraved Heart" is called "The Sinful Life": "God has spoken
to you in the language of paternal kindness and authority, but
how criminally you have shut your ears to his voice. . . . you
have rebelled against the only perfect government in the universe." [29] This is the actual theme of Stephen Crane's poem in
which a creature in the desert gnaws his own heart.

He squats in the desert, the Waste Land traditional in Christian literature as the home of those lacking in Grace. "O the
bitter wrong of sin!" writes Bishop Peck, ". . . It sears, as a
burning fire, the land once lovely with blooming virtue." [30]
The creature—he is unworthy to be called a man—is naked,
bestial, a brute, as we have seen. "I said, 'Is it good, friend?'"
I, the poet, call this vile and wretched thing my friend: I recognize in his posture and lineaments that which is akin to my
own. "It is bitter—bitter. . . . But I like it / Because it is bitter, / And because it is my heart." Loathsome, filled with corruption, the source of all sin and evil, his heart is still good to
him, because it is his. That is his condition, his humanity. And
he would rather taste it, though to do so is to consume himself,
than renounce his humanity for those transcendent goods
which require that more-than-human renunciation. So to will
is to defy God's will. But in both his bestiality and his intransigent self-assertion the "creature" appears to the poet as a
"friend," a kindred spirit.

Crane's poem may thus be read as a denial of the Peck family's relentless insistence upon natural depravity. From his

[29] *What Must I Do*, p. 17.   [30] *Ibid.*, p. 44.

father he may have taken not only the ethical view, as he interpreted it to himself, but also a hint as to the narrative element. In *Holiness the Birthright of All God's Children,* Jonathan Crane recounts his personal acquaintance with "a man who, when convinced of his sin and danger, prayed for a new heart, found pardon and peace." But, as Dr. Crane afterward learned, "when he prayed for a new heart he thought, in his simplicity," that the heart in his breast "had been so long the home of Satan that it must be taken out of his body and a new one substituted." The good Dr. Crane tells this to illustrate that "God's answer was wiser than the prayer"; [31] it is the kind of exemplum, based on personal experience, he would surely have often used in his sermons, and the tale is so odd that young Stephen could hardly have forgotten it. A sinner removes his own heart: this may have been the notion that originally stirred Crane's imagination.[32]

This poem gathers into itself several of Crane's most important themes: rebellion against the wicked God, the kinship of fallen man in his sin, and the insistence upon a human fate—though it be damnation—rather than the transcendent beatitudes that follow superhuman renunciation. These themes account for almost half of the poems in *The Black Riders.* But before we go on to them we must first complete our scrutiny of Crane's poems on the rebellion of man against the vengeful

[31] *Holiness the Birthright,* pp. 116–17.

[32] Yet this poem, or one like it, might have developed from no other source than the Scriptural descriptions of the heart's depravity quoted by Bishop Peck in the passage given above. The Scripture is probably the source of this sestet from a sonnet by Hopkins:

I am gall, I am heartburn. God's most deep decree
Bitter would have me taste: my taste was me;

Jehovah—and his final reconciliation with a more merciful God. It is well at this point to reconstruct the moral universe of the young Stephen Crane, as it was probably given him by motherly and avuncular precept and in the pages of *What Must I Do to Be Saved?*

4

Since Jesse Peck's tract is, half a century later, a scarce book, an extended quotation may prove useful not only for its content but as an example also of the Bishop's hortatory style. The following passage, from a chapter on "The Creature and the Creator," is one of several perorations in the book. Here Peck reiterates in a rhetorical tide his arguments against rebellion, his presentiments of the joys of submitting to the Divine Will;

Whence came your powers of life and motion, of thought and reason, of feeling and will. No finite agency could produce them. Is it right that these noble powers should be turned against the very God who made them? that he should be attacked and insulted by the very organs of speech he has formed to utter his praise? that he should be treated with scorn or neglect by the thinking, feeling, determining mind he has made? that these deathless powers should instigate revolt in the empire of their Creator, bring desolation into his fair heritage, and stir up the world to treason against the only faultless government in the universe? O the bitter wrong of sin! What tears and groans of anguish it has wrung from the

---

Bones built in me, flesh filled, blood brimmed the curse.
  Selfyeast of spirit a dull dough sours. I see
The lost are like this, and their scourge to be
As I am mine, their sweating selves; but worse.

Poems of Gerard Manley Hopkins, ed. by Bridges and Gardner, 3d ed., p. 110.

crushed heart of humanity! What untold misery it has inflicted upon the conscious soul! The blight of death is in it. It turns the very pleasures of life into gall. It sears, as a burning fire, the land once lovely with blooming virtue. It tears down and tramples in the dust the rights of conscience, the rights of God, the hopes of mortals. Its track may be traced in the blood of the slain, in the fainting, writhing, agonizing throng it leaves to curse, and wail, and die beyond the reach of mercy. But you know not even yet of its horrors. You must open the pit of woe, where wrath has come upon souls whose immortality is turned into a fearful curse by this deadly evil. You must hear the language of despair as it comes up from the place where there is "weeping, and wailing, and gnashing of teeth." Nay, you must need feel through every power of your deathless being the undying worm and the burnings of unquenchable fire, to have a just idea of the infinite wrong of sin. But even here you have felt the sentence of death in yourself, because you are a sinner, and you mourn over it as your most humiliating and crushing calamity, that you are a rebel against the Lord of hosts.

On the other hand, how fair and lovely is everything that is still in harmony with the plans of the Creator. . . .[33]

By this time one's ears are so split by the wailing, the gnashing, "the language of despair," that the harmony of the spheres can scarcely be heard above the tumult. Filled though it is with pulpit clichés, the Bishop's description of hell on earth is vivid, sensory in conception, tactile, and terrifying. It is also twice as long as the ensuing description of the joys to be gained only by renouncing the claims of this world:

How sweet are the charms of what yet remains of his earthly paradise! What gladness and delight run through the animal natures that move in harmony with the Creator's plans! What beauty and glory sparkle in the heavens above! What holy rapture glows in the bosoms of those who are saved from the power of sin! What

[33] *What Must I Do*, pp. 43–45.

beatific visions rise before the eyes of faith! What thrills of holy joy,
what shouts of triumph gladden the world of light, where angels
and the ransomed from among men ascribe "glory, honor, and
power, and might, and dominion to Him that sitteth upon the
throne, and to the Lamb forever!" O, this is right. This shows the
just relation of the creature to the Creator. Here is the play of
created powers in the sphere of their original glory. This is the
glad acclaim in which you long to join.[34]

Perhaps. This vision of joy is abstract, bodiless, qualified, un-
convincing; it requires the abnegation of the senses and of the
self—for what? For a clergyman's expostulation, "O, this is
right."

> Supposing that I should have the courage
> To let a red sword of virtue
> Plunge into my heart,
> Letting to the weeds of the ground
> My sinful blood,
> What can you offer me?
> A gardened castle?
> A flowery kingdom?
>
> What? A hope?
> Then hence with your red sword of virtue.   [BR xxx]

Not only is the reward illusory, but the Creator of the latter
part of Bishop Peck's sermon is no less fierce than the terrible
God of the first. Yet, the book insists, the chief end of man is
to make himself worthy, by denying his own nature, of the
approbation of this tyrannical ruler. To rebel is to fling oneself
forever into the burning wilderness.

Crane's poems may well derive their strangely abstract

[34] *Ibid.*, pp. 45–46.

characters from this work, for in the course of repudiating the Bishop's brimstone theology his young nephew adopted some of the unbodied personages from his manual. Chapter headings tell us who they are: in addition to "The Creature and the Creator," we find "The Sinner and the Redeemer," ". . . an Enemy," "The Good and the Wicked," "Sinful Men and Demons," "Good Men and Angels," "The Omniscient God." There are but few parables among the Bishop's exhortations, and in these too the characters are faceless and nameless. Were the Bible the only source of Crane's own parables, would he not have inclined to follow the examples there of delineating individuals as well as types? Crane seems to have combined the structure of the Biblical parable with the disembodied allegorical figure from pulpit oratory and the evangelical tract. (Other influences on his parable form, such as Olive Schreiner and Ambrose Bierce, will be discussed in Chapter Seven.) The sinners, demons, angels, and wrathful gods of the verse—not one of whom is named or given any individualizing features— are creatures from Bishop Peck's own sermon. It is almost as though Crane had taken *What Must I Do to Be Saved?* as his text, and proceeded to write commentaries on what seemed to him the monstrousness and inhumanity of the creed of his mother's family. " 'The wrath of God abideth on you.' Condemned already, already lost!" roars Great-uncle Jesse; [35] Stephen replies,

A god in wrath
Was beating a man:
He cuffed him loudly

[35] *Ibid.*, p. 16.

With thunderous blows
That rang and rolled over the earth.
All people came running.
The man screamed and struggled,
And bit madly at the feet of the god.
The people cried,
"Ah, what a wicked man!"
And—
"Ah, what a redoubtable god!"   [BR xix]

We may imagine which people Crane has in mind: his mother's people. In another poem their God threatens the rebellious
mortal again:

Blustering God,
Stamping across the sky
With loud swagger,
I fear You not.
No, though from Your highest heaven
You plunge Your spear at my heart,
I fear You not.
No, not if the blow
Is as the lightning blasting a tree.
I fear You not, puffing braggart.

Crane does not deny that this God exists, nor that he is powerful; there is such a God, active in malice, and yet the poet de-
fies Him.

Withal, there is One whom I fear;
I fear to see grief upon that face.

                       .   .   .   .

Ah, sooner would I die
Than see tears in those eyes of my soul.   [BR liii]

Crane opposes the "Blustering God" not, like Ingersoll, with
the void of agnosticism, but with another One—whom he

fears, not to be injured by, but to injure. This gentle personal God is vulnerable only to some unstated possible injury He may receive from the man who believes in Him. What would bring "tears in those eyes"? The eyes, we note, are not glaring down from the brows of heaven; they are "of my soul"—in transcendental fashion Crane merges the Divine in himself with the Divinity. Those eyes would weep were he to violate the compassionate nature of the Divinity within him.

It is important to remark that much as Crane opposes the damnatory Methodism of his mother's family, he nowhere denies that man is a fallen sinner. But this fact, accepted from the background against which he rebels, has quite a different significance to Crane's inner God of mercy from what it meant to Bishop Peck. We scarcely need the Bishop to tell us what the "Blustering God" makes of man in his depravity; yet the following passage is useful, since another poem of Crane's is a counterstatement to these admonitory words:

And your sins are remembered. The omniscient God knows every one of them, and will hold you to a stern responsibility. . . . You cannot endure to meet the least of these in the presence of the Judge; but what will you do when in countless numbers they throng your memory, when every one charges upon your soul its infinite wrong, and demands the wrath of your offended Sovereign without mixture of mercy forever. . . . "Depart from me, ye cursed, into everlasting fire. . . ."

The Savior himself has condescended to inform you of the fearful doom which awaits you. You shrink from it with indescribable terror.[36]

The relation of Crane's poem to this passage is made clear by a manuscript in the Columbia collection in which the pro-

[36] *What Must I Do,* pp. 26–27.

nouns "one" in the first line and "he" in the last are capitalized;
the published text, from another manuscript, suppresses these
indications of the Deity and leaves the significance of the
poem ambiguous:

> There was one I met upon the road
> Who looked at me with kind eyes.
> He said, "Show me of your wares."
> And this I did,
> Holding one forth.
> He said, "It is a sin."
> Then held I forth another;
> He said, "It is a sin."
> Then held I forth another;
> He said, "It is a sin."
> And so to the end;
> Always, he said, "It is a sin."
> And finally, I cried out,
> "But I have none other."
> Then did he look at me
> With kinder eyes.
> "Poor soul!" he said.   [BR xxxiii]

The theme of compassion for humility appears again in poem
xvii, where the one who could not remember having done any
good deeds is deemed by God "O best little blade of grass."
In still another poem, "The God of his inner thoughts," as opposed to "The God of many men," regards him "With soft eyes
/ Lit with infinite comprehension," and calls him "My poor
child!" (BR li).

"The God of many men" had a voice that "thundered loudly,
/ Fat with rage, and puffing."

> The livid lightnings flashed in the clouds;
> The leaden thunders crashed.

A worshipper raised his arm.
"Hearken! hearken! The voice of God!"

"Not so," said a man.
"The voice of God whispers in the heart
So softly
That the soul pauses,
Making no noise,
And strives for these melodies,
Distant, sighing, like faintest breath,
And all the being is still to hear." [BR xxxix]

This inner voice of mercy, of direct reverberation with the Love that is God, takes the man who hears it out of the fellowship of Christians assembled in their churches. There, ministers and bishops echo the threats of the other God, menacing in thunder. Bishop Peck, wise in the snares of Satan, had warned Stephen against that alluring voice which softly subverts the Divine Order and the Church by promising forgiveness for human frailty. One chapter of *What Must I Do to Be Saved?* is called "The Whisperings of an Enemy":

There has been another voice within you, a rebel voice, whispering treason against the Lord of lords and King of kings; a voice which has dared to oppose the communication of Divine wisdom, saying: "There is no great harm in this carnal indulgence; there is no immediate danger in a life of pleasure; God is merciful, he will punish you according to your sins, he will still follow you with offers of pardon. . . ." [37]

But Stephen Crane knew very well where he had first heard the voice of mercy that whispers "so softly" that "All the being is still to hear." He had heard it from his father. He knew that his father was "simple and good." And he knew what to make

[37] *Ibid.,* p. 52.

of a creed that heaped such malign threats upon his own. Crane's own creed was that of "a radical, unchurched, de-faithed, Christian gentleman," as the editors of his most reveal-ingly personal letters describe him. "Trained to believe in the great tradition of the Christian gentleman as it had been Americanized in the generations of Jefferson and Emerson and Robert E. Lee, Crane made the tempermentally natural gesture of taking it seriously . . . he was moved in the name of the ideal to revolt desperately against the smothering con-ventionalities of moralism and respectability by which the world evaded the ideal." [38] As Crane put it himself, "The final wall of the wise man's thought . . . is Human Kindness of course. . . . Therefore do I strive to be as kind and as just as may be to those about me and in my meagre success at it, I find the solitary pleasure of life." [39]

Opposed though the Christian ethics of Jonathan Crane were, in Stephen's mind, to the iron rule of Jesse Peck, it is well to emphasize that if his "mother's had been warring with his father's God in Crane's thought," it was a war which nei-ther parent nor maternal grandfather nor great-uncle recog-nized or fought themselves. There is no indication whatever that the Reverend Dr. Crane's mildness was regarded as heret-ical by his wife's family or by any authority of the Methodist Church; indeed, his father-in-law gave Dr. Crane's books the encouragement of four pages of advertising among the fly-leaves of his autobiography. Probably Dr. Crane used George Peck's publisher at the latter's behest. And Jesse Peck, as we have noted, was considered "not bigoted" as regards doctrinal

[38] *Love Letters,* ed. by Cady and Wells, pp. 21–22.   [39] *Ibid.,* p. 35.

differences.[40] Although two such intrepid logicians as the
brothers Peck would certainly have recognized their differences with Jonathan Crane, relations between them seem not
to have been strained. Nor is there evidence that Dr. Crane
and his wife had any serious fallings-out on theological
grounds—or on any other. The conflict became a conflict only
in the mind of their son.

The psychological burden of his inner battle may be reck-
oned from two poems in *The Black Riders*, the longest and the
last. In "I stood musing in a black world" (XLIX), not knowing
where to go, he hears a thousand voices call "Look! look!
There!" A radiance flickers "in the far Sky"—and disappears;
"I hesitated." But the torrent of voices calls again, and he
leaps "unhesitant":

> The hard hills tore my flesh;
> The ways bit my feet.
> At last I looked again.
> No radiance in the far sky,
> Ineffable, divine;
> No vision painted upon a pall;
> And always my eyes ached for the light.

But the torrent again cries "Look! look! There!"—

> And at the blindness of my spirit
> They screamed
> "Fool! fool! fool!"

This theme of faith desperately sought and not found is
paralleled in poem LXVIII, significantly placed as the final
"lines" in the book:

[40] *DAB*, XIV, 380.

> A spirit sped
> Through spaces of the night;
> And as he sped, he called,
> "God! God!"

Seeking "into the plains of space," his calls are mocked by echoes;

> Eventually then, he screamed,
> Mad in denial,
> "Ah, there is no God!"
> A swift hand,
> A sword from the sky
> Smote him,
> And he was dead.

We remember the spear of the "Blustering God" was "as the lightning blasting a tree": the terrible God of wrath is ever-present, most known when most denied. This is the burden of guilt Crane must bear for his temerity. "You must go alone to the bar of God," warned Jesse Peck. "You must answer for your own life of guilt, and you yourself must, if finally impenitent, obey the terrific words, 'Depart, ye cursed, into everlasting fire.' You alone must suffer for your obstinate rebellion." [41]

But Stephen Crane is not in quite the same case as the God-denying spirit of this last poem. Unlike him, Crane, as we have seen, does not at the end of his quest scream "Mad in denial, / 'Ah, there is no God!' " What Crane denies is the God he fears, while he acclaims and seeks the Spirit of Love. Behind the denial we may trace again the ethical vision of his father. In this poem, the controlling image and the unstated logic derive from *Holiness the Birthright,* or from Jonathan Crane's oral repetition of this theme:

[41] *What Must I Do,* p. 34.

God could, if he deemed it best, so reveal himself that unbelief would be impossible. He might write his laws upon the azure skies. . . . He could smite every sinner at the very moment of his transgression with so stern and visible a hand that obedience would have little moral value. . . . That moral liberty may not be destroyed, God withdrew himself from human vision. . . . And because He is not seen, the fool hath said in his heart, *There is no God.*[42]

The spirit in the last poem, then, was a fool. (The speaker in "I stood musing" is called a fool by the faithful, but for his blindness, not his unbelief.) But those whose God is lightning in a swift hand are not so wise. "Not to thrust one's hand into a blazing furnace is not proof of uncommon sagacity. . . . For children to obey when the father stands holding the rod over them, is no proof that they possess the spirit of true obedience." [43] It is from such knowledge that Crane took courage in his own rebellion and in his quest.

5

The death of the faithless spirit concludes *The Black Riders,* but it does not bring to an end Stephen Crane's preoccupation with God in his poems. Two or three poems from that book remain to be mentioned, in which are prefigured themes he takes up again in *War is Kind* or in verse hitherto unpublished. Significantly, there is nothing in his later book as nihilistic as "God fashioned the ship of the world carefully," as embittered as "Well, then, I hate Thee, unrighteous picture." The remaining themes, to state them in rough generalizations, are these: (1) there is one code appropriate for gods and angels, but men live by another; (2) the Church is a fallible institution,

[42] *Holiness the Birthright,* pp. 123–25.   [43] *Ibid.,* p. 124.

not the Body of God; (3) men are brothers in sin; and (4) God is inscrutable.

When Copeland and Day, publishers of *The Black Riders*, conveyed to Crane their reservations about bringing out his manuscript, his reply was typically candid and uncompromising: "It seems to me that you cut all the ethical sense out of the book. All the anarchy, perhaps. It is the anarchy which I particularly insist upon. . . . The ones which refer to God, I believe you condemn altogether. I am obliged to have them in when my book is printed." [44] Although Crane did offer to withdraw "some which I believe unworthy of print," he may have had to drop others in whose worth he believed, for two of the seven omissions he later included in *War is Kind* (III and XVI); but these were not about God. Two which are about God have turned up in the Columbia collection; the other three are still untraced.[45]

Two codes. In what way did Crane see anarchy as essential to "the ethical sense" of his verse? If by anarchy he meant self-determination in defiance of institutions, the connection is plain. It was Crane's fate to find his paternal heritage of integrity, kindness, humanism, and love irreconcilable with the attitudes and institutions his mother's tutelage put before him as the Christian tradition to which he ought to belong. Jona-

[44] Stallman, *Omnibus*, p. 602.

[45] Linson MS, pp. 193–94. The Columbia collection has "A god came to a man" and "One came from the skies," to be discussed below. Untraced are "A god it is said / Marked a sparrow's fall"; "The traveller paused in kindness"; and "Should you stuff me with kindness." Poem III of *War is Kind* is "To the maiden / The sea was a laughing meadow"; XVI is "There was a man with tongue of wood."

than Crane, in his gentleness, had yet made peace with the
same church over which the Pecks presided; indeed, he had
been converted to it at eighteen from his Presbyterian background. But for Stephen the way was harder, perhaps because,
as we have seen, the Peck variety of Methodism was by his
boyhood anachronistic in a long-settled urban society. The
social forces which had made it attractive were no longer
operative.

So it is that when Stephen Crane envisaged the Fall, he
agreed with his father that the "elements of [human] nature
to which appeal was made were holy. . . . There are affections, also, in themselves not only innocent but essential to a
perfect humanity, which may at times impel in the direction
of sin." But Stephen cannot go on to believe that "Man's duty
and safety demand that [his appetites and passions] be subjugated," even as his father believed, for here the gentle voice
of paternal reasonableness is drowned out by the thunderer.
In the following poem, not before available, Crane, like his
father, interprets Genesis. But where the father had absolved
Eve of guilt in being tempted, his son interpolates a human
reply to the commandment to abstain from the fruit (2.16–17).
Stephen implies a question that would never have occurred
to Jonathan Crane: How can God be good if he demands the
impossible of man? For his father, "To ponder that question
[of obedience] is to begin to yield."

> A god came to a man
> And said to him thus,
> "I have a glorious apple
> "It is a glorious apple

"Aye, I swear by my ancestor
Of the eternities before this eternity
"It is an apple that is from
The inner thoughts of heaven's greatest.
And this will I hang here
And then I will adjust thee here
Thus—you may reach it.
And you must stifle your nostrils
And control your hands
And your eyes
And sit for sixty years
But,—leave be the apple.

The man answered in this wise:
"Oh, most interesting God
What folly is this?
Behold, thou hast moulded my desires
Even as thou hast moulded the apple.

How then?
Can I conquer my life
Which is thou?
My desires?
Look you, foolish god
If I thrust behind me
Sixty white years
I am a greater god than god
And then, complacent splendor,
Thou wilt see that the golden angels
That sing pink hymns
Around thy throne-top
Will be lower than my feet.   [Columbia MS]

In another poem the argument is condensed and the presentation, while still allegorical, is made lyrical by a functional refrain:

"It was wrong to do this," said the angel.
"You should live like a flower,
Holding malice like a puppy,
Waging war like a lambkin."

"Not so," quoth the man
Who had no fear of spirits;
"It is only wrong for angels
Who can live like the flowers,
Holding malice like the puppies,
Waging war like the lambkins."   [BR LIV]

Those are ambiguous puppies and lambkins. Even in heaven
these gentle beasts own something of the malice and aggres-
siveness of animal nature.

Irrelevance of the church. After his father's death Stephen
Crane probably never again attended a church in which the
voice of his inner God was heard. In *The Black Riders*, poem
XXXII, we see the irrelevance of the conventional church to the
worship of the true God:

Two or three angels
Came near to the earth.
They saw a fat church.
Little black streams of people
Came and went in continually.
And the angels were puzzled
To know why the people went thus,
And why they stayed so long.

In this new poem, probably written after his trip to Mexico
in the summer of 1895, Crane uses a ruined Indian temple to
symbolize the transience of human creeds: [46]

[46] Crane published "Ancient Capital of Montezuma" in the Philadelphia
Press, July 21, 1895, p. 32, describing a rail trip with "an archaeologist
from Boston."

A row of thick pillars
Consciously bracing for the weight
Of a vanished roof
The bronze light of sunset strikes through them,
And over a floor made for slow rites.
There is no sound of singing
But, aloft, a great and terrible bird
Is watching a cur, beaten and cut,
That crawls to the cool shadows of the pillars
To die.   [Columbia MS]

Here, as in "It was wrong to do this," he concludes with animal images. The "great and terrible bird" is the condor, a huge
and disgusting vulture which prefers carrion to live prey.
Waiting for the "beaten and cut" dog to die in the treacher-
ously inviting shadows, this bird is the only occupant of a
Heaven as vacant as the deserted temple.

Two poems in *War is Kind* carry further the "anarchy" of
Crane's assault on institutionalized religion:

Even the sky and the opulent sea,
The plains and the hills, aloof,
Hear the uproar of all these books.
But it is only a little ink more or less.

This refers to the voluminous clerical writings of Crane's family. The aloofness of nature from man's aspirations we are to
meet again. The poem continues:

What?
You define me God with these trinkets?
Can my misery meal on an ordered walking
Of surpliced numskulls?
And a fanfare of lights?
Or even upon the measured pulpitings

Of the familiar false and true?
Is this God?
Where, then, is hell?
Show me some bastard mushroom
Sprung from a pollution of blood,
It is better.

Where is God? [WK IV]

This poem is a curious jumble of Crane's verse at its best and worst. From the third through the seventh lines above there is a fusion of language, rhythm, and concept. But this requires a psychological distance from the subject; in the rest of the quotation this distance is lost, and with it the verbal control. The result is jejune invective, too self-conscious of its own iconoclasm. The extent of such lapses is shown in Crane's note to Elbert Hubbard, to whom he had submitted this poem: "Oh, Hubbard, mark this well. Mark it well! If it is over-balancing your discretion, inform me." [47] Hubbard must have marked it well indeed, for he never printed the poem. But in April, 1898, the back-wrapper of his *Philistine* carried this terse declaration:

You tell me this is God?
I tell you this is a printed list,
A burning candle, and an ass. [WK x]

Here again Crane has condensed a long poem into a short one. Although "a printed list" may be as good a phrase as "a little ink" (neither is remarkable), surely "a burning candle" lacks the suggestiveness of "a fanfare of lights," while "an ass" is

[47] Written on MS in the Syracuse University Library, on a sheet lacking the first six lines of the poem.

flat and puerile compared to "an ordered walking / Of surpliced numskulls." One danger of Crane's poetic practice—
the result of his condensation and directness—is a tendency
toward flat statement instead of evocative indirection.

Brothers in sin. A dozen poems in *The Black Riders* elaborate one of the implications we have found in the fable of the
heart-eater: the kinship of fallen man in his sin. Most of the
poems of which this is the theme are short and unambiguous:

> I stood upon a high place,
> And saw, below, many devils
> Running, leaping,
> And carousing in sin.
> One looked up, grinning,
> And said, "Comrade! Brother!"   [BR ɪx]

This poem, as Mr. Stallman remarks, "epitomizes Hawthorne's
story *Young Goodman Brown*." [48] But if these lines look backward to Hawthorne's theme and his use of allegory, "Comrade!
Brother!" reminds us also of Baudelaire's "Hypocrite lecteur
—mon semblable—mon frère." Crane does not yet resemble
Baudelaire in poetic strategy; that will come later, as he develops his own means to express attitudes and states of feeling far
more complex than the theme of these early poems. Although
one sixth of his first book is given to categorical fables like the
foregoing, not a single poem in *War is Kind* treats this theme
directly. There is however one manuscript poem—"The patent
of a lord"—that does so, in a way more ambiguous than those
in *The Black Riders*.

The world appears in this group of poems as "a reptile-
swarming place" (BR xxɪx), or "a desert" of sand, heat, and

---

[48] Stallman, *Omnibus*, p. 570.

vacant horizon, despite God's voice assuring him "It is no desert" (XLII). The evil truth of the human heart is envisaged in XLIV:

> I was in the darkness;
> I could not see my words
> Nor the wishes of my heart.
> Then suddenly there was a great light—
>
> "Let me into the darkness again."

Earlier, the poet had summoned a "Mystic shadow" to "tell me—is it fair / Or is the truth bitter as eaten fire? . . . / Fear not that I should quaver. / For I dare—I dare" (BR VII). Now he knows the bitterness of truth: "There was a man who lived a life of fire . . . / Yet when he was dead, / He saw that he had not lived" (LXII). And again, more personally,

> Many red devils ran from my heart
> And out upon the page.
> They were so tiny
> The pen could mash them.
> And many struggled in the ink.
> It was strange
> To write in this red muck
> Of things from my heart.   [BR XLVI]

This confession may explain an unnoticed significance to the title poem of *The Black Riders.* Since this is the only poem in the book in which the action involves horses, why, one wonders, did Crane head the book with it and give the whole collection its name? Crane is so deliberate about such matters as his titles [49] that it must be this: in a metaphorical sense, *all*

[49] Crane was "furious," Berryman records (p. 230) when his story "The Price of the Harness" was retitled "The Woof of Thin Red

the poems are like the black riders that come from the sea (conventionally a symbol of the unconscious), and in them, as in his imagined warriors, there is

> . . . clang and clang of spear and shield,
> And clash and clash of hoof and heel,
> Wild shouts and the wave of hair
> In the rush upon the wind:
> Thus the ride of Sin.

In succeeding chapters we will trace in Crane's verse the themes of sensual life ("the wave of hair") and of war. As in the poems discussed in the present chapter, these too are concerned primarily—obsessively—with Sin.

Knowledge and admission of one's own sinful nature has the immediate effect of isolating one from human kinship, sympathy, and love. Crane's verse shows three directions in which the isolated individual may try to reestablish the love and kinship lost with his innocence. He may recognize that all men are as sinful as he; he may seek to share the sinful love of a fallen woman; and, in two poems only, he presages a triumph of regenerate believers over the agony of mortal life. This vision, in "The Blue Battalions," we will reach at the end of the fifth chapter; his love poems are the subject of the next. But now we have four poems attacking the hypocrisy of pious gestures hiding a heart of shame, for the isolation that follows sin cannot be denied.

In two of these poems (BR L and LVII) the same line, "You

Threads": "Damn Walker . . . . it *is* the price of the harness . . . paid for wearing the military harness . . . and they paid blood, hunger, and fever."

say you are holy," is repeated; in these and in a third (LXIII) the "you" is obviously a clergyman; in the fourth (LVIII) he is a "sage." Mr. Berryman interprets the image this way: ". . . in poems the father-image (sage or seer) is generally on a high place and hypocrisy is the usual charge, suggesting that the original incredulous revulsion on learning that the parent who preaches on Sunday 'does it too' is still governing the poet's fantasies." [50] It may well be that such poems as the following represent masked rivalry against the father:

> There was a great cathedral.
> To solemn songs,
> A white procession
> Moved toward the altar.
> The chief man there
> Was erect, and bore himself proudly.
> Yet some could see him cringe,
> As in a place of danger,
> Throwing frightened glances into the air,
> A-start at threatening faces of the past. [BR LXIII]

Berryman might, in fact, have used this poem to strengthen his case, for *songs* and *chief man* connect with analogous images in Crane's story "The King's Favor"; there the biographer finds them symbolic disguises of self and father-image. [51] Freudian considerations enlighten achievements artistically more interesting in the love poetry. Here, however, there is another possible source for—or at last contributory to—Crane's animus against religious hypocrites in high places.

From one periodic sentence three pages long in Great-uncle

---

[50] Berryman, p. 314.   [51] *Ibid.*, p. 306.

Jesse Peck's tract, I select six clauses on the incapacities of
ministers to win mercy for unrepentent sinners:

Christian ministers can present to you the gracious message from
the lips of Jehovah; . . . they can uncover a life which you would
fain conceal from the world, from angels, and from God; . . . they
can lead you to Sinai trembling to its base under the frown of a
revealing Jehovah . . . they can uncover the pit of endless woe,
where wicked men and devils walk, and curse, and writhe forever-
more; . . . they can range the world of love and wrath for motives
to sway your purpose and bring you to the foot of the cross; they
can do all this, but they cannot yield, or repent, or believe for you.[52]

Now the effect of this passage is to glorify Christian ministers,
not to insist upon the need of repentence. I do not doubt that
Berryman is at least partly right: the "you" of these poems is
Crane's father. But "you" is also, partly, the whole tribe of
preaching Pecks. Phrases in this passage collate neatly with
these poems, which, turned against the ministers, "uncover a
life which you would fain conceal from the world." Where
Crane "stood upon a high place," Bishop Peck leads him to
Sinai. As for the rest, the Bishop with resplendent redundance
restates all the reasons Stephen Crane had to hate his doctrines and to turn them against the sinners who believed in his
damnation but assumed their own perfection in rhetoric as
arrogant as this.

One further poem, a manuscript at Columbia, completes this
group, implying rather than proclaiming the familial ties of
sin:

> If you would seek a friend among men
> Remember: they are crying their wares.

[52] *What Must I Do,* pp. 31–33.

If you would ask of heaven of men
Remember: they are crying their wares.
If you seek the welfare of men
Remember: they are crying their wares
If you would bestow a curse upon men
Remember: they are crying their wares
   Crying their wares
   Crying their wares
If you seek the intention of men
Remember:
Help them or hinder them
   As they cry their wares.   [Columbia MS]

This relates of course to *The Black Riders* xxxiii, in which "One I met upon the road" asked, "Show me of your wares" and all the traveler's wares proved to be sins. There God regarded him "with kinder eyes"; here that compassion is invoked as a code of human conduct. Technically the repetitions are too insistent and monotonous; Crane will later achieve a tense equilibrium between the harshness of his "tongue of wood" and the lyricism of balanced structure, incremental repetition, and refrain.

The Lord is unknowable. The theme in Crane's verse which I represent by this statement is expressed in a group of interesting poems which differ surprisingly in technique and in content. It is stated outright in *The Black Riders,* lix: "Walking the sky, / A man in strange black garb / Encountered a radiant form," but when he bowed to do it reverence, "the Spirit knew him not." More complex is "In the night" (WK xviii), first published in the *Chap-book* for March, 1896. Like many of the poems in *War is Kind,* this one differs from most of those in *The Black Riders* in its stanzaic organization and the use of a refrain. The poem is cyclical, these opening lines being repeated at the end:

> In the night
> Grey heavy clouds muffled the valleys
> And the peaks looked toward God alone.

The thrice-stated refrain consists of their prayers which, with incremental repetition, beg "that we may run swiftly across the world / To huddle in worship at Thy feet"; implore "Give voice to us, we pray, O Lord, / That we may sing Thy goodness to the sun"; and affirm "We bow to Thy wisdom, O Lord— / Humble, idle, futile peaks." The central stanza contrasts to the imperturbable humility of the peaks the daylit bustle of humanity:

> In the morning
> A noise of men at work came the clear blue miles
> And the little black cities were apparent.

But at the end it is night again and "Grey heavy clouds muffle the valleys." Man is enshrouded in darkness, and the mountains, with the wisdom of humble resignation, "looked toward God alone." We are not told that they see Him.

The contrast between the humble serenity of the natural world and the egotistic striving of man for knowledge and personal salvation is made again in two other poems from *War is Kind.* Amy Lowell cited these, apparently on technical grounds, as "Crane's high-water mark in poetry." With respect to the first (WK XIV) she noted "the vigorous handling of colour in the first two lines" and "the noise and tremor whirling

into one stupendous shout." "He had got beyond the stage of
mere expression to where he can . . . make a thing of
beauty." [53] The "thing of beauty" is in this case a Whitman-
like iteration of the purposelessness, the futile noises, of human striving.

> A slant of sun on dull brown walls,
> A forgotten sky of bashful blue.

> Toward God a mighty hymn,
> A song of collisions and cries,
> Rumbling wheels, hoof-beats, bells,
> Welcomes, farewells, love-calls, final moans,
> Voices of joy, idiocy, warning, despair,
> The unknown appeals of brutes,
> The chanting of flowers,
> The screams of cut trees,
> The senseless babble of hens and wise men—
> A cluttered incoherency that says at the stars:
> "O God, save us!"   [WK xiv]

As first published in the *Philistine* for December, 1895, the
last line read "O, God save us!" In any case the plea is directed
not, as the wise men think, "Toward God," but "at the stars."
These, fixed in their orbits, regard the "cluttered incoherency"
without concern. Part of the "senseless babble" is man's own
din, of which this later three-line bit, not included in *Collected
Poems*, is reminiscent:

> Rumbling, buzzing, turning, whirling Wheels,
> Dizzy Wheels!
> Wheels! [54]

[53] Introduction to Crane, *Work*, VI, xxiv.
[54] *Philistine*, VIII (December, 1898), front cover; reprinted by D. H.

But the rest of the babble is the cries of brutes and flowers.
"The screams of cut trees": Nature crying against man's abuse.

In poem xxv of *War is Kind* there is a synaesthetic evocation of natural beauty, regarded as praise of God and proof of His existence. The technique resembles the impressionism and colorfulness of "A slant of sun."

> Each small gleam was a voice,
> A lantern voice—
> In little songs of carmine, violet, green, gold.
> A chorus of colours came over the water;
>
> . . . .
>
> Small glowing pebbles
> Thrown on the dark plane of evening
> Sing good ballads of God
> And eternity, with soul's rest.
> Little priests, little holy fathers,
> None can doubt the truth of your hymning,
> When the marvellous chorus comes over the water,
> Songs of carmine, violet, green, gold.

The point of course is that even this "marvellous chorus" fails to appease man's doubt. In contrast to this sacramentalizing of Nature, Crane elsewhere regards it as a force which "at fateful time" reveals "grim hatred" for man, as we shall see.

Crane's most successful poem on the inscrutability of God is only five lines long, a hitherto unpublished poetic cryptogram on the problem of evil. Nowhere in his published verse did Crane achieve such evocative compression:

> The patent of a lord
> And the bangle of a bandit

Dickason in "Stephen Crane and the *Philistine*," *American Literature*, XV (November, 1943), 283.

        Make argument
        Which God solves
        Only after lighting more candles.   [Columbia MS]

The slightness of dimension is deceptive, as an attempt at paraphrase makes clear. The first three lines are plain enough;
the reality of privilege and plunder raises the question of evil,
for how can such things be if God is good? But what is meant
by the answer implied to the argument "Which God solves /
Only after lighting more candles"? We must first note that the
argument is solved by God, not man; but what signify the
candles He lights? In one sense they signify both light and
enlightenment: God makes light and is the source of our
knowledge. Mere candles then are an ironic comment on how
little light omniscient God, creator of suns and stars, has thus
far given us. But God Himself may be baffled for want of light.
On the other hand, candles are lit for the souls of the dead;
that is to say, God will solve the argument for us only after
death, when He will enlighten our immortal souls on such
points of Divine Truth as lie beyond human sight. The candles
then indicate that more faith than we have now is needed to
"solve" the problem. But with more faith the problem is not
really solved, it simply ceases to exist. The "argument" begins
when man has the temerity to question the Divine Will as it
appears in the world about him. This, to paraphrase Crane's
father on the Fall, is where sin begins. In this poem Crane has
come a long way from his blatant rebuttals in *The Black
Riders* to Great-uncle Jesse's damnation tract. A more absolute
economy of diction, based on an aesthetic of poetry as the
spoken language rather than the sung, would be perhaps impossible to imagine.

6

Crane's personal Redeemer is, as we have seen, a private deity, his own sanctification of an ideal compassion, an ideal love, which he found embodied in neither the world of natural forces man inhabits nor in the world of social forces man creates. As I have intimated throughout this chapter, Crane did, in one important poem, eventually achieve a resolution of the almost unbearable tensions which give his best poems and stories their validity and power. Since that resolution involves not only the war between his mother's and his father's gods, but all of his major themes, I must postpone analysis of "The Blue Battalions" until these other contributory matters have been explored.

There remains to be examined here a group of poems in which the Blustering God wears as his mask the visible forms of Nature. His wrath and rod are our hostile environment; part of our weakness is our illusion that Nature, because occasionally beautiful, has any care for us in the vistas we admire:

> To the maiden
> The sea was a blue meadow,
> Alive with little froth-people
> Singing.
>
> To the sailor, wrecked,
> The sea was dead grey walls
> Superlative in vacancy,
> Upon which nevertheless at fateful time
> Was written
> The grim hatred of nature.   [WK III]

Thus, a year and a half before he watched the snarling waves from an open boat. That experience did not alter his convictions about man's relation to nature; it simply confirmed them. After that ride in the open boat, though, he was to dramatize the hatred of nature in another poem far more subtle and profound than this one, a poem on the coldness of God. The poem quoted above is titled "The Sea—Point of View" in a holograph list of magazine acceptances of his verse. The first point of view, that Nature is beautiful and, implicitly, benificent, Crane attributes to a sensibility not only feminine but virginal: to one inexperienced in what, as the next chapter will show us, was for him the exquisite sin and supreme source of terror in life. Only those innocent of the mysterious terror of sin can be so innocent as not to know the terror of being abhorred by the elements in which we live.

Once, in *The Black Riders*, Crane himself had been almost as innocent as that about his favorite emblem of Nature, the sea:

> The ocean said to me once,
> "Look!
> Yonder on the shore
> Is a woman, weeping. . . .
> Go you and tell her this—
> Her lover I have laid
> In cool green hall.
> There is wealth of golden sand
> And pillars, coral-red:
> Two white fish stand guard at his bier.
>
> . . . .
>
> . . . the king of the seas

Weeps too, old, helpless man.
The bustling fates
Heap his hands with corpses
Until he stands like a child
With surplus of toys."   [BR xxxviii]

Copyright to the volume in which these sentiments appeared was applied for on January 14, 1895. Six weeks later, the author was in Eddyville, Dawson County, Nebraska—far from the ocean, yet learning something of Nature that would never again let him pity the sea as an unwilling slave of the fates, nor let him think that Nature might pity him. Crane describes the oncome of disaster in "Nebraska's Bitter Fight for Life," one of the best of his uncollected sketches:

Then from the southern horizon came the scream of a wind hot as an oven's fury. Its valor was great in the presence of the sun. . . . From day to day, it raged like a pestilence. The leaves of the corn and of the trees turned yellow and sapless like leather. For a time they stood the blasts in the agony of a futile resistance. The farmers, helpless, with no weapon against this terrible and inscrutable wrath of nature, were spectators at the strangling of their hopes, their ambitions, all that they could look to from their labor. It was as if upon the massive altar of the earth, their homes and their families were being offered in sacrifice to the wrath of some blind and pitiless deity.[55]

This is a face of Nature unknown to Emerson, undescribed in Bishop Peck's encomia of the bounteous blessings with which God has furnished the habitations of mankind. We realize with a start that this sketch is datelined February 22: Crane has witnessed not this withering heat but the blizzards of half year later. His imagination has endowed other persons' de-

---

[55] Philadelphia *Press,* February 24, 1895, part III, p. 25.

scriptions of the summer's blight with these forceful metaphors of futile suffering and ritual sacrifice.

Nature's malignity and omnipotence are accentuated in
Crane's work by the gnatlike stature of man. The world has
no need for man, and can readily dispense with his strivings:

> A man said to the universe:
> "Sir, I exist!"
> "However," replied the universe,
> "The fact has not created in me
> A sense of obligation."   [WK xxi]

The individual's disproportionate sense of his own magnitude
is a constant source of Crane's irony. Thus, in *George's Mother*
(written in 1893–94), when the hero perceived "that the earth
was not grateful to him for his presence upon it," he relished
"the delicious revenge of a partial self-destruction. The universe would regret its position when it saw him drunk." [56] In
"The Open Boat" we find the same irony as in the last poem,
but the dialogue device is reversed. Now Nature does not
acknowledge the tiny man's existence with so much as a reply:

> When it occurs to a man that nature does not regard him as
> important, and that she feels she would not maim the universe by
> disposing of him, he at first wishes to throw bricks at the temple,
> and he hates deeply the fact that there are no bricks and no temples.
> Any visible expression of nature would be pelleted with his jeers.
> Then if there be no tangible thing to hoot, he feels, perhaps, the
> desire to confront a personification and indulge in pleas, bowed
> to one knee, and with hands supplicant, saying, "Yes, but I love
> myself."
> A high cold star on a winter's night is the word he feels that
> she says to him. Thereafter he knows the pathos of his situation.[57]

[56] Crane, *Work*, X, 48–49.   [57] *Ibid.*, XII, 51.

Crane has reversed the usual techniques of prose and verse, using personification and dialogue in his poem and elaborating a cluster of symbols in the story. Philosophically the selections are identical, and the implications of such a world-view is the terrible aloneness with which Crane's puny protagonists must face their fates.

7

Where in "The Open Boat" the unconcern of the high cold star revealed the pathos of man's situation, in the last poem we are to read on this theme the destiny of man making his little struggles against the hostility of the universe is heightened instead to tragedy. This poem, "A man adrift on a slim spar," was written before *War is Kind* appeared,[58] yet Crane never published it; first printed posthumously in the *Bookman* (1929), it was appended to the 1930 edition of *Collected Poems.*

"A man adrift" resembles in theme the bitter poems with which this chapter began. But unlike those "Godless" poems, and unlike the poems immediately preceding in which the ocean or the universe reveals its grim hatred in abstract terms, this one reflects Crane's mature experience rather than exclusively his early religious training. Yet personal as is the experience, the poem itself is impersonal, objective, and detached in a way impossible to the younger Crane of *The Black Riders.*

[58] The aforementioned list of magazine acceptances includes ten poems from *War is Kind;* the eleventh is "The Blue Battalions," not yet published when the list was made (it appeared in *Philistine,* III [June, 1898], 9–10). Twelfth is "A man afloat [*sic*] on a slim spar."

Writing of *The Red Badge of Courage,* a work artistically more mature than most of the contemporaneous poems in *The Black Riders,* Crane observed, "Preaching is fatal to art in literature. I try to give readers a slice out of life, and if there is any moral or lesson in it, I do not try to point it out, I let the reader find it for himself. . . . As Emerson said, 'There should be a long logic beneath the story, but it should be kept carefully out of sight.' " [59] The earlier poems allow some justice to Harriet Monroe's complaint that Crane was "tempted to orate, to become cosmic and important, to utter large truths in chanting tones." [60] But "A man adrift" follows the precepts just stated, and they bring Crane to a remarkable success of indirection. In this poem Crane does not need to raise his voice, for "the incessant raise and swing of the sea" is terrifying.

Each poem thus far examined has told a story. In this one there is a narrative implied—implied because nothing of the tale is actually stated. Instead we have a succession of images, most of them visual, of how the drowning man sees his own situation:

> A man adrift on a slim spar
> A horizon smaller than the rim of a bottle
> Tented waves rearing dark lashy points
> The near whine of froth in circles.
> God is cold.

This creation of a point of view identical to that of the suffering character parallels the achievement of "The Open Boat." After another stanza of like impressions, in which "growl after

[59] Stallman, *Omnibus,* p. 673.
[60] "Stephen Crane," *Poetry,* XIV (June, 1919), 149.

growl of crest" suggests the malign animism of the sea, there is a shift from the eyes of the victim to those of an objective observer. His nine-line interpolation remarks some implications of the scene:

> The seas are in the hollow of The Hand;
> Oceans may be turned to a spray
> Raining down through the stars
> Because of a gesture of pity toward a babe.
> Oceans may become grey ashes,
> Die with a long moan and a roar
> Amid the tumult of the fishes
> And the cries of the ships
> Because The Hand beckons the mice.

Without interruption the point of view shifts again to the man on the spar; we see his dying moment through his eyes:

> A horizon smaller than a doomed assassin's cap,
> Inky, surging tumults
> A reeling, drunken sky and no sky
> A pale hand sliding from a polished spar.
>   God is cold.

The final stanza returns to the observer, who like the survivors in "The Open Boat," can be an "interpreter":

> The puff of a coat imprisoning air;
> A face kissing the water-death
> A weary slow sway of a lost hand
> And the sea, the moving sea, the sea.
>   God is cold.

This poem is Crane's most complete denial of God—not only of the God of vengeance, but, worse, of the God of mercy. What the observer interprets is a truth of terrible simplicity;

Nature endures—the triple iteration of that last line *makes* it endure—and the God who, Christian doctrine assures us, is concerned with every sparrow's fall, takes not the slightest heed of "A face kissing the water-death," not even to judge his soul. The man is drowned; the sea goes on forever. The refrain had been until now the despairing lament of the dying man betrayed by his God; but the final "God is cold" is a judgment made by another who survives to interpret his death to the living.[61]

But the poem demands closer attention. For all its grim bravura and the memorableness of such lines as "A horizon smaller than a doomed assassin's cap," is it really a coherent whole? What difficulties the poem presents may be dispelled by an explicatory paraphrase.

The observer interpolates two statements, parallel in structure, conditional in mood,[62] on the possibilities of merciful action open to God if He would but follow them. God holds all creation in His hand; He has the power to transform "Inky, surging tumults" of this menacing ocean into the gentleness of

[61] A manuscript worksheet in the Columbia collection shows that Crane had originally introduced the refrain midway in the observer's first passage (after line 14, which reads in the MS, "By the gesture of pity toward a child."). But "God is cold" is excised, as are "By the" and "child," for which are substituted the final version of the line. That Crane was aware of the significance of having the refrain first spoken by the observer *at the end* is apparent from his rejected overstatement of the irony: in MS the refrain is repeated, then the second "God is cold' is crossed out.

[62] The Columbia MS shows a revision of the two verbs from "Oceans are" to "may be" (line 12) and "The seas turn to" to "Oceans may become" (line 15), making both passages conditional and parallel in structure.

spring rain, were he pitiful. (This accurate allusion to the
water cycle is one of the few images Crane derived from science.) God in His omnipotence could blast the sea to ashes,
bringing consternation to the fishes and the ships (how they
come alive in that line!), if He should care to save even the
mice aboard them.

But, to the man adrift on the slim spar, the horizon is
"smaller than a doomed assassin's cap," doomed [63] because he
is being executed through God's nonintervention just as surely
as though he were a murderer, condemned, unworthy of
mercy. The irony of the epithet "assassin" is turned against
God too, for He in effect murders the man by refusing to save
him, by considering him less worthy of sustenance than the
mice. This term "assassin," which Crane, like Emily Dickinson,
was curiously given to using in nonpolitical contexts,[64] combines in portmanteau fashion the word *sin* with the signification of murder or killing. So the drowning man may be an
assassin after all, since natural depravity, as first inherited by
Cain and by him passed on, led to the murder of a brother.
"Assassin" further suggests the desperation of the victim (the
term derives from *hashish,* smoked in the Orient by hired mur-
derers to induce frenzy); and the cap of a doomed assassin
is a powerful image of what the drowning man sees as the

[63] "Doomed' was a fortunate afterthought. In the MS the phrase originally read "an assassin's cap." (The only other variant from the published text is in line 6, where "of" is written twice and scored out after
"The incessant raise.")

[64] See BR xxvii, lvi; also Hoffman, "Stephen Crane's New Jersey
Ghosts," *Proceedings of the New Jersey Historical Society,* LXXI (October, 1953), 242.

waves close over his head. In the first stanza the waves were "tented," which ironically suggests both land and sleep. Now the tent has shrunk to a fez or stocking cap, contracting the round horizon to the funneled darkness of a diminishing sky no larger, at its widest diameter, than his own headband.

The "lashy dark points" come together above him and break as he surfaces into "A reeling drunken sky," then sinks: "and no sky." He loses his hold on the spar, and nothing remains but the sea. "A weary slow sway of a lost hand" is the drifting of both the hand that has lost its grip and of the man himself— sailors are "hands"—whose soul is lost. The "slim spar" that fails him is the debris of the wreck from which he has been cast adrift: the "ship of the world" which God had abandoned in *The Black Riders* (vi). The slim spar also evokes the correlated images in "The Open Boat," the "thin little oar" of Billy Higgins, the oiler who dies, which "seemed ready to snap"; and "The breaking of a pencil's point" which expresses the correspondent's unconcern with the deaths of others before his initiation into the fellowship of those who do not know the color of the sky.[65]

"There is no probation beyond the cold river." Perhaps Stephen Crane remembered this sentence from the tract that thundered over his boyhood.[66] The coldness of the waters has become the coldness of God, and all that can matter to man is the integrity with which he meets the perils in life and the death from which an uncaring Deity will not save him.

[65] The linkage of these images was first remarked by Stallman in *Omnibus*, p. 419.
[66] J. T. Peck, *What Must I Do?*, p. 25.

Four ∽ *LOVE ON EARTH*

Destined to suffer in an indifferent or hostile universe, exiled by sin from the fellowship of the innocent, what solace for the individual can Crane's dark fatalism propose? Recognizing that all sinful mankind is fallen too, he sees the love of another sinful creature as an ideal to be affirmed despite the coldness of God. In the blasted wilderness of our life we may yet find love. But this human love, this cleaving of two sinners in "a reptile-swarming place," is for Crane determined by somewhat unusual circumstances and choices, and it imposes upon the lover an ideal code not only of devotion but of loyalty. This code is not easy to live up to, for lover and beloved alike are menaced by their own fallen, fallible natures. This human love, so passionately desired, so difficult to live, will in the end prove a redemptory principle in Crane's moral universe. But Stephen Crane habitually sought as ministering spirits to his soul's redemption women who seemed to others the least likely consorts to beatitude the world could offer him.

John Berryman has a theory about the persistence of Crane's amatory adventures, which had, to be sure, some rather outlandish patterns. Crane was again and again attracted to older women, usually married, often of questionable reputation—a

Canadian mother of seven, an ex-actress, another man's mistress, two chorus girls, a streetwalker, a madame. He was in fact obsessive in his attention to prostitutes, both in life and in his writings. The remarkable point of this interest is his desire to *rescue* them. Mr. Berryman's theory attempts to explain all this, and more: it tells us, too, why he was "obliged to spend his life imagining and seeking war," and tries to show us where Crane's greatness as an artist came from; yet Berryman is careful to make the distinction that for greatness itself "no explanation is available." [1] But the poems Crane wrote of love, his biographer's theory, and its application to this verse must wait until we have set down some necessary biographical information.

Robert H. Davis, a journalist who knew Crane, tells a story in his introduction to Volume II of Crane's *Work*—some thirty years after the event—of their having walked together on the Bowery one night when Crane, approached by a streetwalker, "placed his left hand upon his heart, removed his hat, and made a most gallant bow . . . [an] exquisite gesture of chivalry." To her query, "Can you show me anything?" Crane replied, "Yes, I can show you the way out, but if you prefer to remain——." [2] As Berryman remarks, "the way out" in *Maggie* is death; [3] but death is not the only way.

"If it were necessary to avow a marriage to save a girl who is not a prostitute from being arrested as a prostitute, it must be done, although the man suffer eternally," Crane wrote in a hitherto unreported account of his appearance in a New York police court on behalf of a woman arrested for soliciting. On

---

[1] Berryman, p. 298.   [2] *Work*, II, xvii–xix.   [3] Berryman, p. 304.

September 16, 1896, having arranged to write "a series of studies of life in New York" for the *Journal,* Crane spent the day
at the court in Jefferson market; but, the editor's introduction
to his story continues, "The novelist felt. . . . He must know
more of that throng of unfortunates; he must study the police
court victims in their haunts." [4] In this quest he spent the evening in "a Broadway resort" with two "chorus girls" and "a
woman of the streets," looking for trouble, as it were. The girl
whose arrest Crane protested was one Dora Clark, companion
of the woman whose husband he had claimed to be.[5] Dora
Clark, or, to use her real name, Ruby Young, was being cruelly
framed by the police: Crane had been present at the alleged
solicitation, and knew it to be a lie. Little else though he knew
about "Dora Clark," he must take the stand in her behalf.
Crane wrote down his reasons scrupulously for the newspaper
public: were he bound to discretion by such hostages as a job
with a business firm, or a wife, or a titled fiancée, he might not
have the courage to go through with her defense. But none
of these possibly extenuating circumstances at present protects
him from his own conscience, and so he must become "a re-
luctant laggard witness."

[4] "Adventures of a Novelist," New York *Journal,* September 26, 1896,
unpaged clipping in the Columbia collection.

[5] The received account of this affair, as Berryman retells it, goes
that a plainclothesman arrested both women but "at the station let one
of the girls go after she passed into hysterics" (p. 145). From Crane's
article just cited we learn that while the released girl did become
hysterical at headquarters, on the street she had nimbly told the officer
that Crane was her husband. This he could not bring himself to deny;
the officer, reporting the arrest, "did not mention at this time the arrest
and release of the chorus girl."

His first act, then, in defense of the two women was to pretend to be married to one of them—"it must be done, although the man suffer eternally." For his temerity, in testifying in her defense, the New York police force hounded Crane out of the city. He never lived in New York again.

A few years later there is another woman in Crane's life whose status as a prostitute is not even as equivocal as that of Dora Clark or her friend. Once again, he pretended to marry her.

> Thou art my love,
> And thou art the ashes of other men's love,
> And I bury my face in these ashes,
> And I love them—
> Woe is me. [Intrigue 1]

Crane seems in this poem, as in the earlier news story, masochistically to invite suffering. Yet his life with Cora Howarth Taylor Stewart Crane, later McNeill, brought him as close to happiness as he ever came. As though to oblige the Crane biographer's desire for a symbolic nexus of his psychic compulsions, Cora, who actually did marry two husbands before Crane and one more after his death, never solemnized her vows, as the saying goes, with the one man who made her happy.[6] The poems in "Intrigue," however, anticipate no satisfactions; the mood is defeated, the tone nostalgic and sentimental. "In loving me once / Thou gave me an eternal privilege / For I can think of thee," the final poem concludes.

---

[6] Miss Lillian Gilkes, now writing a biography of Cora Crane, informs me that she has searched without success in court and church records of Jacksonville, Florida, and London for the one document missing among the legal evidences of Cora's many marriages.

Through most of "Intrigue" one must agree with Thomas Beer
that "his erotic verse drops into the banal." [7] It is indeed surprising to find such a clutter of "thee's" and "thou's," such
absurdly sentimental outbursts as "I weep and I gnash, / And
I love the little shoe, / The little, little shoe," coming so late
in his career—after *The Black Riders* and at least half of the
poems in *War is Kind*.[8] Amy Lowell concluded that Crane "is
losing his grip . . . poetry is sliding from him . . . it had
been no more with him than a breath of adolescence." [9]

For all that, though, there are occasional moments of power
in "Intrigue":

> I thought of the thunder that lived in my head,
> And I wished to be an ogre,
> And hale and haul my beloved to a castle,
> And there use the happy cruel one cruelly,
> And make her mourn with my mourning.   [iv]

Unlike most of the poem, these lines succeed in finding images
that dramatize the violent emotions felt; elsewhere the tone is
soliloquy or self-pitying rumination. Yet the sado-masochism
of this successful passage suggests that the whole of "Intrigue"
may be of more interest to the investigator of Crane's psyche
than to the analyst of his poetic achievement.

Let us for a moment pursue the psychological inquiry—or
rather, follow Mr. Berryman while he pursues it. Perhaps to
assume that Crane "seems to address" Cora in these poems

[7] Beer, p. 225.

[8] Crane sent "Intrigue" to his agent, Paul Reynolds, on October 20,
1898. Stallman, *Omnibus*, p. 683. By then the thirteen poems from *War
is Kind* which had periodical publication prior to the book had already
appeared. Williams and Starrett, *Stephen Crane: A Bibliography*, pp.
41–42.

[9] Introduction to Crane, *Work*, VI, xxviii.

where "love is a doom" is to oversimplify somewhat a psychological condition baffling in its complexity. Berryman, whose assumption on this particular point [10] I question, demonstrates elsewhere the compulsive repetition of circumstances in which Crane became involved—or deliberately involved himself—with women. For reasons which will in a moment become clear, I think "Intrigue" refers only incidentally to Cora.

Berryman's theory is this: he proposes that Crane fulfills with exactitude the four "conditions of love" described by Freud in his study of "A Special Type of Choice of Objects Made by Men" (1910).[11] The first condition, Freud observes, is "the need for an injured third party," that is to say the woman desired can be "only one in regard to whom another man has some right of possession, whether as husband, betrothed, or near friend." She must in the second place be "more or less sexually discredited"; her "fidelity and loyalty" must be open to "some doubt." This condition may be met "within a significant series" ranging from a flirtatious married woman to an actual prostitute. Third, "a high degree of compulsion . . . sincerity and intensity" characterize the lover, whose "passionate attachments of this kind are frequently repeated many times . . . each an exact replica of the others." External circumstances, "such as changes of residence and environment," may lead "to a long chain of such experiences." And finally, "The trait in this type of lover that is most astonishing to the observer is the desire they express to 'rescue' the beloved." [12]

What is one to make of this disturbing constellation? These

---

[10] Berryman, p. 151.
[11] *Collected Papers*, ed. by Ernest Jones, IV, 192–202.
[12] *Ibid.*, pp. 193–96.

peculiar conditions of choice, Freud avers, "have the same
source as the normal attitude in love." Being derived from "a
fixation of the infantile forms of tenderness for the mother,"
they "represent one of the forms in which this fixation expresses itself." It is evident, Freud says, that the injured third
party "is none other than the father himself." The second condition—sexual debasement of the woman—is said to result
from the child's discovery of his parents' sexual relations and
his consequent "cynical" identification of mother and harlot.
"In the light of this new knowledge he begins to desire the
mother herself and to hate the father anew for standing in
his way; he comes, as we say, under the sway of the Oedipus
complex." The compulsive repetition is explained because
"the pressing desire in the unconscious for some irreplaceable
thing often resolves itself into an endless series . . . [since]
the satisfaction longed for is . . . never found in any surrogate." [13]

The significance of the rescue element is more complex.
Freud takes this to be "an exceptionally felicitous 'rationaliza-
tion' of an unconscious motive":

. . . rescuing the mother acquires the significance of giving her a
child or making one for her—one like himself, of course. The departure from the original meaning of the idea of "saving life" is not
too great. . . . The mother gave him his own life and. . . . The
son shows his gratitude by wishing to have a son by his mother
that shall be like himself; in this rescue fantasy, that is, he identifies
himself completely with the father. All the instincts, the living, the
grateful, the sensual, the defiant, the self-assertive and independent
—all are gratified in the wish to be *the father of himself*. Even the

[13] *Ibid.,* pp. 196–99.

element of danger is not lost in the change of meaning; the experience of birth itself . . . is in fact the first of all dangers to life, as well as the prototype of all the later ones we fear.[14]

If this last intricate tangle of displaced identities and masked wish-fulfillments is at all present in Crane's work it surely remains latent, not manifest. Yet when Berryman has adduced Crane's attachment for, and wish to rescue—from plights sometimes imaginary—the betrothed Helen Trent (1891); Mrs. Lily Brandon Munroe (1894); the street girl reported by Davis, Mrs. Dora Watts Bowen, Dora Clark and her chorus girl friend, and a widowed actress named Amy Leslie (all in 1896), as well as Cora, whom he met late in that year, the probability is strong that the biographer is right in proposing Freud's essay as a "description and explanation of reality"[15] with respect to Crane's psychic make-up. Newly recovered writings by Crane in the Columbia University collection, as well as the readings I offer in the present chapter of his love poems, further incline me to feel that this is the likely case. Such conclusions can at best be only tentative, however, and it should be stated that my only concern with this psychological theory is to take whatever help may be available from it in the interpretation, first, of the poems of Crane's that are now before us, and second, of the sensibility which created them. The value of the Freudian theory is probably greater to Crane's biographer than to the critic of his verse; still, it would seem to explain certain recurrent patterns in both his actions and the images of his writings; it makes possible likely inferences as to the areas of experi-

[14] *Ibid.*, p. 201. [15] Berryman, p. xiii.

ence most available to his imagination; and it suggests the probable limits on some important choices of the materials and metaphors of his art. All this is merely inferential, however; even tentative conclusions must be wrung from the writings themselves.

Helpful as it may be, it is nonetheless inadvisable to rely exclusively on such a psychological approach, for its inherent emphasis upon the configurations of the individual psyche tends to isolate the investigation of an author's work from the cultural currents in terms of which his assumptions about life are also strongly conditioned. Brilliant as are his conjectural linkages of Crane's images, Mr. Berryman seems to me to be in some measure culpable in this respect. His study takes little account of a possibility raised by the foregoing chapter, namely, that Crane's mode of interpreting experience was deeply influenced by the religious doctrines which comprise the chief furniture of his cultural heritage. This I think to be true with respect to his poems on love. To the extent that emotion and metaphor from Crane's religious background control his work, it may be advisable to modify somewhat Berryman's predominantly Freudian interpretation of his writings.

Crane's love poems deal in greater particularity than does his fiction with the situations and feelings his "special type of choice of objects" imposed upon him. They are thus crucially revelatory of an important part of his sensibility, despite the fact that on the whole the imaginative world of his verse is a narrower one than that presented in his stories; in a later chapter we shall try to find the reasons for this limitation. The principal images of Crane's love poetry do not for the most part correspond to the governing metaphors of his prose. It would seem that he reserved certain phases of his experience for poetic treatment, and to deal with them he developed a cluster of imagery to some extent independent of that in the rest of his work.

Crane's main body of fictional metaphors has been eluci-dated by Mr. Berryman's Freudian exploration in the con-cluding chapter of his book. There he asserts that what is usually taken to be fear in Crane's work is actually "something else . . . the possibility of fatal intervention," which he char-acterizes as panic. Conjecturally, he traces this panic back to the primal situations for which all later expressions of panic in Crane are unconscious displacements. There are two such hy-pothesized situations: when twelve years old, Crane, riding his pony, had seen a white girl being stabbed by her Negro lover in the woods; and when he was very young—less than four—he had nightmares of black riders rising from the surf, a dream associated with a still earlier experience of being made by his mother to ride a white horse of which he was terrified.[16] The violence of the stabbing, Berryman suggests, is later gen-eralized under the aspect of war, while its erotic context is preserved in recurrent images of Negroes, knives or razors, which are further linked to Crane's father shaving and to barbers; a conjectured Swedish barber in Crane's home-town supplies a link to Swedes, Dutchmen, and Germans in his work, and the explanation for the name of Henry Fleming in *The Red Badge* and for the nationality of the ineluctable victim in "The Blue Hotel." The Civil War obsesses Crane, Berryman suggests, because it was "precisely *about the Ne-gro*." [17] But the Oedipal situation is a familial civil war in

[16] Berryman, pp. 306; 321, 9.   [17] *Ibid.,* p. 307.

which aggression is directed against surrogates for the father, who are characterized by tenor voices, chieftainship, or priestly rank. Aggression is also incipient in the striking namelessness of Crane's characters, a denial of patronym as well as a masking of identity. Berryman emphasizes Crane's alleged feelings of desertion following his father's early death. The chief image of aggression in Crane's work is the horse.

Images in the love poems are not as elaborately disguised or as intricately linked as the foregoing, nor are they drawn from so varied a range of experiences and associations. Love is characteristically associated with longing, despair, and violence, the latter sometimes manifested in metaphors of war or predation. The woman loved may be represented in synecdoche by her white arms, a maternal image which, when linked to erotic contexts, is accompanied by metaphors of cosmic catastrophe. She may be shown as sexually promiscuous, a feared aggressor; in this connection occur snakes, desert, sin and punishment. Further associations are loyalty and desertion, courage and cowardice. Ever recurrent is the rescue theme, sometimes in contexts involving war and horses.

The poetic effectiveness of these images we shall shortly examine, but we must first return to Stephen Crane's amatory adventures.

2

We have seen the third condition of Freud's hypothesis—compulsive repetition—to be conspicuously applicable to Crane. It would seem that this type of lover is predestined to be "busily seeking in continual change," as a greater poet of love than Crane described it. This would be especially true in Crane's case, since the kind of woman to whom he was drawn by his compulsion would, one expects, hardly be of a character to give such a man as he the satisfactions of lasting companionship. Thus in 1896 he turned with passionate intensity from one to another love "object"—there must have been more than the six we have listed—until at last, by the year's end, he met Cora Howarth Stewart in her bordello at Jacksonville.

A word must be said about Cora. At the time she was conducting her pleasure palace she had left her second husband, Captain Donald William Stewart, C.M.G., son of a former commander-in-chief of the British forces in India and younger brother of Major General Sir Norman Stewart, C.B., who was by 1901 to rise to his father's post. In the Columbia collection two letters of that year from Sir Norman to Cora reveal that she and Donald had never been divorced—he warns her not to see any of the large circle of old friends in London who know her "only as Mrs. Stewart,"—yet he hopes, while dissuading her from seeking an interview with Donald, to see her himself upon his return from India. Sir Norman seems to have taken Cora's part against his family, and likes her still, wishing her happiness in her new life as "Mrs." Crane—unaware, in India, of Crane's death a year earlier.

After the early death of her parents Cora was brought up by her grandfather, George Howarth, who had come to America from England sometime before 1833. After living briefly in Connecticut and New York he settled in Boston in 1837. His practice in restoring oil paintings flourished, and by

1860, five years before Cora's birth, he owned property worth $12,000.[18] Of her father, John Howarth, nothing is known save that he was born on Long Island and was a painter.[19] On her mother's side, a long letter from her Aunt Mary Holder informs her, she was a descendent of Christopher Holder, the Quaker leader who arrived in Boston in 1656.[20] Her maternal grandfather "was the oldest piano maker in New Jersey sent the first piano to San Francisco," and Aunt Mary herself had married E. G. B. Holder, "the popular composer." [21] From these artistic and musical forebears Cora inherited sensitivity and literary ambition, if not actual creative talent. (Her trials

[18] Nothing further seems known about Howarth; Cora, at Brede Place, put her name and address in a booklet he had written—*The Restoration of Oil Paintings,* published in 1858, the date of Jesse Peck's *What Must I Do to Be Saved?* The information as to his movements and properties, from the *Eighth Census, 1860, Mass.,* XXVII, 404, and *New England Business Directory* (1860), advt. p. 17, is given in a forthcoming *Directory of American Artists,* a publication of the New-York Historical Society. I am indebted to the kindness of Miss E. Marie Becker, Reference Librarian of the Society, for making it available to me in advance of publication.

[19] For information on John Howarth I thank Miss Lillian Gilkes.

[20] See Charles F. Holder, *The Holders of Holderness,* for biography of Christopher and genealogy of the Holder family, whose talented members included the naturalists, authors, and historians Joseph Bassett Holder (1824–88) and his son, Charles F. (1851–1915), biographer of Darwin and Agassiz. The latter's genealogy does not include Cora's maternal grandfather Charles (married Sophia Bunn) or her uncle E. G. B. Holder, perhaps because their descendants were not reached by, or failed to answer, his questionnaires. John Greenleaf Whittier was a relative of the Holder family. *The Holders,* p. 226.

[21] According to Trow's *New York City Directory* (1864), p. 416, Eldridge G. B. Holder sold pianos and lived at 188 Spring Street. In that year he married Cora's Aunt Mary, whose letter to Cora of July 29, 1897 is numbered 133 in Columbia's Stephen Crane Collection.

at fiction are conventional and stilted; after Stephen's death her attempt to remain in England as a professional writer was unsuccessful despite efforts of his friends to place her work.)

What is significant here is that in Cora Howarth, Stephen Crane met a woman who seemed made for him. She combined with the peculiar qualifications required for his psychological needs deep sympathy for his literary aims and his ideals of conduct. She, too, was in revolt against a narrow religious upbringing, and, unlike another intelligent young woman whom we have yet to discuss, when Crane presented to her the glaring unorthodoxy of his true opinions about life, she did not hastily put an end to their discourse. To Cora, he must have seemed the fulfillment of all she had dreamed and sought in her curious career of libertinism self-consciously daring. Her manuscript books show her to have been bohemian, sentimental, given to philosophizing on love and unhappiness; there was a vein in her that found its magnet in both the stoicism and the sentimentality of a twenty-five-year-old newspaper correspondent who made his way one night to her bordello in Jacksonville. At about the time of their meeting, she mused in her notebook:

When we come to think about it seriously it is rather absurd for us to expect to have uninterrupted stretches of happiness. Happiness falls to our share in separate detached bits; and those of us who are wise, content ourselves with these broken fragments——

It was doubtless in consonance to sentiments like these that Stephen wrote, on November 4, 1896,

To C. E. S.

Brevity is an element that enters importantly into all pleasures of life, and this is what makes pleasure sad; and so there is no pleasure but only sadness.

Stephen Crane.[22]

In her daring refusal even to pretend to renounce the flesh and in her consequent sense of love as a doom, again she met a kindred soul in Stephen Crane. He might indeed have agreed with this:

There is no spirit of Evil—we are betrayed by our passions & the chief of these passions is love. It is the great Nemesis that stalks through the world, haunting all men, & goading some to great wrong.[23]

This Nemesis had goaded her to break completely with her respectably artistic family, and with her religion. It is a strange fruit of Crane's Methodist heritage that he should have passed as married to a woman of Roman Catholic faith.[24] Despite Cora's past—and the lurid career as directress of

[22] Letter 55 in the Columbia Stephen Crane Collection.

[23] Cora Crane's small red MS book in the Columbia collection, pages unnumbered; these excerpts appear on the 34th and 40th pages. I date these entries at about the time she met Stephen because of the similarities discussed here and below between them and writings of his; and on the 42d page, after the entry "To the evil all things are suggestive," she signs herself still as "C.S." [Cora Stewart].

[24] It is curious too that the descendant of some of the most prominent Quakers in America should have been, or become, a Catholic. We learn of this possibility of her persuasion in a frank letter to her from Stephen's brother William, who had sent his unruly daughter Helen to the couple in England, hoping that Cora's good influence would have an effect upon the adolescent girl. (The Cranes had no idea that Stephen and Cora were not legally married, nor did they know anything of her scandalous past. And indeed, Cora discharged this difficult responsibility with credit.) William writes that he has "no objections to your bringing influence to bear upon Helen to make her a Catholic. Of course, it would be unfortunate to make a bigot of her," this open-minded Methodist goes

still another Florida bordello and wife of the proprietor of a Jacksonville saloon, a murderer, that was to be hers after Stephen's death—she was a truly loving "wife" to him. And as a hostess she was able to meet his literary friends—Conrad, Wells, Frederic, James, Ford—on compatible grounds. But above all her merits as Stephen Crane's presumptive wife were her tender love for him and the similarity of their temperaments. The latter is partly due to their both rebelling against the same, or similar, codes of life. Nothing is known of the Howarth family's religion, but whatever it was, it gave Cora iconoclasms in common with Stephen Crane, as this entry in her manuscript book attests:

> Remember the shriek of the village choir—
> Before Jehovah's awful throne
> Ye nations bow-wow-wow with sacred joy—[25]

That they should have lived "in sin" seems foreordained from Crane's earliest poems of love (addressed in imagination to Helen Trent) and others in which love is damnation. These we will shortly examine, but first there are conclusions about "Intrigue" to which we are almost ready to come.

To say that Cora is the love addressed in these bad poems is, I think, to commit a biographical fallacy. As we have seen, Crane met her at the end of a year of blasted amatory and erotic adventures; the women he tried to "rescue" either took

---

on, "But I do not think there is any danger of that . . ." Reflecting in extreme form the liberality of Jesse Peck on this point, and the tolerance of his and Stephen's father, William concludes, "My own notion is that true religion is the essential and that the form, under which one worships, is largely a matter of circumstance." Letter 114, August 14, 1899, in the Columbia Stephen Crane Collection.

[25] Cora Crane's red MS book, 27th page, in the Columbia collection.

advantage of him, "borrowing" large sums of money (Dora Watts, Amy Leslie), or involved him in public scandal (Dora Clark and his assumptive "wife" in the Bowery). This "highly compulsive series" of unsuccessful rescues had followed his rejection by a young woman who, unlike any of these, fulfilled none of the "conditions of love" set forth by Freud.

Nellie Crouse, whom he had met but once and to whom he wrote seven letters from December 31, 1895, through March 18, 1896, was certainly not "sexually discredited." A belle of good family, she soon afterward married a man she had met at a Harvard prom. There was nothing Crane could rescue her from, except conformity to the social norm. As the editors of his *Love Letters* remark, Crane himself "was moved in the name of the ideal to revolt desperately against the smothering conventionalities of moralism and respectability by which the world evaded the ideal." [26] If there was a Platonist incipient in this quondam lover of harlots, he made his emergence here in self-revealing letters which could only have frightened the attractive and upright young girl who knew not the depths out of which he wrote to her. His sixth letter takes her to task for something written in admiration of "the man of fashion":

Time after time, I have seen the social lion turn to a lamb and fail—fail at precisely the moment when men should not fail. . . .

I swear by the real aristocrat. The man whose forefathers were men of courage, sympathy and wisdom, is usually one who will stand the strain whatever it may be. . . .

[26] *Love Letters,* p. 22.

He goes on to speak of Tolstoy, whose aim is, "I suppose—
I believe—to make himself good." [27] But in her next letter
Nellie Crouse rejected Crane.

His reply, a letter begun in New York on March 1, 1896,
and finished in Washington on March 18, ends, ". . . by this
time I should have recovered enough to be able to write you
a sane letter but I cannot—my pen is dead. I am simply a man
struggling with a life that is no more than a mouthful of dust
to him." [28]

Edwin Cady and Lester Wells, who edited these *Love Letters,* do not take very seriously Crane's "ultimate posture of
permanent despair." They contrast to this three letters to
other friends written at about this time: one to Lily Brandon
Munroe (February 19); another to Viola Allen, an acquaintance of his preparatory school days; and a third to his friend
Willis Hawkins, asking forgiveness for some slight because
"It was a woman! Don't you see?" [29] Writing to "Dear L.B."
(he pointedly refuses to recognize the "M." of her marriage
name), Crane invokes the "little creed of art" which "I developed alone" and "Later . . . discovered that my creed was
identical with the one of Howells and Garland"—surely the
one true thing left him that neither fickleness nor misfortune
could destroy. "The letter to Viola Allen . . . gaily recall-
ing pre-school lights-o'-love is hardly a 'flagons of despair'

[27] *Ibid.,* pp. 48–50.
[28] *Ibid.,* p. 54.
[29] *Ibid.,* pp. 53, 11, 20–21. Letter to Lily Brandon Munroe is in Schoberlin's introduction to *Sullivan County Sketches,* p. 19, and *Omnibus,*
p. 648; to Viola Allen, in *Love Letters,* p. 11; to Hawkins, in *Omnibus,*
p. 649.

screed," write Cady and Wells; [30] but this exaltation of his
own youthful innocence and idealism—if it is indeed gay—
may belie a turmoil in his heart: "Men usually refuse to recognize their school-boy dreams. They blush. I dont. The emotion itself was probably higher, finer, than anything of my
after-life . . ." [31] Two weeks earlier he had begun the last
letter to Nellie Crouse. Perhaps it was on his desk as he wrote
Viola Allen. He had got as far in it as this:

If there is a joy of living I cant find it. The future? The future is
blue with obligations—new trials—conflicts. It was a rare old wine
the gods brewed *for mortals.* Flagons of despair—[32]

Internal evidence in these letters aside, a manuscript in the
Columbia collection suggests that Crane did not take lightly
his dismissal by Nellie Crouse:

> Oh, a rare old wine ye brewed for me
> Flagons of despair
> A deep deep drink of this wine of life
> Flagons of despair.
>   Dreams of riot and blood and screams
>   The rolling white eyes of dying men
>   The terrible heedless courage of babes

Like his last letter to her, the poem is unfinished, unformed;
indeed, we scarcely know what to make of the last three lines,
in which jagged nightmare breaks the despondent lyrical
mood of the first four. What is this battlefield carnage doing in a poem that begins with a phrase in his letter to the
girl who has cast him aside? This is a question we shall come
to.

[30] *Love Letters,* p. 53.   [31] *Ibid.,* p. 11.   [32] *Ibid.,* p. 54.

Now, however, we must pause to note something else. Dismissed by this "good" girl, to whom he had bared his innermost convictions and ideals, within weeks his misadventures with women disreputable and professional begin. Crane must have staked much on Nellie Crouse—as Cady and Wells have shown, he waged a clever and persistent campaign by mail to win her.[33] It is as though she had seemed to him the last chance he would have of deserving the love—or desiring it— of a woman unfallen, not to be rescued, not already possessed. From here on this strange constellation of compulsions obsesses him, and until he lives with Cora all of his affairs, like the one on which he staked so much, are unfulfilled. By the time he met Cora—perhaps even two years later (the date of "Intrigue"), before they had been together in Greece or settled in England—love must have seemed to him by its very nature

> A stupid, simpering, eyeless bungler,
> Breaking the hearts of brave people
> As the snivelling idiot-boy cracks his bowl,   [Intrigue ix]

and all his love-affairs foredoomed bitterness. The self-pity, sentimentality, and bathos of much of "Intrigue" reflects this mood.

What flaws this long poem beyond repair is a fundamental inadequacy of sensibility—an inadequacy, that is, in creating and sustaining a poetic strategy by which to express the emotions felt. The few parts of "Intrigue" which commend themselves to us on grounds other than psychological do so because of a violence of metaphor appropriate to the emotion ex-

[33] *Ibid.*, pp. 17–20.

pressed; yet this violence is controlled by that much of the passion which in the experience described was unfulfilled. That this emotion is usually sadistic or self-destructive is hardly relevant to the poetic success of such passages as "I thought of the thunders that lived in my head." But these thunders do not often escape in "Intrigue"; their obverse, which often does, is a whimpering longing for defeat, the treasuring of memories past, the savoring of hapless suffering. As Yeats was to write about more recent verse on Crane's other favorite subject, war, "passive suffering is not a theme for poetry." [34] Crane's attitude toward war is anything but passive, and we have seen how curiously the imagining of war intrudes upon the mood of his defeat in love in "Flagons of despair." Crane's most ambitious love poem is his largest failure. In some other poems, however, if the suffering was passive its objectification in verse invests it with energy sufficient to give the illusion, essential to art, that the poetic statement controls as well as describes the experience it evokes in the beholder.

3

We may take, for example, a poem (WK vi) whose meaning is similar to that of much of "Intrigue." Developing the theme of brevity in his note to Cora, quoted above, the poem tells us that love is momentary; Crane likens it to "the passing of a ship at night." This is one of his best pieces—Berryman quotes it to illustrate his observation that in *War is Kind* "There swelled . . . if anyone had listened—a strange singing." [35] But before quoting it here I wish to trace the stages in its development. We know so little about the way Crane's imagination

---

[34] *Oxford Book of Modern Verse*, p. xxxiv.   [35] Berryman, p. 242.

worked, so little about what it selected from the improbable events of his life to work on, that an interest attaches to the derivation of those poems whose starting-places we can trace.

The unlikely point of departure for poem VI is this entry in Cora's manuscript book, on the page following her thoughts about the hopelessness of expecting "uninterrupted reaches of happiness":

Ships that pass in the night and speed each other in passing
Only a signal shown, and a distant voice in the darkness,
So, on the ocean of life, we pass and speak one another
Only a look and a voice, then darkness again and a silence.

Cora, whose commonplace book includes excerpts from Byron, Shakespeare, Burns, Keats, Mrs. Browning, *David Copperfield,* Seneca, George Eliot, and the doggerel of one Philander Johnson, knew also these lines from Longfellow's *Tales of a Wayside Inn.* She must have recited them to Crane; for why else would Longfellow's images be transfigured in this note of his to her?

To C. E. S.

Love comes like the tall swift shadow of a ship at night. There is for a moment, the music of the water's turmoil, a bell, perhaps, a man's shout, a row of gleaming yellow lights. Then the slow sinking of this mystic shape. Then silence and a bitter silence—the silence of the sea at night.

Stephen Crane [36]

We can surmise from Crane's little parody of "The Psalm of Life" that Longfellow was hardly his favorite poet. Why should the abstract "Ships that pass in the night" have released

[36] Letter 54 in the Columbia collection. Undated, the note is pasted to an envelope in another hand addressed to Stephen Crane at Hartwood, N.Y., postmarked New York City, January 26 [1897].

in Crane's imagination these vivid concretions, this strange intensification of mood? Perhaps because certain links in Longfellow's passage were already present in Crane's mind. The conjunction of *boat*: *signal light*: *shout*: *darkness*: *silence* (with darkness already intensified to something more menacing) turns up, with the elements in almost exactly this order, in the manuscript of a press dispatch, apparently never printed. This was written in the spring of 1895 while Crane was in Mexico City.[37] He is describing a nocturnal boat ride on the Viga Canal:

The musicians played slumberously. We did not wish to hear any too well. It was better to lie and watch the large stars come out and let the music be merely a tale of the past, a recital from the possessions of one's memory, an invoking of other songs, other nights. For, after all, the important part of these dreamful times to the wanderer is that they cry to him with emotional and tender voices of his past. The yellow glitter of the lantern at the boatman's feet made his shadow to be a black awful thing that hung angrily over us. There was a sudden shrill yell from the darkness. There had almost been a collision. In the blue velvet of the sky, the stars had gathered in thousands.[38]

Some of the sentimentality of "Intrigue" is suggested by the yearnings here, but the threatening images of boatman and collision point ahead to other writings more powerful. From this manuscript comes the key that locked Longfellow's lines

[37] Stallman dates his Mexican trip between February and early June (*Omnibus,* p. 616n.); his published dispatches appeared in the Philadelphia *Press* on May 19, June 30, and August 11, 1895 and on October 18, 1896.

[38] From page 5 of the second of three untitled MS press articles, headed "City of Mexico," in the Columbia collection.

into Crane's imagination: the context of unfulfilled love in association with the images of ship, signal, voice, darkness. And for Crane, love never comes without menace.

It is a temptation to make of his note to Cora a Crane poem, so close are the rhythms of its phrases to those of his "lines." [39] Crane himself soon wrote a poem using this chain of images, but he was to speak quite a different language, and to establish more dramatically a point of view from which the action is recorded. These lines first appeared in the *Bookman* for October, 1896:

> I explain the silvered passing of a ship at night,
> The sweep of each sad lost wave,
> The dwindling of the steel thing's striving,
> The little cry of a man to a man,
> A shadow falling across the greyer night,
> And the sinking of the small star;
> Then the waste, the far waste of waters,
> And the soft lashing of black waves
> For long and in loneliness.
>
> Remember thou, O ship of love,
> Thou leavest a far waste of waters,
> And the soft lashing of black waves
> For long and in loneliness.　　　　　　　　[WK vi]

Now the motion of the ship is fully realized in "sweep," "dwindling," the falling shadow and sinking star. Longfellow's vague "distant voice" had in Crane's note become "a man's shout,"

[39] In 1947 Melvin Schoberlin did make a poem of it, printing 100 copies "Of this original draft of 'I explain the silvered passing'" as a New Year's card (Baltimore: Mogollon Press). Cf. introduction to *Sullivan County Sketches*, p. 13, where he set Crane's prose as verse.

and in the Mexican article, "a sudden shrill yell," but the final
"little cry of a man to a man" best expresses the poignant attempt to break through the silence of isolation to another soul.
A manuscript of this poem at Columbia has "Oh, thou, my
ship in thy stern straight journey" instead of "Remember, thou,
O ship of love." Although the latter suggests perhaps too
closely the didacticism of Longfellow ("Sail on, O Ship of
State") or Holmes, the poem must somewhere specify what it
is all about. Yet once we know that, the rejected alternative is
revealing too: love travels a "stern straight journey"; why this
must be so to Crane we shall shortly see. More intrinsic to the
present poem is the success with which a set of associated concepts has been rendered in concrete objective images, the very
rhythms and sounds of which contribute in the reader's imagination to both the action and the emotion the poet wishes to
create there.

4

"You have the most beautiful arms I ever saw," Crane wrote to
Helen Trent in 1891. "If I could keep your arms nothing else
would count. It would not matter if there was nothing else to
hope for in the world or if there was no more world. In dreams,
don't you ever fall and fall but not be afraid of anything because somebody safe is with you?" But the next day the
twenty-year-old lover was stunned to learn that Miss Trent
would soon be married in London. Nine years later, Beer remarks with felicitous irony,[40] "when an Englishman pointed
out the celebrated Stephen Crane, she saw him across the flare

[40] Beer, pp. 64–65; retold in Berryman, pp. 30–31.

of a London theatre without knowing why he was celebrated.
But in 'The Black Riders,' on the eleventh page:"

> Should the wide world roll away,
> Leaving black terror,
> Limitless night,
> Nor God, nor man, nor place to stand
> Would be to me essential,
> If thou and thy white arms were there,
> And the fall to doom a long way.   [BR x]

In this earliest love poem, love is already a desolation. These
seven lines give us several attitudes and images typical of
Crane's verse on this subject. "Black terror" reminds us of "the
terrible heedless courage of babes"—we find courage and terror continually invoked in contexts of love. Another strange
thing: to symbolize the woman's beauty and erotic attraction
Crane mentions, of all her parts and qualities, only "thy white
arms." Her arms will prove to be a repeated image whose
other appearances bear examination. Finally, although her
arms would save him from "the fall to doom," what the poem
really says is that he is doomed and fallen because he loves
her. Surely this is one of the most joyless love poems ever written. Crane's attitude is paradox, the antithesis of romance; his
ambivalence is partly due to the grim grasp upon his imagination of Bishop Peck's damnatory doctrines. Crane's natural
impulse is deeply, wildly romantic, but he is inhibited by that
"swift hand" from the sky which he hates but has not yet
fended away. Thus "Black terror, / Limitless night" are his
expected portion.

To begin with, why does Crane mention only her arms? We

find in "Intrigue" too the loved one's arms are prominent as a symbol of her erotic spell (iii, vi, x) and of his passive suffering (iii). There are occasional references to lips, face, voice, but none so recurrent as these. Crane's love poems are strangely barren of descriptions of the beloved. What is unusual here is the concentration in *arms,* a maternal image, of significations so intensely erotic. Freud, describing the Oedipal situation, remarks that "the libido has dwelt so long in its attachment to the mother, even after puberty, that the maternal characteristics remain stamped on the love-objects chosen later —so long that they all become easily recognizable as mother-surrogates." [41] Berryman goes on to equate, for Crane, harlot with mother-image.[42] Here it is enough to note that when the arms appear in the poems erotically, the image invokes menacing associations (writhing, frenzy); but when, as in "Should the wide world roll away" and in another poem deferred for later discussion (BR lxvii), the arms are protective, the emotional context is infinitely more tender. But in the identification of the beloved's arms with protectiveness (a maternal function), the imagined action becomes fearsomely self-destructive: in the first instance, God, man, and the world are rolled away; the second begins, "God lay dead in heaven," and ends with "the jaws of the final beast."

Since to love is to be damned, the meditated action in Crane's poems on love takes place in a *paysage moralisé.* In one of them he writes, "I looked here; / I looked there; / Nowhere could I see my love." But at last he finds her: "She was

<hr />

[41] *Collected Papers,* IV, 196.   [42] Berryman, p. 302.

in my heart" (BR vIII). After his meal of a heart in the desert
(BR III), the repetition of "in my heart" sounds ominous. A
later poem is more explicit:

> Love walked alone.
> The rocks cut her tender feet,
> And the brambles tore her fair limbs . . .   [BR xLI]

This is followed by "I walked in the desert" (xLII), which remains a desert to him although "A voice said, 'It is no desert.'"
We remember what the heart-eater was eating: "From within,
out of the heart of men, proceed evil thoughts, adulteries, fornications . . . laciviousness. . . ." Since love, sexual love,
is the epitome of all sin, such paradises as the romantic aspires
to must be abjured:

> Places among the stars,
> Soft gardens near the sun,
> Keep your distant beauty;
>
> .   .   .   .
>
> Since she is here
> In a place of blackness
> Here I stay and wait.   [BR xxIII]

These themes of the waste land, sexual love, and sin are
joined again in poem xI of *War is Kind*. "On the desert" a tribe
"Of hooded men, squat and dumb" watch a woman snake-
dancer:

> . . . mystic things, sinuous, dull with terrible colour,
> Sleepily fondle her body
> Or move at her will . . .
>
> .   .   .   .
>
> Slow, menacing and submissive. . . .

There is no other action in this erotic tableau. But the last lines recall again the heart-eater relishing his bitter feast:

> The dignity of the accursèd;
> The glory of slavery, despair, death,
> Is in the dance of the whispering snakes.

The Arabian houri is an apt image for the type of love we have seen Crane pursue. As the exhibitionistic lover of the many "hooded men" she is sexually discredited. Their hoods may link them with the snakes that fondle her body—cobras no doubt—yet we note that their responsibility for sexual initiative is partly suppressed by the suggestion of sleep, or wholly transferred as the snakes "move at *her* will . . . submissive."

In other poems, too, we find the initiative taken by the woman, who is therefore dangerous. In this context the image of snakes recurs. Linton, hero of "The Squire's Madness," Crane's only story about a "poet," has difficulty completing these lines (not included in *Collected Poems*):

> The garlands of her hair are snakes;
> Black and bitter are her hating eyes.
> A cry the windy death-hall wakes—
> O, love, deliver us.
> The flung cup rolls to her sandal's tip;
> His arm—

Whereupon his thought fumed over the next two lines, coursing like greyhounds after a fugitive vision of writhing lover, with the foam of poison on his lips, dying at the feet of the woman.[43]

[43] *Work*, XI, 295; but I follow Crane's MS in the Columbia collection in substituting "wakes" for "makes" (line 3) and "love" for "Love" (line 4). Cora Crane finished this posthumous story; a scrapbook contains tearsheets of its first appearance in *Crampton's Magazine*, XVI (October,

In this tale the wife thinks her absent-minded and distressed poet insane, and persuades him to see a brain specialist. But the diagnosis is: *"It is your Wife who is Mad! Mad as a Hatter!"* Truer than the observed reality of the prose—his distracted air and practical incompetence—were the fears expressed in his poem.[44]

Earlier, in "Intrigue," the same combination appears of woman as feared aggressor, doom, and snake:

> Thou art my love,
> And thou art a priestess,
> And in thy hand is a bloody dagger,
> And my doom comes to me surely—
> Woe is me.
>
> Thou art my love,
> And thou art a skull with ruby eyes,
> And I love thee— [Intrigue i]

The significance of the usually phallic snake is ambiguous in these poems. We may better understand it after consulting Crane's story, "The Snake" (1896), in which a man and a snake confront each other with "hatred and fear":

1900), 93–99, with her notation, "This is a bad copy they did not send me proofs to correct." *Crampton's* has "makes" (line 3), "O love, deliver us" (line 4) and no punctuation at the ends of lines 1–3.

[44] In the story his lover is normalized to wife—most likely Cora, who finished the tale in all innocence of this implication. Linton is lord of "a manor-house in Sussex," locale also of Brede Place. The MS shows that Crane wrote as far as line 6, p. 297 (*Work*, Vol. XI). On verso of corresponding MS sheet, in Cora's hand: "Wife thinks husband mad—makes him think he is mad—he goes with her to a doctor to see if it's true & Dr. says wife is mad . . ." which I take to be her notes as to Crane's intentions for the denouement.

Individuals who do not participate in this strife incur the investigations of scientists. Once there was a man and a snake who were friends, and at the end the man lay dead with the marks of the snake's caress just over his East Indian heart.[45]

One might take the rest of this sketch to be realism, or, perhaps in view of a passage on snakes in hell, a theological parable. But the two sentences just cited point in another direction. Along with hatred and fear of snakes, Crane feels an inescapable fascination—not to know it is to be unnatural, an object of puzzled scientific scrutiny. And the second sentence, itself a fable complete, brings us back to the whispering snakes in the desert: again we are in the Orient, and the snake caresses the lover's heart. Hidden beneath the narrative level of the sketch, contributing to its almost unbearable intensity, is this masked sexual anxiety. It is well to remember how shocked Crane's good father had been at such milder sins as drinking, dicing, and cards; how zealous a Methodist was his mother; how ascetic the ethics of *What Must I Do to Be Saved?* It is likely that Crane approached sex with tremendous inhibitions and guilt. Part of the explanation for his attachment to harlots may have been a conviction that if the "sexually discredited" woman initiates sexual activity, her lover may be partly absolved of the guilt. The snake image in these poems and tales is also to be taken in its theological signification as the agent of man's fall, the inciter to sin. Thus the lover, in the Squire's poem, taking the poisoned cup of sin (a flagon of despair) from his snake-haired Medusa (possibly a mother image), becomes a viper himself, and dies. This fate,

[45] *Work*, XI, 246–47.

however, is what human nature has in store for us, "The dignity of the accursèd" which Crane has celebrated in his poem
about the heart-eater and in "A god came to a man" in the
Garden of Eden.

5

Another group of poems on this theme shows Crane's technical
versatility in the handling of his obsessive materials. We may
begin with a curiously terse, seemingly uncommunicative
poem from *War is Kind:*

> The chatter of a death-demon from a tree-top.
>
> Blood—blood and torn grass—
> Had marked the rise of his agony—
> This lone hunter.
> The grey-green woods impassive
> Had watched the threshing of his limbs.
>
> A canoe with flashing paddle,
> A girl with soft searching eyes,
> A call: "John!"
>
> .   .   .   .
>
> Come, arise, hunter!
> Can you not hear?
>
> The chatter of a death-demon from a tree-top.   [xix]

Perhaps because so much is demanded, so little apparently
given, no critic of Crane's verse has discussed this poem since
it first appeared in Elbert Hubbard's *Philistine* (August, 1895)
and *Roycroft Quarterly* (May, 1896). Were the action in this
poem ungrounded in an intended narrative it would be unique
among Crane's verse, yet what that narrative is may not be

at once apparent. I take it there are three *personae* in the story
of which this poem is a synopsis in the intensifying shorthand
of symbolism. These are the death-demon, a "lone hunter"
named John, and a girl. But how are we to read the right connection between "the threshing of his limbs" in the woods,
and the girl in a canoe? It is possible at this point to introduce
some evidence not available to other readers who may have
felt this poem deserving of interpretation. We can infer from
manuscripts in the Columbia collection that "The chatter of a
death-demon" is the syncretion of two other unpublished
poems. One is about "a grey thing that lives in the treetops";
the other concerns "a lad and a maid in a canoe."

The first of these is a death-song, perhaps reminiscent of
Poe's tales in its mood of mystery and horror:

> There is a grey thing that lives in the tree-tops
> None knows the horror of its sight
> Save those who meet death in the wilderness
> But one is enabled to see
> To see branches move at its passing
> To hear at times the wail of black laughter
> And to come often upon mystic places
> Places where the thing has just been.   [Columbia MS]

This is, I think, a rather effective evocation of ambient
dread. The "grey thing" is a felt presence, menacingly invisible
to all "Save those who meet death in the wilderness." This
wilderness (or desert) we have seen to be a conventional image of the sinful life. Nothing more is specified in this poem, a
sustained imagistic concretion of an intangible emotion. Two
halting repetitions intensify the mood.

The second manuscript is also a song, apparently a love song:

> A lad and a maid at a curve in the stream
> And a shine of soft silken waters
> Where the moon-beams fall through a hemlock's boughs
> Oh, night dismal, night glorious.
>
> A lad and a maid at the rail of a bridge
> With two long shadows adrift on the water
> And the wind sings low in the grass on the shore.
>   Oh, night dismal, night glorious.
>
> A lad and a maid in a canoe
> And a paddle making silver turmoil   [Columbia MS]

And here the manuscript breaks off.[46]

Incomplete though it is, what does it tell us? Most noticeable is the lyrical rhythm, so unlike either the elliptical terseness of the "death-demon" poem or the slower movement in the sustained image of the "grey thing." We can deduce what action and thematic development are probably intended from the changing images in the second line of each stanza: shine, shadows, turmoil. Taking these in conjunction with "night dismal, night glorious," we see in the stanzas an inferrable pro-

[46] There may have survived another copy in more complete form, for Crane included the title "Oh night dismal, night glorious" in a list of twelve poems, of which the first eight and the tenth ("I explain the path [*sic*] of a ship") appear in *War is Kind*. "Chatter of a Death-Demon in a tree top" is seventh; the last four titles are separated by a dash from the foregoing, as though it indicate that Crane was less certain of including them. It would seem, then, that he considered this poem complete, but certainly the copy transcribed above is unconcluded. (List in Columbia collection, not to be confused with magazine acceptance list mentioned earlier.)

gression from glory toward chaos, but in the refrain this direction is reversed. Nothing is effectively developed in this fragment, but the sensuous imagery surrounding the lad and maid
in their moonlit canoe mildly suggests an erotic situation.
From the refrain and "silver turmoil" one might infer a certain sense of foreboding.

Now let us see what happens when Crane combines these
two rather simple poems into "The chatter of a death-demon
from a tree-top." It is perhaps possible that all we have is an
imagistic presentation of the accidental death of a young
hunter and the pathos of his girl's search for him. But I do not
think this simple view accounts for the visible residues of
meaning from the two unpublished poems, nor does it explain
the question toward the end nor the persistent chattering of
the death-demon. Where each of the manuscript poems had
presented a single mood, in poem xix of *War is Kind* we find
the violence of "Blood—blood and torn grass" juxtaposed to
the sensuousness of "A girl with soft searching eyes." The
menacing mystery of the grey thing and its slowly developed
image have given way to abbreviated images of agony and
tenderness, but the ominous note reappears in the last three
lines. This is another instance of the recurrent tension between
love and annihilation, more effective in this poem than in the
earlier fragmentary "Flagons of despair." Taking account of
the two contributory drafts, we may provisionally propose that
the theme of this poem is the fear and guilt which accompany
consummated love.

Although the chattering death-demon is an image inferior
to the frightening indistinctness of the "grey thing," it has

a particularity needed to enclose the poem. It is not physical danger merely, or vague menace, but a visitation of death sent up from hell. The image suggested is ape or monkey, with the consequent revulsion against the atavistic creature whose ugly form is a mockery of man's and God's. The death-demon does not stalk his prey, as the "lone hunter" must; he waits in "the grey-green woods" among colors emblematic of death and life. He is part of the natural world which is "impassive" to the human "agony" enacted upon it.

The narrative of that human action might run something like this. The lad and his maid have landed their canoe in the grassy wilderness under the tree-top, and have lain together in a "mystic place" over which the presiding death-demon chatters expectantly. The lad is now a "hunter," aggressive, predatory, and "lone" even in the moment of union. The "blood," the "torn grass," the "threshing of his limbs" would seem to imply a violent sexual act.[47] What in the lad and maid poem was his "night glorious" is here an "agony," rising to climax as sexual union is approached and found illusory. In this fearful love-dream of a sensibility in almost unbearable isolation,

> The grey-green woods impassive
> Had watched the threshing of his limbs.

In this moment of stillness after union the death-demon springs from the tree-top. The "lone hunter" is now the lone victim of his hunting.

[47] In the early story, "Killing His Bear," the hunter steels himself to "mad emotions, powerful to rock worlds" as he pulls the trigger. "A mad froth lay in the animal's open mouth, and his limbs were twisted from agony." As the hunter approaches the dead beast, "Upon his face was the smile of the successful lover." *Sullivan County Sketches,* p. 54.

The next three lines may indicate the awakening of the lovers. "A canoe with flashing paddle" I take to be the first image to swirl across his consciousness, an image both of drowning and of rebirth. The girl tenderly calls his name, a summons to live again. The next lines, however, are not spoken by his beloved; an observer, impassive as the woods, yet mocking, calls him too:

> Come, arise, hunter!
> Can you not hear?

Awaking, he hears not the girl but the chatter once more of the death-demon. Having sprung upon him in fearful images of blood, tearing, agony, threshing, the demon now releases him to live again.

If this reading of the poem has any merit, it would appear to be as unjoyful an example of romantic nihilism as one could think of. The interpretation just suggested seems consistent with Crane's other writings on each of the two themes joined here, and, as has been remarked, their conjunction is characteristic too. Apart from its subject, however, the poem is interesting technically. The broken rhythms, the furtive ellipses, the unlinked presentation of vivid impressions seems an attempt to make the mode of presentation contribute to the tensions of the poem. The nondiscursive method parallels "A man adrift on a slim spar" (a better articulated poem, however), and other verse to be examined in succeeding chapters. Had Crane sustained this style consistently, suppressing narrative to gain intensity, his verse—on technical grounds at least—might have won for itself a less equivocal place in the history of recent poetry. In so far as Crane does practice such a style as I have just described, his technical means resemble to some degree those of the French Symbolist poets and the later Imagists.

6

We are now approaching the answer to a question raised some pages ago, as to why images of war intrude upon the love-lament in "Flagons of despair." There are further poems combining war and love which remain to be examined, but on the way toward them another group must now detain us. Only one of these has the intensity of the poems just examined, but as stages in the tracing of Crane's subconscious image-linking they all contribute to the interpretation of his better work. In them the situation of love: sin: punishment creates a context for the exploration of a curious ethical issue. Loyalty and courage are the minimal requirements of the lover, but desertion and cowardice may be the poor best he can give.

In *The Black Riders*, poem XL, there is a lovers' argument. "You are, then, cold coward," she upbraids him, and he replies, "Ay." But, he goes on, he is "Caught in the stubble of the world" when he tries to come to her; "Man's opinions, a thousand thickets" detain him. Yet he would love her, but he remains a coward. In another poem the situation is more complex:

> There was a man and woman
> Who sinned.
> Then did the man heap the punishment
> All upon the head of her
> And went away gayly.

But this accords with neither human chivalry nor divine retribution. It is an escape-fantasy, immediately contradicted: Again the man and woman sin,

> And the man stood with her,
> As upon her head, so upon his,
> Fell blow upon blow
> And all people screaming, "Fool!"
> He was a brave heart.

Here is the ethical desideratum, defiance of God and man in loyalty to love. But we have seen how often in the imagery of his writing, as in his predilection for loose women in life, Crane sought to transfer sexual initiative and guilt to the woman. We can infer that perhaps the loyalty epitomized here is another fantasy of escape—from the feelings of guilt and inadequacy expressed in these closing lines:

> He was a brave heart.
> Would you speak with him, friend?
> Well, he is dead
>
> .   .   .   .
>
> And your opportunity gone;
> For, in that, you were a coward.   [BR LXI]

A manuscript poem, rejected from *The Black Riders* by Copeland and Day, makes the sin specifically an adulterous love affair, and more frankly than any in the published canon expresses the rescue motif:

> One came from the skies
> —They said—
> And with a band he bound them
> A man and a woman.
> Now to the man

The band was gold
And to another, iron
And to the woman, iron.
But this second man,
He took his opinion and went away
But, by heavens,
He was none too wise.

Three lines more, crossed out in pencil, associate cowardice with his failure to "rescue" the willing woman:

For shackles fit apes.
He is not brave
Who leaves the iron on doves.   [Columbia MS]

The next-to-last poem in *The Black Riders* develops the cosmic desolation of "Should the wide world roll away." Ironically juxtaposed to the final poem (in which an unbelieving spirit is smitten dead by God's sword), this one begins,

God lay dead in heaven;
Angels sang the hymn of the end . . .

The earth turns black and sinks, and then

From the far caverns
of dead sins
Came monsters, livid with desire.

The last four lines were suggested, says Thomas Beer, by this experience: "In the bowery he had seen a young streetwalker cover the head of a drunken procurer with her body while the fellow's assailants were trying to stamp his face to pieces; Crane ran to bring help and the police arrested the girl for cursing." [48]

[48] Beer, p. 122.

But of all sadness this was sad—
A woman's arms tried to shield
The head of a sleeping man
From the jaws of the final beast.   [BR lxvii]

Here is a bold transfiguration of the observed impression—
horrible in its brutality, the loyalty pathetic in lovers so sordid
and degraded—into a set of images whose horror is universalized. The streetwalker and her drunken pimp are become
Man and Woman. This generalization of the now-disguised
specifics is accomplished partly through the invocation of an
apocalyptic framework. But the sense of inexplicable terror
of the conclusion derives elsewhere. It comes from Crane's extremely personal attitudes toward love, sin, and the exacting
requirements that life implacably demands. The element of
intense pathos is not so much that a gang of ruffians has been
transposed into "monsters, livid with desire," or that these
have become "the jaws of the final beast"; it is that the
woman's action—the most sad thing—is a *reversal* of Crane's
theme of harlot-rescue. The man, asleep, is helpless, menaced
by the dream-monsters of his own desires. Life, for Crane, demanded courage above all else; yet this man is paralyzed in
"sleep," and it is the woman who tried to shield his head. The
monsters "Wrangled over the world, / A morsel." They will
devour him despite her. Even though, as in the other poems,
she takes the initiative, he is damned, damned utterly. But as
we have seen the only fate acceptable to Crane is loyalty to
one's partner in the damnation that is love, that is life. In this
poem the man is incapable of loyalty, but the woman is supremely, maternally loyal. His doom is more terrible than ever.

7

Love, for Crane, is no unequivocal romantic ecstasy. Intrinsic to the emotion itself, to the relationship, are his sense of guilt, sin, and doom. Required above all are loyalty and courage; consummated love is metaphorically a death, and its imaging evokes associations of violence, fears of desertion, and cowardice. It is not, after all, so great a leap of his imagination to link with love the images of another situation in which most of these emotions are fearfully involved. In war, the predicament of the individual is generalized into the condition of society. Crane does not rail against war, terrible and wasteful though he recognizes it to be; he accepts it as a part of nature—blizzards, floods, and the coldness of the sea are similarly lamentable, but all are parts of the given universe. In so far as the images of war are associated in his poems with those of love, we have a fusion of what were for Crane the two supreme experiences of the individual at the highest pitch of psychological stress. Fear, anxiety, panic, the achievement of glory and the realization that glory is nothing—all these, and death, are characteristic to him of love and war.

In an allegorized section of "Intrigue" (vii) Crane sees himself and love alone "at midnight . . . like two creatures by a dead camp-fire." This is an image of his defeat, suffered passively; the ashes are those of a deserted army encampment. In "Flagons of despair" we saw a more active suffering of defeated love:

> Dreams of riot and blood and screams
> The rolling white eyes of dying men
> The terrible heedless courage of babes.

This is inchoate, yet the army at least has not surrendered.
Courage is still possible, though it be terrible and heedless,
possible only to the innocent. Again, in "Intrigue," he longs
for the warrior's courage—to make him worthy as a lover:

> God give me medals,
> God give me loud honours,
> That I may strut before you, sweetheart,

—this is self-deprecatory, a protection against the guilt that
accompanies his violent desires:

> Now let me crunch you
> With full weight of affrighted love.   [Intrigue ɪɪ]

Crane does not envision satisfaction without fear.

Nowhere in "Intrigue," but in one poem from *War is Kind,*
Crane does see the lover as active, warlike, loyal, and brave.
The governing metaphor is appropriately chivalric, for it is
part of the knightly code to rescue the beloved:

> Fast rode the knight
> With spurs, hot and reeking.
> Ever waving an eager sword,
> "To save my lady!"
> Fast rode the knight,
> And leaped from saddle to war.
> Men of steel flickered and gleamed
> Like riot of silver lights,
> And the gold of the knight's good banner
> Still waved on a castle wall.
>
>   .   .   .   .
>
> A horse,
> Blowing, staggering, bloody thing,
> Forgotten at foot of castle wall.

A horse,
Dead at foot of castle wall.   [WK viii]

The lady is saved—but forgotten, as in the second part our
attention is fixed on the death of a horse. The apparent lack
of connection between the narrative first section and the imagistic second is baffling; one does not forget this poem. The
simplicity of the concluding image is the source of its power.
No comment, no explanation, but the seemingly naive directness would not, as Berryman remarks, be seen again. "His
poetry has the inimitable sincerity of a frightened savage
anxious to learn what his dream means." [49] Stallman proposes
that the meaning is the contrast of "illusion versus reality," [50]
another of Crane's ironic prickings of the glory of war. But
the conjunction here of a zealous warrior, rescue (explicitly),
violence, and horse suggests that war may not be the subject
itself but one of a series of metaphors expressing that subject.
Berryman has noted the unusual proliferation in Crane's fiction of the horse image (and associated concepts—hooves,
hocks, and the like) in contexts of fearsome violence, and
these he identifies as key images expressive of Crane's Oedipal
hostilities against both parents.[51] Yet one notes with surprise
that although Crane named his first book of verse *The Black
Riders* there are no horses in it at all—only the riders of the
title poem; in *War is Kind* there are but two horse images, in
"Fast rode the knight" and again in the title poem. Horses occur again in *War is Kind* in xxvii, omitted by Crane from the
book, and indirectly in xii. Only one of the new poems in the
Columbia collection mentions horses (see "A grey and boiling

---

[49] Berryman, p. 277.   [50] *Omnibus,* p. 572.   [51] Berryman, pp. 320–22.

street" in the Appendix, below). The scarcity of horse images
is the more remarkable in view of Crane's explicit treatment
of erotic emotion in his verse, a circumstance which, one
would think, might foster the hostile feelings Berryman alleges
to be at the source of Crane's fascination with horses. It is
possible, however, that an element other than the Freudian
enters importantly into the associations the horse image held
for Crane.

When we think of the only earlier poem involving warlike
horsemen we recall that amid the "clang and clang of spear
and shield," the "Black riders came from the sea," and that
Crane specified, "Thus the ride of Sin." It is possible that in
"Fast rode the knight," despite the conscious rescue motif this
knight too is a black rider, and his leap "from saddle to war"
is again the ride of Sin. In fact his ride may be sinful exactly
because his errand is a rescue of the kind we have seen it to
be Crane's fate to imagine and to perform. As was true in the
poems examined earlier in this chapter, we may expect that
his rescue, performed as an act of love, produces feelings of
guilt and fears of punishment. But what means the violent
death of "a horse"?

For Crane, as for Yeats, to ride a fine horse well was one of
the noblest acts of man. Riding may, as Mr. Berryman maintains, be "a conventional sexual symbol," [52] yet to ride well a
spirited mount means to control by discipline and will an animal whose God-given power is the reason a man should prize
it. Horse and rider, combined centaur-like into a single being,
exemplify huge strength and violent passion reined in by di-

[52] Berryman, p. 321.

rected human will. The resulting action is exhilarating, beautiful. "A good saddle horse is the one blessing of life," Crane wrote to one correspondent; to another he exulted in "a slim-limbed thoroughbred's dauntless spirit." It was the struggle of will with an unbroken horse that he loved: "What can be finer than a frosty morning, a runaway horse, and only the still hills to watch?" [53]

As it happens, a like prescription for the control of animal nature, itself a Divine endowment, by "the intellect and the conscience and . . . the will" is explicitly the ethical view of Jonathan Townley Crane,[54] who, like his son, was exceptionally solicitous of horses.[55] Whether Mr. Berryman is right in finding Oedipal rivalry and death-wish against the father in his work, Stephen Crane does make of horse-and-rider a compacted symbol combining sensuality with stern control, violence with discipline. This complex image thus comes into prominence in contexts involving not only war but love and sin. There one of its functions is to measure the nobility of the life imagined. In this poem the steed has been cruelly abused and left to die by a knight who proves, despite his title and presumptive chivalry, ignoble.

[53] *Omnibus*, p. 647; *Love Letters*, p. 10.
[54] *Holiness the Birthright*, p. 100.
[55] *Omnibus*, p. 693; Berryman, pp. 8, 317.

Five ⌇ *RED WINDS OF BATTLE*

For Crane the natural state of man is conflict, against a cruel God, an indifferent nature, an ironic fate. Love is the loyalty of two doomed souls to one another. In a world devoid of moral purpose, life without human loyalties is a senseless protraction of suffering. Confronting huge amoral forces, the individual hews the solitary path of his own unimportant life. His life may be a futile one, but if it has been loyal, kind, or, supremely, sacrificial, he may take comfort from it when all striving is done.

In such a world the natural condition of society is war. From the first, for Crane, war was not a willed human action but a given condition, an aspect of nature. One of Crane's earliest writings, hitherto unreported, illustrates some years before *The Red Badge of Courage* and the poems his preoccupation with what Henry James called "the imagination of disaster." A news story filed during his brief tenure at Syracuse University reports the emergence of a plague of beetles from a rock quarry. Attracted by a floodlight over a railway spur, they swarm across the ties; squashed insects grease the tracks, halting a train. All of the metaphors in this dispatch of 1891 are terms of war: insects at the edge of the swarm are "pickets or skirmishers"; they "died with a crackling sound like the successive explosions of toy torpedoes" as the locomotive crushes their "turtle-like armor." [1] Of all the ways to describe this extraordinary scene, Crane chose to consider it a conflict between the insects and the locomotive. Unsure as is this early sketch, a more dramatic prefiguration of his later concern with the emotions of such pickets in the swarming armies as Henry Fleming could hardly be adduced. Already war is a fantastically unequal combat, the enemy a machine, the army a senseless swarm, the skirmishers attracted psychomechanically by the glare of battle. It remains only to humanize the beetles.

It is surprising, however, to discover how few of Crane's poems treat explicitly the ostensible subject of most of his major fiction. Only three poems in *The Black Riders* and two in *War is Kind* deal with war; one other published poem to do so is the rhymed epigraph to "The Clan of No-Name," his story of valor in battle and betrayal in love. Three manuscripts, newly recovered, add longer, more ambitious ventures to this short list. But interesting as these are in clarifying Crane's attitude toward war, it is still to the fiction that we must look for his most significant and artistically successful treatment of this theme. We remember that Crane considered *The Black*

[1] "Great Bugs in Onondaga," New York *Tribune,* June 1, 1891, p. 1. This item was located by Ames W. Williams, Crane's bibliographer, in whose scrapbook of Crane photostats I found it in the Syracuse University Library. But "Great Bugs" was omitted from the *Bibliography* —"reluctantly," Mr. Williams writes me, because he had "no proof of authorship" (letter of July 17, 1955). Williams now agrees that my comments indicate Crane's authorship, and adds, "It was the only bit I found to confirm the legend of his being a Syracuse correspondent for the NY papers" (letter of November 29, 1955).

Riders as "a more ambitious effort" than *The Red Badge,* which he termed "a mere episode in life, an amplification." [2] What flaws these longer poems of war is his attempt to make them too ambitious, to generalize about moral conduct rather than, as in the prose, to concentrate upon "a mere episode" and compel the moral principle to develop in the reader's mind as the inevitable result of his scrutiny of a particular action.

"I have got the poetic spout so that I can turn it on or off," Crane wrote to Garland in May, 1894.[3] He had offered the newly completed *Red Badge of Courage* to McClure's syndicate, and was writing poems in a fever of productivity. Soon he would submit *The Black Riders* to Copeland and Day; meanwhile, he was scratching a precarious livelihood from newspaper feature-writing. His letter to Garland continues, "I wrote a Decoration Day thing for the Press which aroused them to enthusiasm. They said in about a minute, though, that I was firing over the heads of the soldiers." The manuscript the *Press* rejected [4] is in the Columbia collection, headed by a hitherto unpublished poem. Verse and article are of particular interest in giving us poetic and explicit statements of Crane's attitudes toward some of the themes in *The Red Badge of Courage:*

---

[2] Stallman, *Omnibus,* p. 628.

[3] *Ibid.,* p. 600.

[4] The New York *Press* ran five articles on Decoration Day during the last week of May, 1894, but assuredly none of these pieces of pedestrian reportage is by Crane: "First Memorial Day," May 27, part v, p. 2; "Veterans in Line," *ibid.;* "Day of Heroes Dead," May 30, p. 2; "Dead on the Field of Honor" [editorial], *ibid.,* p. 4; "Veterans' Ranks Thinner by a Year," May 31, pp. 1–2.

A soldier, young in years, young in ambitions
Alive as no grey-beard is alive
Laid his heart and his hopes before duty
And went staunchly into the tempest of war.
There did the bitter red winds of battle
Swirl 'gainst his youth, beat upon his ambitions,
Drink his cool clear blood of manhood
Until at coming forth time
He was alive merely as the grey-beard is alive.
And for this—
The nation rendered to him a flower
A little thing—a flower
Aye, but yet not so little
For this flower grew in the nation's heart
A wet, soft blossom
From tears of her who loved her son
Even when the black battle rages
Made his face the face of furious urchin,
And this she cherished
And finally laid it, upon the breast of him.
A little thing—this flower?
No—it was the flower of duty
That inhales black smoke-clouds
And fastens its roots in bloody sod
And yet comes forth so fair, so fragrant—
Its birth is sunlight in grimest, darkest place.

As in the later "Intrigue," Crane had not here sustained an objective point of view or developed a poetic strategy commensurate with the requirements of his theme. These he defines in his article:

. . . we can expect that when the last veteran has vanished there will come a time of great monuments, eulogies, tears. Then the boy in blue will have grown to heroic size, and painters, sculptors and writers, will have been finally impressed, and strive to royally celebrate the deeds of the brave, simple, quiet men who crowded upon the opposing bayonets of their country's enemies. . . . In the tremendous roll of events the pages and paragraphs of future histories are nothing. Our obligation exists in the present, and it is fit that we leave not too much to future historians.[5]

Here heroism is considered without the irony which surrounds it in *The Red Badge of Courage*. It is among the very few means man has of achieving magnificence, and of these few, this is the one Crane preferred. The "deeds of the brave, simple, quiet men" are heroic because sacrificial; what makes the ironies of Henry's search for courage in *The Red Badge* cohere is the measuring of all his illusions against the possibility that he might really prove heroic, a sacrificial victim, himself. The flower in the above poem is analogous to the Flag in the novel, an heraldic symbol rather than an intrinsic image. The poem is spoiled by the shift from the youth who "went staunchly" into "the bitter red winds of battle" to the all-too-allegorical blossom of duty. When Henry rescues the Flag in Chapter XIX, we feel a similar intrusion of something arbitrary. But this is almost the novel's only structural flaw. Crane had learned in prose how to handle complexities with which he was still awkward in verse. In his later war poems he would become more elliptical, and his view of the significance of battle would confirm the beginning, not the end, of this poem on sacrifice and duty.

[5] Columbia MS, "The Gratitude of a Nation to Her Soldiers." This article is printed in its entirety in Crane, *The Red Badge of Courage and Other Stories*, ed. by Hoffman, pp. 187–89.

2

According to one of the fables in *The Black Riders*, "Once there came a man" who desired to range "all the men of the world in rows." But at once there was a clamor, quarrel, bloodshed, world-wide and age-long, between those who would stand in rows and those who would not.

> Eventually, the man went to death, weeping.
> And those who stayed in bloody scuffle
> Knew not the great simplicity. [BR v]

The great simplicity, one infers, is some platonic vision of perfectability achieved, one which makes no greater demand upon mankind than that they "stand in rows." But even this is too great, and even those who "pined" to follow the prophet "stayed in bloody scuffle."

A later poem begins when war has been long under way:

> There was crimson clash of war.
> Lands turn black and bare;
> Women wept;
> Babes ran, wondering.
> There came one who understood not these things
> He said, "Why is this?"
> Whereupon a million strove to answer him.
> There was such intricate clamour of tongues
> That still the reason was not. [BR xiv]

By now the original "great simplicity" has become a snarling confusion. In the midst of such chaos, one hopes, remembering Crane's fiction, that heroism at least may redeem the individual from the futility of the race. But this little poem offers no such consolations:

"Tell brave deeds of war."

Then they recounted tales—
"There were stern stands
And bitter runs for glory."

"Ah, I think there were braver deeds."   [BR xv]

Yet in a later story, "The Clan of No-Name," and in the
poem which is its prefix, fidelity to courage as a code of life
is all that gives meaning to the death of Manolo Prat. Life, in
this context, means "battle as a condition of existence." [6] The
story begins and ends in the garden and parlor of Margharita,
Manolo's sweetheart in Tampa; she is receiving another lover,
one Mr. Smith, a civilian. "It was part of his love to believe
in the absolute treachery of his adored one." [7] Learning of
Manolo's death in Cuba two months earlier, Margharita accepts Smith's proposal and burns her soldier's photograph.
But the story itself concerns the last half-hour of Manolo's life;
in his first battle he proves to himself that he is brave, and, in
an insignificant skirmish, dies.

The story, as Berryman justly remarks, is a turning-point in
the development of Crane's prose style, introducing for the
first time the envelope structure; "together with familiar elements there is an interest here in prose movement and syntax
which is new." [8] First published in the posthumous *Wounds in
the Rain,* "The Clan of No-Name" contains a third innovation
which, like the others, Crane did not live to use again. This is
a verse epigraph:

[6] Crane, *Work,* II, 156.   [7] *Ibid.,* p. 172.   [8] Berryman, p. 255.

Unwind my riddle.
Cruel as hawks the hours fly;
Wounded men seldom come home to die;
The hard waves see an arm flung high;
Scorn hits strong because of a lie;
Yet there exists a mystic tie.
Unwind my riddle.   [*Work*, II, 151]

Why should Crane have used this new device here? Seeking connections between epigraph and tale, we recognize at once that the poem too is enclosed, by the repetition of the first line at the end. (The pattern, suggestive of Whitman, is common in Crane's verse, however.) The insistent single rhyme and oracular tone mark this as not one of Crane's better efforts, yet it is an interesting key to the ensuing tale. For if the reader can unwind the riddle of the "mystic tie" he can understand the meaning of Lieutenant Manolo Prat's death, of Margharita's pledged love. Reading the story with the riddle in mind, we feel the force of the second line. After Manolo has been cut to pieces by a Negro guerilla, who has given his victim's photo of Margharita to a Spanish officer, "High over the green earth, in the dizzy blue heights, some great birds were slowly circling with down-turned beaks." [9] The next line refers directly to Manolo's situation: his war is being fought between Cuban insurgents and the traitorous native guerillas, a fratricidal combat more terribly visualized than is the Civil War in *The Red Badge*. There is no quarter here.

But in the next line the riddle fails to correspond with the tale. There is no sea in the story; "The hard waves" that "see

[9] Crane, *Work*, II, 171.

an arm flung high" are those around the open boat, the waves
closing over the man adrift on a slim spar. The two situations
were equivalents in Crane's mind, war and sea ("the grim
hatred of nature") as two confrontations of death. The "lie" is
Margharita's inscription on the back of the photo Manolo had
tried to lift from his pocket to read as he lay wounded, await-
ing the final machete: "One lesson in English I will give you—
this: I love you."

"Yet there exists a mystic tie," a tie that will not break under
the blows of scorn of love's betrayal. This is the ethical center
of "The Clan of No-Name." Manolo has just leapt into an outpost held by dead and wounded comrades:

> He knew that he was thrusting himself into a trap whose door,
> once closed, opened only when the black hand knocked; and every
> part of him seemed to be in panic-stricken revolt. But something
> . . . moved him inexorably in one direction; he perfectly under-
> stood, but he was only sad, sad with a serene dignity, with the
> countenance of a mournful young prince. He was of a kind . . . and
> the men of his kind, . . . through all wine and want, through all
> lies and unfamiliar truth, dark or light—the men of his kind were
> governed by their gods, and each man knew the law and yet could
> not give tongue to it, but it was the law; and if the spirits of the
> men of his kind were all sitting in critical judgment upon him even
> then in the sky, he could not have bettered his conduct; he needs
> must obey the law, and always with the law there is only one way.
> But . . . through wine and want, through all lies and unfamiliar
> truth, dark or light, he heard breathed to him the approval and the
> benediction of his brethren.[10]

"The benediction of his brethren" has a sacramental ring
which will resound again as Crane's vision of war as the crisis

---

[10] *Ibid.,* pp. 167–68.

of the soul is fulfilled in his poetry. Here this benediction must suffice for Manolo; we have learned, just before he deliberately closes the trap, that "In reality the men barely needed the presence of their officers." [11] The men knew what they must do whether or not he be there. Militarily his death is futile. Its only significance is in the testing of his spirit.

3

War tests the spirit of nations as well as of individual soldiers. In his tribute to the veterans of the Civil War Crane invoked with patriotic rhetoric a half-legendary historic grandeur:

When they are gone, American society has lost its most valuable element for they have paid the price of patriotism, they know the meaning of patriotism, and stars shot from guns would not hinder their devotion to the flag which they rescued from dust and oblivion.[12]

Although Crane had little to learn from actual experience under fire of the psychology of the individual in battle, his participation as correspondent in the Spanish-American War four years later did modify his view of war as a manifestation of national life and policy. Of course 1898 was not the same sort of war as the fratricidal battles of 1865; it is significant, however, that Crane's stories of the Spanish-American conflict collected in *Tales of Two Wars* (*Work*, vol. II) treat it as though it too were civil. We have noted the emphasis in "The Clan of No-Name" upon the divided Cuban combatants, revolutionists against guerillas; the conflict in "The Second Genera-

[11] *Ibid.*, p. 166.
[12] "Gratitude of a Nation," Columbia MS.

tion" is explicitly between father and son, that in "Virtue in
War" between parental and filial surrogates (Major Gates and
Lige, the civilian-soldier who must be initiated into the professional's code of duty). And in "The Little Regiment" (about
the Civil War) the rivalry is between two brothers on the same
side.

But for all that Crane recognized a different quality of spirit
among the populace clamoring for bigger battles in the war of
imperialistic expansion from that which had united the North
in the bloody tragedy a generation earlier. In this manuscript
poem Crane rages against the bloodthirsty civilians eager for
battles in which other men fight and die, their appetite for
carnage whetted by such jingo journals as the Hearst papers
(Crane sent twenty dispatches from this war to Hearst's New
York *Journal*):

> There exists the eternal fact of conflict
> And—next—a mere sense of locality.
> Afterward, we derive sustenance from the winds.
> Afterward we become patriots.
> The godly vice of patriotism makes us slaves,
> And—let us surrender to this falsity
> Let us be patriots.
>
> Then welcome us the practical men
> Thrumming on a thousand drums
> The practical men, God help us.
>   They cry aloud to be led to war
>   Ah—
>   They have been poltroons on a thousand fields
>   And the sad sacked city of New York is their record
>   Furious to face the Spaniard, these people
>   And crawling worms before their task

They name serfs and send charity in bulk to better men
They play at being free, these people of New York
Who are too well-dressed to protest against infamy.

[Columbia MS]

The Spanish-American War stirred America's bards to different kinds of song. Richard Hovey, of recent *Vagabondia* fame, in "Unmanifest destiny" extolled "My country" and "Its dark command"; opposing this easy jingoism, William Vaughn Moody wrote in "On a Soldier Fallen in the Philippines,"

Did we wrong this parted soul?

. . . .

Let him never dream that his bullet's scream went wide of its
island mark,
Home to the heart of his darling land where she stumbled and
sinned in the dark.[13]

Crane, unlike these poets, was himself a witness of this war—on one occasion, for which he was cited in a Marine Corps dispatch, he became a participant. His imperfect poem is even bitterer than Moody's restrained despair. The "infamy" against which the well-dressed civilians failed to protest is the miserable mismanagement and corruption of the army command, the inadequate supplies and inedible food sent to the front, the political interference with soldierly conduct of the war. Crane, who prized the soldier's code of obligation and duty, was appalled by these things; in the latter part of this poem his emotions run uncontrolled by aesthetic discipline.

The first seven lines, however, are implacable in the logic of their ambiguous definitions. We are patriots only because the winds (of rhetoric and chance) blow over us in a certain

[13] *The Poems and Plays of William Vaughn Moody*, I, 29–30.

locality. This is a secondary property of war, whose essence is "the eternal fact of conflict." Patriotism is now seen as a vice —but it is "godly," and we therefore "surrender to this falsity." But Crane, speaking in the voice of such soldiers as Manolo Prat who died, or the "Marines Signalling Under Fire at Guantanamo," [14] beholds his civilian fellow-patriots with disgust and scorn. Unlike his soldiers, the "people of New York" have not "paid the price of patriotism," and they degrade its meaning. Both this poem and "A youth, young in years" begin with strength and assurance but end in rhetoric, the first sentimental, the second furious. Had Crane rewritten them to sustain the level of their openings we would have had two worthy poems; but extensive revision was seldom his practice in either verse or prose.

4

The last of Crane's poems explicitly on war is his longest and most ambitious attempt to define in verse the significance of combat. Never published, it was however submitted posthumously to some magazines, probably in England, by Cora Crane, with the note "The ms. . . . has just been discovered in saddle-bags used by Stephen Crane during the late war with Spain." Two copies, one typewritten, the other in Cora's hand, are in the Columbia collection; no holograph manuscript appears to have survived.

The Battle Hymn

> All-feeling God, hear in the war-night
> The rolling voice of a nation:
> Through dusky billows of darkness

[14] *Work,* Vol. IX.

See the flash, the under-light of bared swords—
—Whirling gleams like wee shells
Deep in the streams of the universe—
Bend and see a people, O, God,
A people rebuked, accursed,
By him of the many lungs
And by him of the bruised weary war-drum
(The chanting disintegrate and the two-faced eagle)
Bend and mark our steps, O, God.
Mark well, mark well, the new path, lead awry
Then in the forest of the lost standards
Suffer us to grope and bleed apace
For the wisdom is Thine.
Bend and see a people, O, God,
A people applauded, acclaimed,
By him of the raw red shoulders
The manacle-marked, the thin victim
(He lies white amid the smoking cane)
—And if the path, the new path, leads straight—
Then—O, God—then bare the great bronze arm;
Swing high the blaze of the chained stars
And let them look and heed
(The chanting disintegrate and the two-faced eagle)
For we go, we go in a lunge of a long blue corps
And—to Thee we commit our lifeless sons.
The convulsed and furious dead
(They shall be white amid the smoking cane)
For, the seas shall not bar us;
The capped mountains shall not hold us back
We shall sweep and swarm through jungle and pool,
Then let the savage one bend his high chin
To see on his breast, the sullen glow of death-medals
For we know and we say our gift.
His prize is death, deep doom.
(He shall be white amid the smoking cane.)

This is an unexpected performance by the poet whose seeming agnosticism we examined in the second chapter. The very title suggests the combination throughout "The Battle Hymn" of Crane's dual ancestral heritage: a joining in his mind of war and of religious emotion, his inheritance from Cranes-at-arms in the Revolution, from circuit-riding Pecks adumbrating Judgment Day in forest clearings.

We have noted his concentration upon sacrificial suffering and death as the ethical justification of war. "There exists the eternal fact of conflict," which Crane does not question; given that fact, how does a man act so that he may not despise himself at the end? We remember Henry, in *The Red Badge*, salving his self-esteem with the reflection, after he had flung a pine cone at a squirrel, that every creature in Nature runs away when it is menaced. But the falsity of that position is obvious: man alone has the power to will himself to courage, to not run away, to suffer and if need be die in common cause with his fellows. Thus "in the forest of the lost standards" where we may not even know or remember what cause it is with which patriotism proposed to bind us, we "grope and bleed apace" in the common bond of our kinship with our comrades. If we fail, they will die. (Similarly, in Chapter XIX of *The Red Badge*, Henry "wondered, afterward" of the moment of his real heroism, "what reasons he could have had for being there." [15]) The people, "rebuked, accursed, / By him of the many lungs"— the war-god, a Blusterer—are "applauded, acclaimed, / By

[15] *Omnibus,* p. 339. (The text of *The Red Badge of Courage* which Mr. Stallman has assembled in the *Omnibus,* restoring to the first American edition uncanceled passages from the final manuscript, supersedes as authoritative the reprinting of the 1895 edition in *Work,* Vol. I.)

him of the raw red shoulders / The manacle-marked, the thin
victim." This seems best explicable as an intended allusion to
the sufferings of Jesus. "He lies white amid the smoking cane"
would then equate the death of a soldier fallen in Cuba—
Manolo Prat, perhaps, now regarded in an apocalyptic light
—with the sacrifice of God's Son. Such an identification is prefigured by the initials, bearing, and stigmata of Jim Conklin
in *The Red Badge of Courage*.[16] The ensuing lines plead "if
the path, the new path, leads straight," then let the stars in
their chains heed the "lunge of a long blue corps" of victorious
combatants. Neither seas nor mountains, Crane's images of Nature's hostility to man, shall deter this army, but we, the survivors, leave behind our "convulsed and furious dead" whose
sacrifice even the savage war-god must honor. "His prize is
death, deep doom," but "our gift" is the mystery of heroism:
at the end, "(He shall be white amid the smoking cane)" indicates that Jesus' spirit is reborn in each heroic death of ours,
and where the war-god offers "deep doom" we partake of the
Sacrifice. Having gone this far, the Resurrection is clearly implied.

Valuable as is "The Battle Hymn" in clarifying Crane's attitude toward his major subject, its thematic unity does not protect the poem from stylistic flaws. The tone is more oracular
than may be desirable even in a "Hymn," and such diction as
"wee shells," the repeated "O, God," "Mark well, mark well"
detracts from the genuineness of feeling in the rest of the

[16] See Stallman's introduction to *The Red Badge* in *Omnibus*, pp. 197–
99, and my introduction to *The Red Badge of Courage and Other Stories*,
pp. xv–xxiv, for discussion of Jim Conklin as a surrogate for Jesus Christ.

poem. Nor is the grammatical confusion admissible in "The chanting disintegrate and the two-faced eagle." Against these objections, however, we may set the suggestive, incantatory movement of incremental parallelism and functional refrain.

It is needless to remark, in view of Crane's bitterness in "There exists the eternal fact of conflict," that nothing could be further from his mind in "The Battle Hymn" than the *Gott mit uns* patriotism of Richard Hovey. Take out "blue corps" and "the smoking cane," and the poem refers to any war, not only to the war of our Manifest Destiny. In that context, however, the "two-faced eagle" is properly ambiguous, for its white face appears on the Great Seal of the United States, its black visage on that of Spain.

"The Battle Hymn" is Crane's attempt to sacramentalize the character of heroism. Admirable though this is, there is yet a discrepancy between the occasion of the poem and its outcome. Crane's attempt to attribute to war alone the solemnity of sacrificial heroism is at once the strength and the limitation of his special sensibility.

If Crane were ever to succeed in writing a poem commensurate with his apocalyptic ethical vision, it would require metaphors more widely implicated in life than these. One would think, too, that such a poem, offering a final resolution of all the tensions which prepossessed him, must come after his near-miss in "The Battle Hymn." Crane did write such a poem—paradoxically not later, but long before "The Battle Hymn"; indeed although it abounds in the imagery of war, long before he had seen a war.

This poem, "The Blue Battalions," did not appear until the June, 1898, issue of the *Philistine*, but it had been written by

April of 1896.[17] The poem is inexplicably absent from *War is Kind*. Amy Lowell, in her reprinting of Crane's two books in his *Work*, Vol. VI, misleadingly and without comment inserted "The Blue Battalions" as the last of the short lyrics in *War is Kind* (xxvii), followed only by "Intrigue." There it remains in *Collected Poems*. It has been anthologized only once, in the year of its original publication, when it appeared in *Spanish-American War Songs*.[18] Neither of Crane's biographers so much as mentions it, nor does any critic of his verse. Yet this is his most significant poem.

5

"The Blue Battalions" combines the narrative-allegorical method with indirection in a fusion of the two modes of presentation which Crane had mastered in "A man adrift on a slim spar," which, curiously, he had also omitted from *War is Kind*. There is a richness of implication here, and a lyrical power that can be seen developing in the later poems in *The Black Riders* and throughout *War is Kind*.

> When a people reach the top of a hill,
> Then does God lean toward them,
> Shortens tongues and lengthens arms.
> A vision of their dead comes to the weak.

[17] The holograph list of magazine acceptances of Crane's verse referred to above includes "The Blue Battalions" as number 11; numbers 10 and 12, "The Candid Man" (WK ix) and "A man afloat [*sic*] on a slim spar," like number 11 had not been accepted and are followed by blanks. The latest acceptance was "The Sea–Point of View" (WK iii) which had appeared in the *Philistine* for April, 1896. Poems in *War is Kind* first published after that date are absent from the list, e.g., "I explain the silvered passing of a ship at night," published in the *Bookman*, October, 1896.

[18] Edited and published in Detroit by Sidney A. Witherbee, this was

The moon shall not be too old
Before the new battalions rise,
   Blue battalions.
The moon shall not be too old
When the children of change shall fall
Before the new battalions,
   The blue battalions.

Mistakes and virtues will be trampled deep.
A church and a thief shall fall together.
A sword will come at the bidding of the eyeless,
The God-led, turning only to beckon,
   Swinging a creed like a censer
   At the head of the new battalions,
      Blue battalions.
   March the tools of nature's impulse,
   Men born of wrong, men born of right,
   Men of the new battalions,
      The blue battalions.

The clang of swords is Thy wisdom,
The wounded make gestures like Thy Son's;
The feet of mad horses is one part—
Ay, another is the hand of a mother on the brow of a youth.
   Then, swift as they charge through a shadow,
   The men of the new battalions,
      Blue battalions—
   God lead them high, God lead them far,
   God lead them far, God lead them high,
   These new battalions,
      The blue battalions.

"A Complete Collection of Newspaper Verse During the Recent War with Spain"; Williams and Starrett, *Stephen Crane: A Bibliography,* p. 38.

Nowhere else in his writings does Crane so strikingly envisage the triumph of man over the fated misery of life. This militant vision of a New Jerusalem manifests the ethical coherence of Crane's ultimate belief; here he has overcome his fears of the vengeful God, and he identifies his inner God of pity with the heroism and sufferings of Jesus. The debt of his ethical sensibility to his father is great, yet his apocalyptic fervor most likely derives equally from the evangelism of his mother's family.

A close reading should make evident the degree to which Crane synthesized most of his controlling metaphors successfully in this prophetic testament. Only his sinful love-and-rescue theme is not included among the images of climbing, seeing, blindness, battle, religious doctrine and ritual, mad horses, and maternal pity. Although the poem is organized into a rather complex stanzaic form, the absence of rhyme and the curious metrical irregularity may for some readers diffuse the intensity of feeling with which these metaphors are charged. Perhaps, when their implications are made explicit, the value of Crane's metaphors in unifying his poetic statement will become more apparent.

First stanza. The opening image, "When a people reach the top of a hill," generalizes the traditional symbol of ascent as an approach to truth or Grace which Crane had used in *The Black Riders,* poems XXVI, XXXV, XXXVII, and XLIX, and in *War is Kind,* poems XV, XVIII, and XXII. In each of these poems it is "I" or "a man" who climbs the hill, mountain, or rooftop; here it is *a people.* The envisaged blessed time will come only when all mankind has reached the heights from which alone truth

can be seen. That a single seer cannot bring about the apocalypse is clear from poem xxvi of *The Black Riders;* climbing
"Through regions of snow" to the "summit-view" of "a mighty
hill,"

> It seemed that my labour
> Had been to see gardens
> Lying at impossible distances.

At such time, when all men have climbed as high as their
mortality permits, "does God lean toward them," meeting
them halfway. Only then do they merit His help.

What help does He give? He "Shortens tongues and lengthens arms": we remember "A little ink more or less! / It surely
can't matter" (WK iv) as disparaging the endless din of religious persuasions. And we remember, too, that to Crane brevity was an important aesthetic principle, and his aesthetic he
once summed up in this remark: ". . . art is man's substitute
for nature and we are most successful in art when we approach
nearest to nature and truth." [19] He would rip away the foggy
clamor of language with which men—even some of the authors he admired—had obscured and falsified the truths of
nature. "Lengthens arms" suggests action, militant action, as
"battalions" three lines below makes clear.

When men, then, have received this much encouragement
from God, "the weak" are further heartened by "A vision of
their dead." What they see may be inferred by citing some
of Crane's references to his own dead, his ancestors. Those
who loom behind "my little life . . . my tiny throes and struggles" (BR xiii) were pioneers, founders of cities, heroes. "Dur-

---

[19] Stallman, *Omnibus,* p. 648.

ing the Revolution the Cranes were pretty hot people," he wrote to a Newark editor in 1896.[20] A letter of 1900 recounts their exploits with pride.

The youngest son [of Crane's great grandfather Stephen, for whom he was named] . . . was captured by some Hessians, and upon his refusing to tell the road by which they intended to surprise a certain American outpost, they beat him with their muskets, and then having stabbed him with their bayonets, they left him dead in the road.

The sacrificial heroism of this youthful forebear living and dying by his code of honor obviously meant much to the author of *The Red Badge of Courage* and the poems which are our concern. The letter continues with another passage already cited: "In those olden times the family did its duty. Upon my mother's side everybody . . . became a Methodist clergyman. . . ."[21] The phrase about the duty of the family links his account of the Cranes in war with that of the Pecks in their pulpits. In the past his family, on both sides, did its duty. "As for myself," he concludes—and he lists the schools from which he did not graduate, the books he has written.

These four lines, then, set the ethical conditions to be fulfilled and invoke the strength of heroic ancestors, antecedent to the revelation of the poem. "The moon shall not be too old / Before the new battalions rise" suggests that these are "things which must shortly come to pass" (Revelations 1.1). The apocalypse is immanent. The arrival of the new battalions is prefigured in an earlier poem (WK xv), which I here re-

[20] *Ibid.*, p. 651.

[21] *Ibid.*, pp. 689–90; see also *Love Letters,* ed. by Cady and Wells, p. 50.

produce from a manuscript in the Columbia collection. There are several phrases at variance with the published text:

> Once a man clambering to the housetops
> Appealed to the empty heavens.
> With strong voice he called to the imperturbable stars;
> A warrior's shout he raised to the higher suns.
> Lo, at last, there was an indication, a dot,
> Then—finally—God—the sky was filled with armies.

The images of climbing high, warrior, and armies in the sky were to be used to better advantage in "The Blue Battalions."

But the armies in the sky are prefigured, too, by a passage from Crane's Decoration Day article in 1894:

> The men who fought in the great war for freedom and union are disappearing. They are upon their last great march, a march that ceases to be seen at the horizon and whose end is death. . . . A vast body of them have thronged to the grave, regiment by regiment, brigade by brigade, and the others are hurrying after their fellows who have marched into the Hereafter. There, every company is gradually getting its men, no soldier but what will be there to answer his name. . . . Let us not wait to celebrate but consider that there are now before us the belated ones of the army that is marching over the horizon, off from the earth, into the sky, into history and tradition.[22]

So battalions. Blue, as it happens, was the color of the United States Army field and dress uniforms, respectively, in the Civil and Spanish-American wars. Henry, in *The Red Badge*, had to learn to regard himself as nothing more than a part of "a blue demonstration." But blue is also the color of heaven. "None of them knew the color of the sky," begins "The Open Boat," in

[22] "Gratitude of a Nation," Columbia MS.

which one of four must pay the sacrificial price of mortality before the others can look up to see the color—blue.

"When the children of change shall fall / Before the new battalions": There shall be war in heaven and earth—this is the theme of the following stanzas, in which the redemptory ethics of Jonathan Crane is asserted with a militancy reflecting the evangelical zeal of the Pecks. "The children of change" are the fallible mortals who in their unwisdom rule the earth, and "change" is the false god they praise. This battle is heralded in a posthumously published poem, a war song in two voices. The first is that of the children of change, a song we have heard before:

> Chant you loud of punishments,
> Of the twisting of the heart's poor strings
> Of the crash of the lightning's fierce revenge.

The blue battalions are limned in this reply:

> Then sing I of the supple-souled men
> And the strong, strong gods
> That shall meet in times hereafter
> And the amaze of the gods
> At the strength of the men.
> —The strong, strong gods—
> —And the supple-souled men—   [*Collected Poems,* p. 131]

Middle stanza. So great an upheaval will be the regeneration of mankind, signified by the triumph of the blue battalions, that all our mortal values and institutions will be irrelevant. Like "the children of change," "A church and a thief shall fall together." In the New Dispensation of Eternity, the church of the old way, where they chanted "loud of punishments," must be thrown down. As for the thief, where "Mistakes and virtues will be trampled deep" his transgressions—even the theft of an apple—will be indistinguishable from the merits of others. The juxtaposition of "church" and "thief" of course suggests the Crucifixion too, the church being the Body of Christ. There, too, "church" and thief fell together, Christ to rise and give hope of salvation to all thieves and sinners. So the "church" that "falls" may be the Body of Christ, the promise of Redemption of the Second Adam, as well as the vindictive institution that denies divine and human love and falls never to rise again. This promise of salvation is the creed which "The God-led" are "swinging like a censer." Now an ecclesiastical censer is swung to quicken the burning of the incense within. The swinging motion suggests also the rhythmic march of the blue battalions: their heavenward advance intensifies the ardor of their belief, and scents the sky with sweetness.

The battalions find their weapons when "A sword will come at the bidding of the eyeless." (In a Columbia manuscript this line reads, "A sword looms at the bidding of the blind.") What is meant is perhaps a rejection of seeing, which so often in Crane's poems brings the seer illusion instead of reality, or knowledge different from that which he sought, or it leads him into the wilderness instead of to the true way (as in BR XX, XLII, XLIV, XLIX, L, LVII; WK III, VII, XIII, XII). But another view of blindness is suggested in a letter to Nellie Crouse, blindness as a symbol of an ethical life: "Tolstoy's aim is, I suppose—I believe—to make himself good. It is an incomparably quixotic task for any man to undertake. He will not suc-

ceed; but he will even succeed more than he can ever himself
know, and so at his nearest point to success, he will be propor-
tionately blind. This is the pay of this kind of greatness." [23] If
this has any bearing on the poem, we may interpolate, "A
sword will come at the bidding of the wholly good."

"The tools of nature's impulse, / Men born of wrong, men
born of right" march in these blue battalions. This is a certain
echo of Jonathan Crane's views on the regeneration of believers in *Holiness the Birthright of All God's Children*. To him
"nature's impulse," we remember, was blameless. Impulse,
"the force which opposes conscience and honor is in itself innocent; and so long as conscience maintains perfect suprem-
acy there is not a taint of sin." Christ, fasting in the desert,
"was in all points tempted like as we are"—through his natural
impulses—*"yet without sin."* [24] So it is that "Men born of
wrong" can march in the blue battalions; "Everyone indeed,
who is born of God has attained an exalted state. He is the
King's son's. Let him not undervalue his birthright." [25] All believers are regenerate.

Final stanza. The opening lines are a climactic ingathering
of Crane's controlling images and major themes. Here at last
integrity, fear, courage, pity, and pain are reconciled to the
cosmic forces and societal injunctions which baffle innocence
and make inhuman demands of humanity:

> The clang of swords is Thy wisdom,
> The wounded make gestures like Thy Son's;
> The feet of mad horses is one part—
> Ay, another is the hand of a mother on the brow of a youth.

---

[23] *Love Letters*, p. 52.   [24] *Holiness the Birthright*, p. 97.
[25] *Ibid.*, p. 137.

In the title poem of *The Black Riders* the "clang and clang of spear and shield, / And clash and clash of hoof and heel," the tumultuous "shouts and the wave of hair" was the "ride of Sin." Now "The clang of swords is Thy wisdom," it is the Divine Will that war and suffering be man's portion. Crane accepts this, not with ironical reluctance as in the final poem in *War is Kind* (xxvi) but with the humility and resignation he had hitherto attributed only to the pebbles (xxv) and the mountain peaks (xviii). "The wounded make gestures like Thy Son's" symbolizes the ever-recurring sacrificial death: that of Billy Higgins in "The Open Boat"; of Jim Conklin, the surrogate for Jesus Christ in *The Red Badge;* of the corpse "amid the smoking cane" in "The Battle Hymn." It is the knowledge of this line, won only through suffering, which makes possible any conciliation with the agonies and injustices of life. We see that the code Crane's characters must seek and live by is an acceptance of the fearful responsibility and pain that is the dignity of mankind. That is why Henry Fleming, who thinks he must discover whether he is brave, learns that what he seeks to know is the nature of courage itself: "a temporary but sublime absence of selfishness." Courage is more than human; when the regiment falters, "They were become men again." [26] To win this knowledge for us that suffering is tolerable only when it is sacrificial, and then it is man's greatest testament to his own humanity, Billy Higgins must die, and leave the interpretation—the artistic statement—of his death to others; this is the ethical reason for the correspondent's presence in the open boat.

[26] Stallman, *Omnibus,* p. 339.

The foregoing may seem a simple truth, obvious in Christian doctrine; but the Methodism of the Pecks was an Old Testament creed swung like a spear, not a censer. The value of his poems to Crane as statements of his "thoughts about life" was that in them he fought the theological battles that had to be won before he could write "The Blue Battalions" or his greatest fiction. Only here and in "The Battle Hymn," at the highest pitch of intensity, is Crane able to identify his inner god of pity with Jesus suffering for mankind rather than with God the Father.

Another part of God's wisdom "is the hand of a mother on the brow of a youth." This image of compassion, reminiscent of the mother who loved "A soldier, young in years," of Henry's mother putting socks in his bundle, and of the "Mother whose heart hung humble as a button" in the title poem of *War is Kind,* is no longer contradicted by "The feet of mad horses." John Berryman has shown how images of horses pervade Crane's fiction. There are fantasies of trampling in *The Red Badge,* the idiot Negro's assumption of a horse's identity in *The Monster,* and the sacrificial heroism of "The Veteran" who dies trying to save colts from a burning stable. And there are the black riders. At the end of the last chapter we mentioned Berryman's psychoanalytic interpretation of these resonant images as parts of a complex of themes involving sexual conflict, Oedipal rivalry against the father, aggression, courage. The contexts in which Crane's horses appear show the validity of some of Berryman's assumptions; enough at any rate to recognize in those horses Crane's commonest image of panic, when we see them "Blowing, stagger-

ing, bloody" (WK vmi) or "affrighted" (WK i), great noble
beasts driven mad with fright and pain by man's monstrous
conflicts. "The feet of mad horses," then, links the present context of acceptance to all the others in which the image appears.
It is Crane's key symbol of conflict, danger, death, the opposite
of his associated images of the horse as fellow-creature and object of compassion.

The blue battalions, "swift as they charge through a
shadow," evoke the courage of Henry's regiment in *The Red
Badge of Courage* routing the chimeras that had been their
fears. They evoke also that roll-call of the regiments of dead
heroes in whose honor the young Crane wrote his Decoration
Day article and poem in 1894. Like them, the blue battalions
are fearless and immortal now; and as we have seen, fearless-
ness is "the sublime absence of selfishness." With the final
invocation, "God lead them far, God lead them high," the Blue
Battalions' battles have been won. The trials of earthly life had
been endured, accepted, overcome. "God-led," they march—
higher than "the top of a hill."

Six

THE IMPACT OF
A MILLION DOLLARS

Despite his febrile intensity, Crane was anything but Protean in the range of subjects in his imaginative writing. For him man's relations to God, to his beloved, and to his fellow-man were so intrinsically linked as to call forth in his poetry associated images time and again in each of these contexts. This consistency and coherence is won at the cost of variety. It is surprising on two counts that only a small proportion of his verse concerns itself with objective reality to a degree any greater than do the poems we have thus far examined. We should not suspect, from them, that Crane was a pioneer in the naturalistic novel; nor should we think he shared, with Whitman, Twain, Howells, and Garland, an apprenticeship to literature as a practicing journalist. True, Crane committed his life to a search for experience—even, at times, for sensation. He was occasionally rewarded, as in the sinking of the *Commodore* or his pursuit by Mexican bandits, with impressions obtained at a pitch of intensity high enough to avail him in transforming the skimble-skamble stuff of life into the stoical view of fate which is the hallmark of his writings. His religious training had led him to consider most important the moral fortitude of the individual man, whatever his temporal circumstances. Crane consequently considered secondary the sort of social problems which the radical young Garland and the older socialistic Howells made the subjects of their fiction.

In the same letter to Garland which mentioned his Decoration Day article, Crane wrote, "That poem, 'The Reformer,' which I showed you in behind Daly's Theatre, was lost somehow, so I don't think we can ever send it to the *Arena*. I can't remember a line of it." [1] The poem was probably written at Garland's suggestion, for the more established writer had sent some of Crane's newspaper sketches to B. O. Flower for republication in that liberal review. But Crane seems not to have cared enough about this poem, or about appearing there, to recall his own lines. Later, he would write to Nellie Crouse, "When I speak of a battle I do not mean want, and those similar spectres. I mean myself and the inherent indolence and cowardice which is the lot of all men." Reading praises of *The Black Riders,* he "began to be afraid, afraid that I would be content with myself. . . ."

For the first time I saw the majestic forces which are arrayed against man's true success—not the world—the world is silly, changeable, any of it's [*sic*] decisions can be reversed—but man's own colossal impulses more strong than chains, and I perceived that the fight was not going to be with the world but with myself.[2]

It is the struggle against these inner forces, inherent indolence and cowardice, which engages Crane. Social forces operate in his world of course, but he can fear and hate the in-

---

[1] Stallman, *Omnibus,* p. 599.
[2] *Love Letters,* ed. by Cady and Wells, pp. 43–44.

justices of life without proposing dogmas or espousing panaceas to ameliorate them. In a prose sketch on the lot of a social outcast—in true Zolaesque tradition he decked himself as a hobo and spent a night in a flophouse to write "An Experiment in Misery"—he simply presents what he sees. There is no alternative offered, no plea for any ameliorative measures. To another correspondent he wrote of this story, "I tried to make plain that the root of Bowery life is a sort of cowardice. Perhaps I mean a lack of ambition or to willingly be knocked flat and accept the licking." [3]

Crane's inscription in three presentation copies of *Maggie* avows that the book "tries to show that environment is a tremendous thing in the world." [4] Yet a careful reading should make clear that the power of that novel resides not so much in its subject as in its style, and the style has practically nothing in common with the style of any other naturalistic novelist. The subject, as Marcus Cunliffe cogently remarks, may have been new to fiction in 1893 but was long known to readers of such religious and charitable reformers as the Reverend Lyman Abbott, Edward Townsend, and Mrs. Helen Campbell, among whom we may assuredly number Mrs. Helen Crane and her son Stephen. [5] But what is there in *Maggie* of social philosophy, what thought of reform? We see the oppressed poor as "Withered persons, in curious postures of submission to something." [6]

[3] Beer, pp. 312–13; Stallman, *Omnibus*, p. 655.
[4] *Omnibus*, pp. 594–95, 610–11.
[5] "Stephen Crane and the American Background of *Maggie*," *American Quarterly*, VII (Spring, 1955), 31–44.
[6] Crane, *Work*, X, 141.

In considering the poems Crane wrote on man's relation to society we may begin with one which alludes to his own place in the economic structure. His profession was newspaper reporting.

> A newspaper is a collection of half-injustices
> Which, bawled by boys from mile to mile,
> Spreads its curious opinion
> To a million merciful and sneering men,
> While families cuddle the joys of the fireside
> When spurred by tale of dire lone agony.

So begins poem XII of *War is Kind*. We must remember that it was only in Crane's generation that the metropolitan daily emerged in its present form. This was the era of Hearst and Pulitzer, and it saw the transformation of the nineteenth-century newspaper into the modern medium of mass communication. In the Gilded Age the exploitation of vulgarity and sensation, the invasion of personal privacy by the press, and the journalistic demagogy in politics became the rule rather than the exception. These were the developments which Howells sorrowfully chronicled in *A Modern Instance* (1881); Henry James, too, looked with horror upon the new journalism in *The Bostonians* (1886). Howells, devoted to journalism, contrasts to his spineless reporter and corrupt publisher the admirable editor Ricker. But in this newspaper poem Crane is no protagonist of the honor of the press.

> A newspaper is a court
> Where every one is kindly and unfairly tried
> By a squalor of honest men.
> A newspaper is a market
> Where wisdom sells its freedom
> And melons are crowned by the crowd. . . .

Thus far the poem offers a link, technically, between the additive incantations of Whitman and the prosier parallelisms of Sandburg; perhaps it was this side of Crane that the latter admired in his "Letters to Dead Imagists." But the final definition of a newspaper is, in both its explicit allegorism and the ensuing language, wholly Crane's own:

> A newspaper is a symbol;
> It is feckless life's chronicle,
> A collection of loud tales
> Concentrating eternal stupidities
> That in remote ages lived unhaltered
> Roaming through a fenceless world.

Even here the omnipresent key image of tension in Crane's work makes an indirectly metaphoric appearance.[7]

In "feckless life's chronicle" citizens who abhorred the nasty fictions of *Maggie* and the uncivil agnosticism of *The Black Riders* could feed their appetite for facts and truths with many an account of real fallen women, with many a dispatch on the unequal struggles of men against their fates. A poem which Crane strategically placed at the end of the first edition of *War is Kind* (followed only by "Intrigue") takes his usual cosmic

---

[7] An earlier poem (BR XI) describes a sage reading a newspaper in a lonely place. "He accosted me: / 'Sir, what is this?' / . . . / 'Old, old man, it is the wisdom of the age.' / The sage looked upon me with admiration." But to this we must contrast XXXVI, wherein a seer holds "The book of wisdom" and calls his interlocutor, who is curious to read it, a child. "Think not that I am a child, / for already I know much / Of that which you hold . . ." but when he opens the book, "Strange that I should have grown so suddenly blind." These poems are more concerned with the relationship of son to father-figure than with the truths of journalism, but do illustrate that Crane shared with the above-mentioned novelists the conviction that the newspaper would prove the subliterary symbol of the present age.

view of such inequities as may seem characteristic of life.
Paradox being the natural condition of Crane's mind, he places
"The trees in the garden rained flowers" directly after the af-
firmative lantern-song of the little pebbles (WK xxv), as he
had in the earlier book preceded the final poem on the spirit
smitten for disbelief in God with another beginning "God lay
dead in heaven." In xxvi, a "spindling little tutor" protests to
"the father" the unjust distribution of blessings among the
children. But the father replies,

> Not so, small sage!
> This thing is just.
> For, look you,
> Are not they who possess the flowers
> Stronger, bolder, shrewder
> Then they who have none?

"My lord," admits the tutor, "The stars are displaced / By this
towering wisdom." An allegory complete, in this last poem the
spindling tutor is Crane himself.[8] While his reply does not
suggest that he accepts without demur the unjust verdict of
Natural Law, the irony is muted as he recognizes that the verdict holds whether he accepts it or not. No longer does he bite
"madly at the feet of the god."

2

Poverty, wealth, and charity are the themes of Crane's verse
on social subjects. Of these he knew the first at first hand, yet
despite his creed of impressionistic realism most of the poems
dealing explicitly with economic injustice are bathetic. It is

---

[8] In physique he was "slight . . . about five six and weighed only
one hundred twenty pounds or less." Berryman, p. 21.

the subject of his earliest surviving poem, a jocular piece of juvenilia preserved by Corwin Knapp Linson, who writes that it gives "witness to a state of mind to which Steve was daily subject for weeks at a time." [9] Linson dates this piece of verse, "Ah, haggard purse," from about December, 1892. (The poem is reproduced in the Appendix, page 283.) A later manuscript poem, "My cross!" (Appendix, page 284) also alludes to his poverty. These attempts are artistically inept. The theme little appealed to Crane for verse. The tensions in his best work are always produced by the discrepancy between a man's ideals and the poor fumbling acts of which he is capable. Poverty as a theme implies a different tension, that of man versus the economic system. In an article which only an idealistic youth could imagine would be printed in a newspaper—this one never was—Crane wrote,

A man has the right to rebel if he is not given a fair opportunity to be virtuous. Inversely, then, if he possesses this opportunity, he cannot rebel, he has no complaint. I am of the opinion that poverty of itself is no cause. It is something above and beyond. For example, there is Collis P. Huntington and William D. Rockafeller [sic]—as virtuous as these gentlemen are, I would not say that their virtue is any ways superior to mine for instance. Their opportunities are no greater. They can give more in quantity but not relatively. We can each give all that we possess and there I am at once their equal.

I do not think however that they would be capable of sacrifices that would be possible to me. So then I envy them nothing.[10]

This emphasis on personal ethics and the irrelevance of wealth and station to its exercise explains the bitterness of Crane's attack on millionaires in two poems in *War is Kind*.

[9] Linson MS, p. 11.

[10] From the first of three manuscript untitled press dispatches headed "City of Mexico," in the Columbia collection.

The impact of a million dollars
Is a crash of flunkeys,
And yawning emblems of Persia
Cheeked against oak, France, and a sabre,
The outcry of old beauty
Whored by pimping merchants
To submission before wine and chatter.
Silly rich peasants stamp the carpets of men
Dead men who dreamed fragrance and light
Into their woof, their lives. . . .   [WK xx]

Meaningless to the millionaire hat manufacturer is the heritage
of artifact and idealism with which he has stuffed his mansion.
In the second poem the irony is heavier:

The successful man has thrust himself
Through the water of the years,
Reeking wet with mistakes—
Bloody mistakes;
Slimed victories over the lesser,
A figure thankful on the shore of money.

                    .   .   .   .

In guiltless ignorance, in ignorant guilt,
He delivered his secrets to the riven multitude.
"Thus I defended; Thus I wrought."
Complacent, smiling,
He stands heavily on the dead.
Erect on a pillar of skulls
He declaims his trampling of babes;
Smirking, fat, dripping,
He makes speech in guiltless ignorance,
Innocence.   [WK xvii]

This ends in caricature and bombast; social satire was not
Crane's *métier*.

Charity, as Crane saw it, was the balm with which Success would soothe its guilt.[11] In poem xvi of *The Black Riders* he writes, "Charity, thou art a lie, / A toy of women, / A pleasure of certain men." His diatribe against the civilian patriots in the Spanish-American War accused them of sending "charity in bulk to better men." An unpublished poem elaborates this theme:

On the brown trail
We hear the grinding of your carts
To our villages
Laden with food
Laden with food
We know you are come to our help
But—
Why do you impress upon us
Your foreign happiness?
     We know it not.

(Hark!
(Carts laden with food
(Laden with food)
We weep because we don't understand
But your gifts form into a yoke
The food turns into a yoke
(Hark!
(Carts laden with food
(Laden with food)
It is our mission to vanish

[11] But Crane once wrote to a Miss Catherine Harris in 1896, "The missions for children are another thing and if you will have Mr. Rockefeller give me a hundred street cars and some money I will load all the babes off to some pink world where cows can lick their noses and they will never see their families any more. . . ." *Omnibus,* pp. 655–56.

Grateful because of full mouths
Destiny—Darkness
Time understands
And ye—ye bigoted men of a moment—
—Wait—
Await your turn.   [Columbia MS]

These poems do violence to Crane's own aesthetic creed, being made of opinions rather than the truths of observation. Yet his verse on economic wrongs is interesting in what it suggests of Crane's view of the class divisions in society. Such divisions, as Henry James remarks in his essay on Hawthorne, are necessary to the novelist in his delineation of character. Crane's fiction, however, is like his verse; there is hardly a sense of society surrounding his characters.

As regards social realism, we do indeed feel that the slum in *Maggie* is a real slum, although Crane describes it in animistic terms in language of such energy as to make the pathetic fallacy seem a law of the universe in Rum Alley. This we do not feel about the caricatured successful man; he is not alive in the midst of his baggage of skulls and corpses. Nor are the images of the food-laden carts in sharp enough focus to move us down their trail.

In one unpublished poem, however, he is more successful than in any of the foregoing in finding objective correlatives to his observations of social inequity and the feelings these observations evoke:

Bottles and bottles and bottles
In a merry den
And the wan smiles of women
Untruthing license and joy.
Countless lights

Making oblique and confusing multiplication
In mirrors
And the light returns again to the faces.

. . . .

A cellar, and a pale death-child,
A woman
Ministering commonly, degradedly,
Without manners,
A murmur and a silence
Or silence and a murmur
And then a finished silence
The moon beats practically upon the cheap bed.

An hour, with its million trinkets of joy or pain
Matters little in a cellar or merry den
Since all is death.   [Columbia MS]

Here Crane combines the pictorial realism of the naturalistic
slice-of-life presentation with an obliquity of statement as to
the consequences of the two scenes he puts before us. These
are in obvious contrast, yet the contrast is redoubled as we
first feel, then realize, that the slices of life are subtly linked
by parallels of structure in the two eight-line stanzas. Each begins with a triple iteration, in each women are shown in action
the significance of which is rendered in terms of a single sense
impression, light and silence. The light image is picked up
again by "The moon beats practically upon the cheap bed,"
an irony intensified by contrasting to the "confusing multiplication" of cabaret lights and mirrors the unexpected practicality of the moon in a tenement lacking gas or candle. Metrically, too, this is one of his best-controlled poems. In the final
three lines, however, Crane revealed that he did not know
when to stop. It is hard to imagine his putting "Since all is

death" into the same poem with "Countless lights / Making oblique and confusing multiplications . . . / And the light returns again to the faces," yet there it is.

The reader may have noticed that several of the newly recovered poems show similar disparities between the objectivity of their openings, firm and assured, and the literal obviousness of their endings. Such was the case in "A row of thick pillars," in "A soldier, young in years," in "There exists the eternal fact of conflict." As for the previously published poems, their inconsistencies have usually been regarded as proof of Crane's immaturity or lack of discipline. Yet it may be observed that when Crane's verse is bad, it is bad in a way that is distinctly his own. When Crane appears deliberately to spoil with heavy hand a poem that seemed well on its way toward becoming a unified construct of metaphor and indirection, he reveals the difficulties which beset a stylistic pioneer. His successes are hard-won. All too often he proves unable to sustain the distinctive style he has evolved to best define his own sensibility; he then betrays his own work by literary dependency to influences he has in fact outgrown.

Thus far, although I have found occasions to demonstrate how Crane makes his poems do their work, my emphasis has been mainly upon his themes, their sources, and their development. Now it is time to look at the stylistic influences which contribute to his verse, to see what they were, how he assimilated them, how he outgrew some and amalgamated others into an idiom strange and new. Then at last we can hazard an attempt to fix Crane's place in the development of modern poetry.

Seven ⮷ *STYLE, SOURCES, SYMBOLS*

I have been suggesting that some of Crane's unsuccessful poems are flawed by a serious inconsistency in treatment and language. A line from his "Battle Hymn" may aphorize this dilemma: "The chanting disintegrate and the two-faced eagle." If we may adopt a conventional metaphor of the poet as a singing or soaring bird (not inappropriate to a Crane), we may suggest that the chant disintegrates because the eagle-like flight of the poetic imagination is indeed trying to move in two directions at once.

The first of these is toward a wry, ironic, seemingly collo-quial diction in which the structure of the verse is achieved through the indirect means of associated images, rhythmic ten-sions, and parallels which we have observed in the first six-teen lines of "Bottles and bottles and bottles," in "The Blue Battalions," in "A man adrift on a slim spar." The second direc-tion is toward an apparently crude sort of allegory, in which x in life is equated exactly with y in verse. What complicates the study of Crane's technique is that while he began as an allegorist and moved toward a kind of symbolism, his progress is not that simple, as the flawed poems in the last chapter re-veal. And, as we have seen, he had already achieved in "The

Blue Battalions" (1896) what he attempted with less success in "The Battle Hymn" (1898). Yet despite these inconsistencies we can trace several patterns in the working-out of his verse techniques.

I refrain from saying the development, or the perfecting, of his techniques because in some ways Crane at the beginning of his short career was in no need of developing what he wished to do. He could already write certain kinds of poems as well as he ever would. Since these were his simplest allegories and epigrams—the heart-eater, "God fashioned the ship of the world carefully," "I stood upon a high place, / And saw below, many devils"—which have proved to be among his anthologists' favorites, Crane's critics have often asserted that his verse did not develop at all.[1] Such critics apparently have been content to regard as typical of his second book the nine or ten poems which correspond in method to those of the first.[2] While most in *The Black Riders* are relatively simple, even in the title poem Crane had achieved the subtlety, ambiguity, and economy of the best of his later work. But there are two changes, one in method, the other in style, which a careful consideration of the total body of his verse reveals.

[1] E.g., *Nation*, LXIX (November 16, 1899), 378; Amy Lowell, introduction to Crane, *Work*, VI, xxvii; Grant C. Knight, *The Critical Period in American Literature*, p. 154; Louise Bogan, *Achievement in American Poetry*, p. 17.

[2] "To the maiden" (WK III); "Have you ever made a just man?" (v); "Forth went the candid man" (IX); "You tell me this is God?" (x); "The wayfarer, / Perceiving the pathway to truth" (XIII); "There was a man with tongue of wood" (XVI); "A man said to the universe" (XXI); "When the prophet, a complacent fat man" (XXII); "There was a land where lived no violets" (XXIII); "Ay, workman, make me a dream" (XXIV).

The first has been alluded to above, his shift from allegory to symbolism, from direct correspondences to far richer constructs of indirections; this we shall shortly investigate in further detail. The second change, in his style, is the concomitant of the first as Crane enlarged the scope of his poems to treat experiences and states of feeling more complex than the simple attitudes of the allegorical poems.

Stylistically he developed in several ways. Parallelism of statement is characteristic of his verse throughout, but he moves from the ironic repetition of statements to the stanza-and-refrain structure of a more conventional lyric form than that with which he began. In diction he tries several tongues, and not all by any means are wooden. He essays the clip-clapper with its verbal economy and dissonance, as in "The patent of a lord"; yet at the same time he is working toward the flat, colloquial understatement of "A newspaper is a collection of half-injustices," toward the terse compression of "The chatter of a death-demon." In the title poem of *War is Kind* he achieves his ironic effects partly through juxtaposition of two of these styles, here shaped to the special purposes of that poem:

> Do not weep, maiden, for war is kind.
> Because your lover threw wild hands toward the sky
> And the affrighted steed ran on alone,
> Do not weep.
> War is kind.

This is the diction of ironic understatement, plain, unpretentious, and accurate. But the intercalary choruses speak in a different voice:

> Hoarse, booming drums of the regiment,
> Little souls who thirst for fight,
> These men were born to drill and die.
> The unexplained glory flies above them,
> Great is the battle-god, great, and his kingdom
> A field where a thousand corpses lie.[3]

Here we have contrasting overstatement, rhetorical and incantatory, with compelling rhythmic regularity—and rhyme. Mr. Berryman has expertly shown that "the poem is based on the letter *i* in the word 'kind,' " and that "the poem takes place in the successful war of the *prose* ('unexplained,' 'gulped,' and so on) *against* the poetic appearance of lament." He remarks on the power of the first line in the concluding stanza, in which the *i* sound is conspicuously absent.[4]

> Mother whose heart hung humble as a button
> On the bright splendid shroud of your son,
> Do not weep,
> War is kind.

To these perceptive comments we may add the observation that Crane, understanding the power of recapitulation and contrast, intrudes in "the bright splendid shroud" phrase the high style of the choruses in a way designed to demonstrate the hollowness of the heroic pose. The power of the poem is in its style. Crane's style was a more flexible instrument than most critics of his poetry have allowed.

[3] A true holograph copy of this poem, dated August 17, 1895, is on the third flyleaf of the copy of *The Red Badge of Courage* which Crane presented to Howells. The book is now in the Berg Collection, New York Public Library. For an explanation of seeming inconsistencies in the date see Berryman, p. 120.

[4] Berryman, p. 272.

Two circumstances have made it difficult for Crane's verse to find its proper place. The first is the very diversity of styles we have just examined. Developing so many tongues, using each successfully in so few poems, Crane failed to leave us a sizable body of work distinguished for the same virtues. The impression a poet leaves—and perhaps on the whole this is rightly so—is that created by the bulk of his work. We tend to invite the weight of his performance to impose upon our estimation of his quality. Since the majority of Crane's poems are not in his indirect symbolistic vein, his critics have apparently based their estimates upon the epigrammatic allegories which dominate *The Black Riders*. The second circumstance contributing to their opinion is that some of Crane's best poetry of indirection was not available until long after his death: "The Blue Battalions" in 1926, "A man adrift" in 1929, and of the seventeen new poems first presented here several exhibit the subtler virtues of which I speak. The delayed presentation of these poems may help to explain why Crane's work was so little known to many of the early Imagists who, Amy Lowell admitted, could well have benefited from his example.

2

Crane, as we have seen, repudiated the conventions of poetic form and diction practiced by other poets of his time; our problem now is to try to discover where he found other hints and clues from which to develop a new formal basis for his verse. When *The Black Riders* appeared in 1895, Crane's "lines" seemed a bizarre departure from any verse the world had seen; Emily Dickinson and Walt Whitman—two other eccentrics—were then and since suggested as inevitable influences. The merits of these claims we shall soon examine. But let us begin here with Crane's earliest acknowledged literary enthusiasms; in them we may find suggestions as to ways of making statments which were not lost on him. In addition to the influence of the Bible remarked by Amy Lowell there were two secular influences as well. "He had just been reading Olive Schreiner's 'Story of an African Farm,'" Corwin Knapp Linson recalls. "'She is a woman of sense and an artist,' he said with warmth. He had no liking for the somber moods of Ambrose Bierce." [5] We have the right authors but the wrong works— "somber moods" suggests Bierce's fiction; later, Horace Gregory would mention *The Devil's Dictionary*. It was neither of these that helped Crane shape his poems, but he found in *Fantastic Fables* a technique which Stallman has called the "structure of ironic reversal." [6] As for Schreiner, it was not her autobiographical novel but her later volume of didactic allegories, *Dreams* (1891) which gave Crane contemporary examples of the oldest literary genre for the inculcation of morality.

But his first debt was to the Bible. It is of course immense, as the debt to it of every author of parables must be. The notion of the short parable as a suitable subject for a single poetic statement Crane must surely have taken from his own reading of the Bible and from the uses made of the Gospel in the Sun-

[5] Linson MS, p. 34. But compare Crane's words "I deeply admire some short stories by Mr. Bierce . . . ," quoted in Berryman, p. 284.

[6] Stallman, *Omnibus*, p. 568, but Stallman suggests as a model Bierce's "Moral Principle and Material Interest," which was not published until December, 1926 (in the *Golden Book*), when Crane had been dead for a quarter of a century. Joseph Gaer, *Ambrose Gwinnet Bierce*, p. 27.

day sermons which almost all of his male forebears delivered
each week. Yet when he uses a Bible *story* directly, he revises
the Word with savage sarcasm and irony. "God fashioned the
ship of the world carefully" is a bitter parody of the first chapter of Genesis. "A god came to man" is his rebuttal to the
words of the Lord in Genesis 2.15–17, and "Well then, I hate
thee, unrighteous picture" his defiant rejoinder to Exodus 20.5.
Thomas F. O'Donnell finds several passages in the poems
which use actual phrases from the Bible—not as many as one
might suppose, however.[7] The Eighteenth Psalm appears to
have been Crane's favorite; e.g., "The Lord is my rock, my
fortress" (Ps. 18.2) becomes

> "Truth," said a traveller,
> "Is a rock, a mighty fortress;"   [BR xxviii]

Less convincing a parallel is "The Lord also thundered in the
heavens, and the Highest gave his voice; hail stones and coals
of fire . . ." (Ps. 18.13) and

> . . . the Deity thundered loudly,
> Fat with rage, and puffing   [BR li]

But there is a more tangible connection between "For thou
wilt light my candle; the Lord my god will enlighten my darkness" (Ps. 18.28) and "I was in the darkness; / I could not see
my words / Nor the wishes of my heart. / Then suddenly there
was a great light— / "Let me into the darkness again" (BR
xliv). This twenty-eighth verse undoubtedly contributes also
to the manuscript poem, "The patent of a lord."

With the exception of "The Battle Hymn" and "The Blue

[7] O'Donnell, "An Analysis of the Poetry of Stephen Crane," pp. 14–16.

Battalions," the New Testament is absent from his verse; but in *The Red Badge* and "The Blue Hotel" image and context are taken freely from the Gospels.[8]

It is not surprising that Crane's early favorites, Bierce and Schreiner, should have resembled him in that both were provincial authors who, rebelling against the grimness of inherited Puritan and Calvinistic creeds, yet adapted to their own needs the parable form characteristic of the didactic preachings they opposed. Bierce's reputation as a mordant ironist survives, but except for a handful of stories and a score of quotable epigrams he remains unread today despite Clifton Fadiman's claim that in an age intimidated by the atom bomb he "solicits our attention" as "a minor prophet of hopelessness." [9] We do not read Bierce today because his nihilism, evoking terror without pity, is unremittingly devoid of purgation. Prodigiously prolific in his long journalistic career, Bierce was in the decades of Crane's boyhood read and reprinted widely in newspapers across the country. It is inconceivable that Bierce's epigrams, fables, definitions, and sketches did not turn up as fillers in the newspaper exchanges that came each week to Townley Crane's news bureau in Asbury Park, or that Stephen was not thoroughly familiar with the writings of the most celebrated journalistic wit of his time. The evidence is not only circumstantial; parallels between their writings will

[8] See my introduction to *The Red Badge of Courage and Other Stories,* pp. xiii, xv–xxiv; Stallman's introduction in *Omnibus,* pp. 187–200; and, on "The Blue Hotel," Helen W. Goldberg, "Techniques and Attitudes in the Fiction of Stephen Crane," pp. 86–92.

[9] "Ambrose Bierce, Portrait of a Misanthrope," introduction to *The Collected Writings of Ambrose Bierce,* p. xiv.

be shortly offered, as well as an account of Bierce's changing
attitude toward his young admirer. But first a word about
Crane's other favorite.

Olive Schreiner (1855–1920), today all but forgotten except
in her native South Africa, in the 1880's won world-wide renown as the author of a local-color autobiography whose locale
was truly barbarous and bizarre; she continued to be a force
in the movement for women's rights into the twentieth century.
Her father, a German missionary, had married an English Nonconformist, and Olive grew up in a landscape of wild beauty,
drought, and heat, amid a Boer population Calvinistic and
dour. Where Bierce's fables are sardonic or macabre, hers are
unfailingly sentimental. Verbosity they share, but in attitude
they are indeed continents apart. This is from the first chapter in *Dreams:*

When on the sharp stones Life cut her feet he [Joy, the issue of
Life and Love] wiped the blood upon his garments, and kissed the
wounded feet with his little lips. When in the desert Love lay
down faint (for Love itself grows faint), he ran over the hot sands
with his little naked feet, and even there in the desert found water in
the holes in the rocks to moisten Love's lips with. . . .[10]

What, one wonders, could Stephen Crane have learned from
that? It is surely a far cry from the sparse language and unen-
chanted vision of his poems. But Schreiner's cloying *Dreams*
did give him clues and hints which, as was true of his "use"
of the Bible, he inverted to express his own sensibility. Ignorant of *Piers Ploughman* or *Le Romaunt de la Rose*—even,
it seems, of *Pilgrim's Progress*—Crane found in this ill-written

[10] *Dreams,* p. 17.

fantasy his first example of secular allegory. Personified abstractions move in human guise, not to terrorize him as had
Bishop Peck's figures of guilt and doom, but to express a view
of life compatible with that of the Reverend Jonathan Crane.
When Stephen Crane drew images and situations from
Schreiner, however, the resulting lines were not dreams she
would have dreamed:

> Love walked alone.
> The rocks cut her tender feet,
> And the brambles tore her fair limbs.
> There came a companion to her,
> But, alas, he was no help,
> For his name was heart's pain.   [BR xli]

Again, in "Intrigue," Crane personifies love in a way reminiscent of *Dreams:*

> Alone with love,
> Poor shivering love,
> And he, little sprite,
> Came to watch with me. . . .   [Intrigue vii]

The value of Schreiner's *Dreams* to Crane was, first, to show
him that the allegorical personifications of abstractions could be
used in literary statements as well as in ecclesiastical writings;
second, to suggest to him patterns or frameworks of allegorized action, which Crane invariably turned upside-down to his
own uses; and third, to suggest the images of desert, draught,
climbing mountains as a path to truth, seeking the light and
seeing it not, which abound in the poems in *The Black Riders.*
These images are all characteristically Biblical, but Crane
probably learned to handle them from Olive Schreiner rather

than from the Bible itself. Of course, he used them far better than she, squeezing her prolix and sentimental fancies to yield hard and ironic nuggets of verse. The correspondences between them are consequently indirect. For instance, a passage from one of her "Three Dreams in a Desert," written in attempted Biblical style, probably suggested to Crane the pattern for a poem which uses some of the same elements—desert dialogue form, confusion of appearance and reality—to make quite a different fable:

I saw a desert and I saw a woman coming out of it. And she came to the bank of a dark river; and the bank was steep and high. And on it an old man met her, who had a long white beard; and a stick that curled was in his hand, and on it was written Reason. And he asked her what she wanted; and she said, "I am woman; and I am seeking for the land of Freedom."

And he said, "It is before you."

And she said, "I see nothing before me but a dark flowing river, and a bank steep and high, and cuttings here and there with heavy sand in them."

And he said, "And beyond that?"

She said, "I see nothing, but sometimes, when I shade my eyes with my hand, I think that I see on the further bank trees and hills, and the sun shining on them!" [11]

> I walked in a desert
> And I cried,
> "Ah, God, take me from this place!"
> A voice said, "It is no desert."
> I cried, "Well, but—
> The sand, the heat, the vacant horizon."
> A voice said, "It is no desert."   [BR XLII]

[11] *Dreams,* pp. 75–76.

Edmund Wilson once remarked that he had "learned from another source than the biography of Mr. Beer" that Crane "sometimes amused himself by trying to cut down specimens of contemporary American poetry to the minimum of idea or emotion that, on scrutiny, he found them to contain." [12] Here the essential minimum of idea is the individual in the desert not seeing the goal before his eyes; all of Schreiner's attempts at verisimilitude are excised, and her slackening of tension in "but sometimes . . . I think that I see . . ." is sternly eliminated.

Another of her *Dreams*, "The Hunter," concerns a man who searches for the great white bird of Truth, persists through many false trails and discouragements, climbs an interminable mountain, builds a stair, and at last dies wizened and bent, clutching a white feather. Crane wrote no poem according in detail with this trite story, but the basic situation of the truth-seeker and its associated images appear in several guises:

> There was set before me a mighty hill,
> And long days I climbed
> Through regions of snow.

As usual, Crane ironically inverts Olive Schreiner's sentimental optimism:

> When I had before me the summit-view,
> It seemed that my labour
> Had been to see gardens
> Lying at impossible distances.   [BR xxvi]

[12] *New Republic*, January 2, 1924, reprinted in *The Shores of Light* (New York, 1952), p. 113.

In poem XIII of *War is Kind* a wayfarer perceives "the pathway to truth," but finding it overgrown—"each weed / Was a singular knife,"—concludes "Doubtless there are other roads." Another poem of search and failure is "I stood musing in a black world" (BR XLIX), cited above in Chapter Three.

Both Schreiner and Bierce offer passages possibly suggestive to Crane of one of his best-known poems. Schreiner's comes from "The Hunter":

"Look down into the crevices at your feet," they said. "See what lies there—white bones! As brave and strong a man as you climbed to these rocks." And he looked up. He saw there was no use in striving; he would never hold Truth, never see her, never find her. . . .

He laughed fiercely, and the Echoes of Despair slunk away, for the laugh of a brave, strong heart is as a death-blow to them.

Nevertheless they crept out again and looked at him.

"Do you know that your hair is white?" they said, "that your hands begin to tremble like a child's? Do you see that the point of your shuttle is gone?—it is cracked already. If you should ever climb this stair," they said, "it will be your last. You will never climb another."

And he answered, *"I know it!"* and worked on.[13]

"The minimum of idea or emotion" here is the futility of pursuit of a self-willed ideal, a concept Schreiner introduces only to disprove it. With a toughness she would never have, Crane makes this fable anew:

> I saw a man pursuing the horizon;
> Round and round they sped.

[13] *Dreams*, pp. 46–48.

I was disturbed at this;
I accosted the man.
"It is futile," I said,
"You can never—"
"You lie," he cried,
And ran on.   [BR xxiv]

But contributory to this epigram may also be three of Bierce's
Fantastic Fables, which likewise propound the commitment to
a willed course by an individual blinded by his own self-
importance:

A Jackal in pursuit of a Deer was about to seize it, when an
earthquake opened a broad and deep chasm between him and his
prey.
"This," he said, "is a pernicious interference with the laws of
Nature. I refuse to recognize any such irregularity."
So he resumed the chase, endeavouring to cross the abyss in two
leaps.[14]

Precise dating of most of Bierce's fugitive snippets proved
too difficult for his bibliographer [15] but we do know that this
fable first appeared in the London *Fun* in 1872 or 1873; since
Bierce reprinted everything he wrote whenever possible it is
not unlikely that his Jackal was known to young Stephen
Crane. His *Fantastic Fables* were not collected into a book
until 1899 but such items as these, too, had been ephemerally
in print much earlier:

A Man Running for Office was overtaken by Lightning.
"You see," said the Lightning, as it crept past him inch by inch,
"I can travel considerably faster than you."

[14] *Collected Writings of Ambrose Bierce,* p. 636.
[15] Gaer, *Ambrose Gwinnet Bierce,* p. 3.

"Yes," the Man Running for Office replied, "but think how much longer I keep going!"

Another:

A Dog that had been engaged in pursuit of his own tail abandoned the chase and lying down curled up for repose. In his new posture he found his tail within easy reach of his teeth and seized it with avidity, but immediately released it, wincing with pain.

"After all," he said, "there is more joy in pursuit than in possession."

More succinct than these is another fable on futility:

"See these valuable golden eggs," said a Man that owned a Goose. "Surely a Goose that can lay such eggs must have a gold mine inside her."

So he killed the Goose and cut her open, but found that she was just like any other goose. Moreover, on examining the eggs that she had laid he found they were just like any other eggs.[16]

Crane may have appropriated the structural device of ironic surprise from such a model in his poem,

> A man saw a ball of gold in the sky.
> He climbed for it,
> And eventually he achieved it—
> It was clay.
>
> Now this is the strange part:
> When the man went to earth
> And looked again,
> Lo, there was the ball of gold.
> Now this is the strange part:
> It was a ball of gold.
> Ay, by the heavens it was a ball of gold.   [BR xxxv]

[16] *Collected Writings of Ambrose Bierce*, pp. 551, 662, 645.

The authority of the heavens, by which he swears at the end, has been undermined by his foregoing experience, an irony also apparent in the manuscript poem "One came from the skies."

Crane, reducing to the essential minimum these cynicisms of Bierce, is appropriating more of the older author's structure than his content, more of his attitude than his images. Bierce was indeed, as Fadiman remarks, "a pessimism-machine . . . a Swift minus true intellectual power"; [17] it is the machinery which Crane appropriates, the techniques of ironic reversal, of statement and deflation, while he invests Bierce's parable structures with greater significance. As was true of his adaptations of Schreiner, Crane replaces essentially trivial concretions with suggestions of more general application. Thus Bierce's "Man and Goose" is limited to cupidity, while Crane's ball in the sky can represent any ideal, or all ideals. In another instance, Bierce gives us merely "The All-Dog":

A Lion seeing a Poodle fell into laughter at the ridiculous spectacle.

"Who ever saw so small a beast?" he said.

"It is very true," said the Poodle, with austere dignity, "that I am small; but, sir, I beg you to observe that I am all dog." [18]

This assuredly suggests "A man said to the universe, / 'Sir, I exist!'" (WK xxi). It took boldness beyond Bierce's cynicism directly to address so overwhelming an interlocutor.

In assessing Bierce's influence on Crane we must observe a change in the fableist's attitude toward the younger celebrity. Robert H. Davis reports Bierce as commenting in September, 1895 on the author of *The Red Badge of Courage*, "This young

---

[17] *Ibid.*, p. xv.   [18] *Ibid.*, p. 567.

man has the power to feel. He knows nothing of war, yet he is drenched in blood. Most beginners who deal with this subject spatter themselves merely with ink." [19] But nine months later the New York *Press* carried a vitriolic attack by Bierce on Percival Pollard, editor of the *Echo,* and on Crane:

That hardy and ingenious explorer, that sun-eyed searcher of the intense inane, that robber baron invader of literature's loud oblivion, that painstaking chiffonier of fame's eternal dumping ground, has dragged to upper day two worse writers than Stephen Crane and names them out loud. I had thought there could be only two worse writers than Stephen Crane, namely, two Stephen Cranes.[20]

Why this sudden animus? Bierce, we remember, defined the verb *plagiarize* as "To take the thought or style of another writer whom one has never, never read." In the interim between his praise of *The Red Badge* and the above sarcasm, *The Black Riders* had appeared. But even in attacking Crane, poor Bierce reveals the limiting redundancy of his own imagination, for he had defined the noun *clarionet* as "An instrument of torture operated by a person with cotton in his ears. There are two instruments that are worse than a clarionet— two clarionets." [21] Bierce remains the technician of ironic statement, a victim of his own dehumanized cynicism. Crane, a true

[19] Introduction to Crane, *Work,* II, x.

[20] New York *Press,* July 25, 1896 (unpaged clipping in Columbia collection). Paul Fatout prints this passage in *Ambrose Bierce, the Devil's Lexicographer,* p. 220, attributing it to the San Francisco *Examiner* of the following day; Fatout makes nothing of Bierce's antagonism to Crane. Another undated clipping at Columbia, from the Atlantic *Constitution,* also alludes to Bierce's animus: "Ambrose Bierce, who is now writing for the New York *Journal,* is hot on the track of Stephen Crane." (This may refer to the syndicated item from the *Press,* clip No. 465 from the Author's Clipping Bureau; the *Constitution* bit is No. 483.)

[21] *The Devil's Dictionary.*

idealist, is master of Bierce's technique without becoming the slave of his themes.

3

When *The Black Riders* appeared a review in the *Nation* proposed two other literary influences with which all critics of Crane's verse have since had to contend. The reviewer presented Crane as "a condensed Whitman or an amplified Emily Dickinson. . . . He grasps his thought as nakedly and simply" as Dickinson does hers, and shares her "terseness." [22] It was natural enough to discuss together the three most idiosyncratic poets known to the decade; but where the *Nation* suggests similarities later critics see strong influences. It has been claimed by one critic that Crane is in Dickinson's debt for his "unrhymed verse patterns," while another attributes to her Crane's ironic outlook and vividness of imagery. Amy Lowell thought her the source of his "use of suggestion," while Berryman claims that "the notion of very short-line poems" came from Dickinson, and Stallman finds Crane's verse to be "Inspired . . . but not modeled upon" hers, and sees in both poets "unorthodox sentiments . . . metaphor . . . delight in paradox." [23]

[22] "Recent Poetry," *Nation*, LXI (October 24, 1895), 296.
[23] Donald Richie, "Stephen Crane," *The Study of Current English* (Tokyo), X (October, 1955), 37; Henry Lüdeke, "Stephen Cranes Gedichte," *Anglia*, LXII (1938), 414; Lowell, introduction to Crane, *Work*, VI, xviii; Berryman, p. 274; Stallman, *Omnibus*, p. 568. See also R. E. Lucky, "Apreciación del Poeta Stephen Crane," *Revista iberoamericana*, V (October, 1942), 334: "Conocía y admiraba la obra de Emily Dickinson y sus poesías lo inspiraron a experimentar él mismo"; and W. M. Gibson's introduction to *Stephen Crane: Selected Prose and Poetry*, pp. xiv–xv.

But is all this true?

We know that Crane was acquainted with Emily Dickinson's work from John D. Barry's report that Howells had read from her *Poems* to the impoverished youth who came to call one night in 1893.[24] A comparison of the poems in her first collection with Crane's reveals only one instance of direct indebtedness; this is rather striking, and we will come to it in a moment. Crane found nothing he could use in the Dickinson poems arranged by her editors under the conventional headings "Nature" and "Love," but the last section of her book —"Time and Eternity"—probably proved more interesting to Crane. His metaphors of death do not ordinarily correspond to hers—for him death is not a conferral of status, an entrance to immortality, a sublime suitor; nor does Crane envisage God as a banker, a merchant, a gentleman. In one instance, however, Crane found suggested another metaphor of death which he appropriated in a poem we have already examined. Emily Dickinson is of course a much greater poet than Crane, but in this case his poem surpasses hers in intensity and power. Here is the one Dickinson poem which specifically influenced Crane:

> Two swimmers wrestled on the spar
> Until the morning sun,
> When one turned smiling to the land.
> O God, the other one!
>
> The stray ships passing spied a face
> Upon the waters borne,

[24] "A Note on Stephen Crane," *Bookman*, XIII (April, 1901), 448. Eight unpublished letters from Howells to Crane allude to his poetry but not to hers (Columbia Crane collection). See items 12–15 in *Stephen Crane (1871–1900): An Exhibition*, by Joan H. Baum, for a description of Howells's letters.

With eyes in death still begging raised,
And hands beseeching thrown.[25]

This is one of the least successful poems in the Dickinson volume, yet Crane almost certainly found in it images he used to better advantage in "A man adrift on a slim spar." Perhaps Emily Dickinson sees the soul as divided, and the immersion of one part in the destructive unknown is necessary for the survival of the other, which wills its own return "smiling to the land." But the tone of the poem is really too sentimental to support this implication. The drowned man is seen as a pathetic spectacle; his predicament is observed from the safety of shore and ship, not, as in Crane's poem, through his own eyes. Not only in point of view but in vividness of imagery, in range of metaphoric associations and contrasts, and in emotional conviction Crane's poem is superior to Emily Dickinson's. This is not to say, however, that Crane anywhere achieves a poetic power comparable to her best work. On the very next page after "Two swimmers wrestled on the spar" he may have read "Because I could not stop for Death / He kindly stopped for me." Crane has no poem comparable to this one, for his sensibility cannot respond to the sportive intensity of Emily Dickinson's best work.

As for Crane's debt to Dickinson for techniques, as well as for images or themes, he may indeed have taken the idea of short-line poems from Dickinson, but the prevalence of metrical and stanzaic regularity in her *Poems* makes this hypothetical. As for Emily Dickinson being the source, or *a* source, of Crane's irony, this seems hardly likely. He is chiefly in Bierce's debt for the means by which his innately ironic out-

[25] Emily Dickinson, *Poems,* ed. by Higginson and Todd, p. 137.

look is expressed. Here is paragraph from *Maggie,* written before he had heard Howells read Dickinson:

He clad his soul in armor by means of happening hilariously in at
a mission church where a man composed his sermons of "you's."
Once a philosopher asked this man why he did not say "we" instead
of "you." The man replied, "What?" [26]

It is similarly unlikely that Emily Dickinson is the source of
Crane's use of suggestion, for this technique too he had developed earlier than in his verse. In *Maggie* (1893) he had mastered the use of animistic imagery, color, and situational parallels to suggest far more than he states. An interviewer in
1896 reported, "It is Mr. Crane's contention that any one can
describe any sensation if he uses his experience, because suggestion creates so many sensations," [27] this with respect to
The Red Badge, the first draft of which was completed before
he finished *The Black Riders.* Were Emily Dickinson's work as
a whole influential on Crane there would be many more parallels than the one poem cited above.

A family resemblance has been made to seem a direct de-
scent. "The poems of Emily Dickinson . . . glittered like fire-
flies in the poetic twilight, but they were to have no heirs except Crane's ironic verses in their own century," wrote Carl
Van Doren.[28] But Crane is not so much Emily Dickinson's
heir as were both the beneficiaries of a condition in American
culture which was propitious for the kind of verse they were
to write. This condition has been called by Allen Tate "the

[26] Crane, *Work,* X, 151.
[27] Herbert P. William, "Mr. Crane as a Literary Artist," New York
Illustrated American, July 18, 1896 (unpaged clipping in the Columbia
Crane collection).
[28] "Stephen Crane," *American Mercury,* I (January 1924), 11.

perfect literary situation," in which "the spiritual community
is breaking up," a condition that makes possible "the fusion of
sensibility and thought." "The important thing to remember
about the puritan theocracy," Tate writes, "is that it . . . gave
an heroic proportion and a tragic mode to the experience of
the individual." What was true of the break-up of Puritanism
for Dickinson was similarly true for Crane in the failure of the
Methodist theocracy represented by his maternal forebears.
Given these parallel circumstances—and genius twice—it is
all but inevitable that there should be similarities in their
poetic responses to a world in which the autocratic gods are
crumbling. What Tate says of Dickinson is true of Crane in
his more limited way a generation later: writing as the moment of dissolution of the culture whose symbols her poetry
appropriates, in her verse "the world order is assimilated . . .
to the poetic vision; it is brought down from abstraction to
personal sensibility." [29]

4

"Is there room for a second Walt Whitman?" asked the *Literary Digest* in 1896, offering in lieu of an answer "Do not weep,
maiden, for war is kind," reprinted from the February *Bookman.* The preceding year the *Nation,* as we have seen, had
called Crane "a condensed Whitman," but had claimed the
similarity between them to be merely formlessness; "in other
respects [Crane's lines] are the antipodes of his; while Whitman dilutes mercilessly, Crane condenses almost as formid-
ably." Harry Thurston Peck, in his important review of *The*

[29] *The Man of Letters in the Modern World,* pp. 221, 220, 212–13, 222.

Black Riders, had bracketed the two poets in a different way: "If Whitman had been caught young and subjected to aesthetic influences, it is likely that he would have mellowed his barbaric yawp to some such note as that which sounds in the poems that are now before us." [30]

What Peck is suggesting in his impressionistic way is that Crane and Whitman share, to some degree, the same sensibility. Critics since the 1890's have been more narrowly concerned to find in Whitman a source behind Crane's techniques, and I deal first with their contentions before returning to the larger question of whether or not Crane's sensibility does indeed resemble Whitman's. One would think that without such a resemblance his debt will not be great.

"If we think of style rather than content, it is hard to say just whom Whitman has affected fruitfully," writes F. O. Matthiessen.[31] Whether or not Whitman's presumed influence was fruitful in Crane's case, several critics have proposed it with more or less conviction. Crane's poems, says Stallman, "have a family kinship with the free verse of W. E. Henley, Emily Dickinson, and Walt Whitman. . . . Some of Crane's poems echo Whitman's in phrase ('making cunning noiseless travel down the ways')." Berryman suggests that Crane "probably" took from Whitman "the notion of writing irregularly." Lüdeke finds their metrics to be opposed, with a predominance in Whitman of regular iambics despite the irregularity of his lines, while the obverse is true of Crane; on the other

---

[30] "Lyrics of the Day," *Literary Digest,* XII (February 29, 1896), 520; "Recent Verse," *Nation,* LXI (October 24, 1895), 296; Peck, "Some Recent Volumes of Verse," *Bookman,* I (May, 1895), 255.

[31] *American Renaissance,* p. 592.

hand, O'Donnell proposes that "The debt to Whitman, if there is one, lies in the secret of Crane's prosody," and finds four kinds of parallelism Crane might have learned from *Leaves of Grass:* synonymous, internal, antithetical, and cumulative.[32] But, as O'Donnell observes, Whitman's source for these was the Bible, which Crane is known to have known.[33] Any writer devoted to incremental repetition is probably bound to produce variations similar to these. A more important resemblance to Whitman, however, is in Crane's recurring use of the envelope structure. This device is characteristic of his early verse, but it does not appear in his fiction until the late story, "The Clan of No-Name," a circumstance which suggests the probability that he had adapted the pattern from a verse rather than a prose model. It would be hard to think of a more likely model than Whitman's poems.

Although Berryman mentions Whitman among the few authors Crane is presumed to have read,[34] neither in his biography nor elsewhere have I found any but inferential evidence that Crane was actually familiar with *Leaves of Grass.* The probability is strong that he was, yet if this is so we may be struck less by the resemblances between the two New Jersey authors than by all the possible uses Crane might have made

[32] Stallman, *Omnibus,* p. 568; Berryman, p. 274; Lüdeke, "Stephen Cranes Gedichte," *Anglia,* LXII (1938), 413; O'Donnell, "An Analysis of the Poetry of Stephen Crane," pp. 52, 54–58.

[33] Not only because of his clerical family but because Bible study was a required discipline in each year's course at Claverack College and Hudson River Institute, which Crane attended from January 4, 1888, to some time in 1890. See Lyndon Upson Pratt, "The Formal Education of Stephen Crane," *American Literature,* X (January, 1930), 461–63.

[34] Berryman, pp. 24, 264.

of Whitman's great precedents but which he absolutely forgoes to follow. In discussing Crane's debts to Bierce and Schreiner we have seen him to be a skillful borrower, economizing to good effect their diffuseness and verbosity. One might accordingly expect him to be, as the *Nation* intimated, a condenser of Whitman's exuberant catalogues. But this is not at all the case. Crane resembles Whitman in a few respects, but he would seem to have taken over so little of Whitman's thought and diction as to raise the possibilities either that he had read very little of Whitman's verse, or that what similarities exist between that verse and his own may result not from direct influence but from analogous responses to certain comparable aspects of their cultural situations and personal endowments. Whatever the case, a comparison to Whitman may prove helpful in defining more exactly the nature of Crane's gifts and limitations.

According to the "List of Books, Brede Place" Crane owned no book of Whitman's, yet there is evidence in the Columbia collection of his interest in the older author. Carefully pasted into a scrapbook of British reviews of Crane's writings are two notices of R. M. Bucke's edition of Whitman's letters to his mother from the army hospital where he had nursed the injured with incomparable tenderness. Aside from these, the only reviews in the scrapbook of works not by Crane are several clippings on his friends Conrad and Frederic and some on books of war reportage whose authors are compared unfavorably to Crane. *The Red Badge of Courage* is mentioned in the review of *The Wound Dresser* from the *Daily Chronicle*, but Whitman is here adduced as a contributor of "the naked

horror of facts, or the sheer pity of them" which "far transcends anything which could be achieved by a 'literary presentation.'"[35] The "Books and Bookmen" columnist of the
Manchester *Guardian* went further still:

It seems to be pretty clear that those who have joined in praise of
the "unprecedented realism of Mr. Stephen Crane's sketches of the
American Civil War, for instance, can never have read Whitman's
"Specimen Days," or they would know that the thing had been
done before and—with no disparagement to Mr. Crane's indubitable
talent—done better.[36]

Crane, who believed that art must be close to the truths of life,
remained unconfident of the truth of his own *Red Badge* until
he had himself been in battle; to an author so honest this
praise of Whitman could have seemed only just. But *The
Wound Dresser* had no effect upon Crane's verse, appearing
after all but a dozen of the poems in *War is Kind* were written.
Of Crane's opinion of Whitman's poetry we have no record.

The kinship we feel between Crane's poems and certain of
those in *Leaves of Grass* cannot be explained by structural
resemblances alone. What we have here to deal with is the
fact that one aspect of Whitman's sensibility closely resembles Crane's characteristic attitude toward his major themes.
Richard Chase most succinctly defines this aspect as the "sensibility of annihilation." This Whitman best exhibits in his
Civil War notes in *Specimen Days,* but it is apparent in his
poetry too:

[35] Unpaged clipping of March 7, 1898.
[36] Unpaged clipping of March 26, 1898.

Not much interested in taking sides, the writer studies violence and suffering in themselves. So that his style and his attitude toward what he is writing entitle Whitman to be called the first of the legendary war reporters, the literary ancestor of Ambrose Bierce, Stephen Crane, and Ernest Hemingway. Many of the realistic passages in *The Red Badge of Courage* are anticipated in *Specimen Days.* . . . It should be clear, however, that although the War seemed to Whitman "the distinguishing event of my time," he did not either in his war notes or elsewhere, come to understand life in terms of violence, as did Bierce, Crane, and Hemingway. For various personal and historical reasons, his fascination with war and death was not, like theirs, overt, flamboyant, and active; it remained passive, mystical, and sacrificial. But like the later war correspondents he prided himself on being able to say, "I am the man, I suffer'd, I was there." [37]

Beyond this, is there any justice to H. T. Peck's assertion that Whitman, had he been "subjected to aesthetic influences," might have written poems like Crane's? There are, it is true, fugitive parallels in several attitudes the authors apparently share, but certainly Peck's enthusiasm for the poet he had discovered outweighed his sense of proportion. Crane, if we suppose that he had read "Song of Myself," for example, would have sensed something kindred to his own feelings in Whitman's invitation, "This is the meal equally set—this the meat for natural hunger; / It is for the wicked just the same as the righteous." A passage closer to Crane obsessive harlot-rescue theme is this one:

> The bride unrumples her white dress, the minute-hand of the
> clock moves slowly,

[37] Richard Chase, *Walt Whitman Reconsidered,* pp. 126, 167–68.

The opium-eater reclines with rigid head and just-open'd lips,
The prostitute draggles her shawl, her bonnet bobs on her
                          tipsy and pimpled neck,
The crowd laugh at her blackguard oaths, the men jeer and
                          wink to each other,
(Miserable! I do not laugh at your oaths, nor jeer you;) [38]

Crane's "Mother whose heart hung humble as a button" (WK
i) and his mother whose hand caressed "the brow of a youth"
in "The Blue Battalions" are perhaps suggestive, too, of Whitman's recurrent images of maternal tenderness. The associations we have noted in Crane's mind of a woman's white arms
with maternal, erotic, and fearful emotions is paralleled in at
least one prominent image of Whitman's, "The white arms out
in the breakers tirelessly tossing" in "Out of the Cradle, End-
lessly Rocking." Here, as Mr. Chase remarks, "the image [is]
of the maternal sea, the 'savage old mother' who is at once so
immeasurably attractive and so terrible . . . incessantly whispering . . . the 'low and delicious word death.'" [39]

It is evident that in his own way Crane too is a poet of
death, but his way is assuredly not Whitman's. Crane's conception of death in his poems does not offer him the opportunity
of developing metaphors as richly implicated in life as does
Whitman's. Speaking of "Out of the Cradle," Chase observes
that

Whitman grasps at the most poignant center of experience, and it
is characteristic of him that where other poets would be likely to
derive the meaning of life and the origin of the imagination from

[38] *Walt Whitman: Complete Poetry and Selected Prose and Letters,*
ed. by Emory Holloway, pp. 43, 40; hereafter cited as *Complete Poetry.*
[39] *Walt Whitman Reconsidered,* p. 123.

God (or God manifested in nature) and man's relation to Him, Whitman, like Emily Dickinson, derives them from death. Implicit in the work of both poets there is the recognition that death may be taken as the ultimate metaphor of democracy, that only this metaphor can perfectly express the principle of equality.[40]

This cannot be said of Crane's poetry. Only in the exceptional "The Blue Battalions" and "The Battle Hymn" does Crane suggest an identification similar to Whitman's merger of "One's self . . . a simple separate person" with "the word Democratic, the word En-Masse." This is the more surprising because in Crane's fiction, death, or more accurately, the confrontation of death, is indeed a metaphor of equality. We find this to be true of Henry in *The Red Badge*, who "felt the subtle brotherhood . . . a mysterious fraternity born of the . . . danger of death," just as Manolo Prat "heard breathed to him . . . the benediction of his brethren," and in "The Open Boat" a "subtle brotherhood of men . . . was here established on the seas." [41] The recognition of this brotherhood, established under common adversities which obliterate the claims of the individual self, is what raises Crane's prose to tragic dignity. But Crane's best poem, "A man adrift on a slim spar," gives us the quite different dimension of death more characteristic of his verse. There death is a metaphor of man's ultimate isolation.

Perhaps the crucial reason for the difference between the metaphors of death in Crane's verse and in Whitman's is that while Crane interprets life almost solely in terms of necessity,

[40] *Ibid.*

[41] *Omnibus*, p. 261; "The Clan of No-Name," *Work*, II, 168; *Work*, XII, 36.

one is tempted to call Whitman the poet of the absolutely free will. The conflict between these two points of view is, Mr. Chase suggests, the only philosophical problem of which American literature has been aware. This limitation results from our Calvinist heritage and the egalitarian commitment "which has so sharply set the individual off against society" and which, as De Tocqueville had predicted, has denied us the concepts, natural to aristocratic cultures, of agencies mediating between man, the state, and God.[42] Consequently, the sense of the individual's isolation has been strongly developed in the American sensibility.

In Crane we see the isolato in a deterministic world: man is made infinitesimal by the hugeness of natural forces against which he struggles, not to impose his will, but to live in accordance with a code that allows him dignity despite his insignificance. Death is the terminus of a life lived in continual menace; it is an end of fear and suffering, but death is not in itself a good except that it provides a final opportunity for the assumption of tragic dignity. Only if the individual chooses immolation, for the sake of the fellows from whom in life he has been divided, can his death be other than futile and dishonored. Only if he has loved can he have tasted joy, but how equivocal Crane's view of this joy is we have seen.

Whitman, on the other hand, shows us the isolato in a world where necessity is absent and the will is free—free to reassert the power of the self to reenter the world from which it would seem to have been barred by the very forces which isolated it.

[42] *Walt Whitman Reconsidered,* pp. 103–4.

Where Crane is driven either to solitude, to self-sacrifice, or to his joyless love, Whitman can confidently avow, "There was a child went forth every day, / And the first object he look'd upon, that object he became." [43] Although the child stands alone in Nature, he confronts not the malign forces Crane perceived there, but extensions of his own being.

In comparing Crane to the better-educated poets of his own generation I have mentioned the unavailability to him of the great word-hoards of history, the sources of metaphor and myth central to the world traditions of culture. Whitman, too, had foregone most of the mythic and metaphoric resources of Western literature as belonging to the ages of feudalism and as not conforming to the needs of a democratic art. "Having given up so much—so much more, indeed, than his democratic situation forced him to give up—Whitman is reduced to two principal stratagems of mediation—his use of words in a mythic-semantic manner. . . . and his one grand narrative and metaphorical image of the self with its dialectical powers and its eternal vitality and significance." [44] Whitman's image of the self is the means by which he makes all experience accessible to his poetry—indeed, he proclaims that the self, its experiences, and the poems which celebrate them are indistinguishable. For his presumed disciple Crane, however, the alienated self is impoverished, not enriched, by its isolation. If love adds to its range of experience, it adds equally to its sufferings.

[43] *Complete Poetry*, p. 332.
[44] Chase, *Walt Whitman Reconsidered*, p. 92.

But Whitman proclaims, "In me the caresser of life wherever moving, backward as well as foreward sluing." [45] He and experience merge into one another through the power of love. Mark Van Doren puts it best when he says, "Whitman is a great love poet because love is necessary to his understanding of the universe." [46] It may be said however that so far as his program is concerned—and Whitman's poetry cannot be divorced from his program—he makes an atypical, inverted love the basis for a theory of society. This is surely unrealistic, but without the passive qualities of his sexual make-up it is unlikely that Whitman could have possessed a sensibility so accessible to experience. His "fluidity of sexual sympathy made possible Whitman's fallow receptivity to life." [47] Yet this fluidity, this receptivity, is at the same time the source of his "peculiar estrangement from the world" in which the only personal relations apparently possible for him were those "strongly susceptible of abstract and ideal meaning"; his alienation impelled him "to resort to symbolic and ideal forms of reattachment." [48]

One way of defining the incomparable advantage of Whitman's richer sensibility over Crane's is to note that the tensions in his work between alienation and reattachment, between the "simple separate person" and the "Camerado," lead Whitman to enlarge the world in which his imagination participates until he can exult, "The orchestra whirls me wider than Uranus flies, / It wrenches such ardors from me, I did not know I

[45] *Complete Poetry*, p. 37.
[46] *The Portable Walt Whitman*, ed. by Mark Van Doren, p. 16.
[47] Matthiessen, *American Renaissance*, p. 535.
[48] Chase, *Walt Whitman Reconsidered*, pp. 45–46.

possess'd them." If one can participate with such intensity in an experiential world of such magnitude, one can only with greatest difficulty maintain the sense of his own identity. A few lines later we find the poet overwhelmed by the immensity of all that he has merged with himself: "I lose my breath, / Steep'd amid honey'd morphine, my windpipe throttled in fakes of death." Thus Whitman defines "that we call Being." [49]

For Crane however, the tension lies between isolato and self-immolator, and it leads to an obsessive concentration upon only a few possibilities open to either the unconscious or the will. Death becomes for Whitman "the ultimate metaphor of democracy," a representation of perfect equality and of one stage in the ever recurring cycle of "the procreant urge of the world." [50] But in Crane's verse the concept of death, being a terminus rather than a new beginning, cannot liberate his imagination from the limits within which his psychic pattern and his cultural situation have confined it.

If Whitman is reduced to two stratagems of mediation (his use of words and his image of the self), Crane's resources would seem to be still further restricted. Crane must depend upon his metaphoric imagination alone. For Crane does not celebrate the self. He regards it in his firmest work with pitiless irony, and he mocks the assertiveness of the ego with a detachment not untinged with cruelty. Language must be the sole resource of his poetry. We would expect him, then, to make full use of metaphor with its synoptic and intensifying powers; yet we find this to be true only intermittently, in relatively few of his poems. It is in his prose that metaphor best

[49] *Complete Poetry*, p. 53.   [50] *Ibid.*, p. 28.

expands and controls his imaginative grasp of experience. The enigma of Crane's apparently "prosaic" verse and "poetic" fiction interposes itself here, and we must for a moment give that problem our consideration. Walt Whitman may have a part in the explanation of this paradox in Crane.

Should the hypotheses regarding Crane's sensibility proposed above be valid, they will, I think, apply equally to his fiction as to his verse. Crane does not change his convictions about man's place in the universe when he writes in prose, yet in the best of his stories there are consistently present certain valuable qualities lacking to all but a few of his poems: vivid, metaphoric diction, sustained complexity of organization, superb control of the rhythms of language. There are perhaps two factors which help explain Crane's ability better to project his exceptional qualities in prose than in verse. One of these is his attitude toward the literary forms he is using. His denial of the conventions of poetic diction, stanzaic form, regular rhyme and meter place him in the position of having to provide substitutes for the structural devices he has rejected. As A. G. Lehmann observes, "Art abhors a formal vacuum as ardently as Nature abhors a material one." [51] Writing empirically, with neither an articulate body of theory nor the stimulation that discussion with like-minded poets and critics might provide, Crane tried out one device after another in his attempts to reconstitute the formal elements he could not accept from extant poetic convention. Consequently his successes are sporadic and discontinuous; their excellences, not being of the same kind, do not reinforce one another.

[51] *The Symbolist Aesthetic,* p. 182.

In fiction, however, Crane's progress toward sustained achievement and originality was perhaps facilitated by the fact that he was never in a comparable rebellion against novelistic or short story form. It is true that he wrote to his friend Lily Brandon Munroe in 1896, "When I left you [1892], I renounced the clever school in literature. . . . If I had kept to my clever Rudyard-Kipling style, the road might have been shorter but, ah, it wouldn't be the true road." [52] Yet Crane never repudiated what he had learned from Kipling of the skillful organization of action and incident and of the pacing of the story. There may be a debt here to Stevenson too, whose work Crane often mentioned with an antipathy so pronounced as to suggest the possibility of his once having been under its influence. Crane's other early models were Mark Twain's mastery of colloquial speech and humor, Bierce's irony, and Poe's concentration and control of atmosphere.

It was probably in Zola that he first saw the fictional presentation of a naturalistic world view, and in Tolstoy perhaps he encountered models for his assured handling of panoramic action.[53] Crane's fiction, based as it is on the assimilation of a variety of qualities from excellent models, thus evolved in a manner more encouraging to organic development and consistency of effort than did his poetry.

Crane's special contribution to the development of fiction is his concentrated use of the metaphoric and symbolic aspects of language to advance the action and to extend the implications of his themes. This significant technical resource is used

[52] Stallman, *Omnibus*, p. 648.
[53] For the debts of *The Red Badge of Courage* to Zola, Kipling, and Tolstoy, see my introduction, pp. ix–xiv.

in his stories to reinforce the more conventional structure of
plot which he conserved from his "clever Rudyard-Kipling
style." The second advantage inhering in his prose style is that
Crane's metaphoric imagination can operate under much freer
conditions in fiction than those his poems allowed. Variety of
situation, the presentation of character, and the invention of
incident make necessary a salutary concreteness in the fiction
writer's conception of his materials. His language will, if successful, reflect this concreteness; and if, like Crane, he has a
primarily sensuous response to experience, his metaphors will
combine passion with immediacy of perception. These are
qualities, however, which in many of his poems Crane would
seem to have gone to some lengths to deny himself. Yet the
limitations in his verse are present partly because of his use
there of a narrative technique.

What is finally interposed as a further difficulty toward his
having created a body of good poetry comparable in consistency to his best prose is that Crane's poems are, as he put it,
committed to dealing with his "thoughts . . . about life in
general." [54] That is to say, they deal with large abstractions,
and Crane was unprepared either by native gifts or training
to deal effectively with abstract ideas, as his disinclination to
speculate on the theoretical principles on which his literary
practice is based suggests. With a sensuous rather than an
analytical imagination, Crane deals with abstractions only in
terms of narrative, his habitual mode of thought. All of his
poems we have found to be based on narrative situations,
whether explicit or implied. The narrative presentation of ab-

[54] *Omnibus,* p. 628.

stract ideas produces allegory. In tracing his debts to the Bible, his family's religious writings, and to Bierce and Schreiner, we saw that Crane was familiar with the allegorical mode from childhood, although, as his secular models indicate, he was conspicuously unfamiliar with allegory at a high level of literary excellence. Yet T. S. Eliot's remarks on the style best suited to allegory apply not only to Dante but to all writings in that mode; since allegory is itself an extended metaphor, "there is hardly any place for metaphor in the detail of it." [55] Crane's propensity for the abbreviated allegory cuts off such poems from the metaphorical resources of his sensuous imagination. Lacking the richness and resonance which reverberate in his best prose, many of those poems do not have the virtues of good allegorical style either. Where that style is concrete, Crane tends to be abstract and portentous. When he does treat his allegorical subjects directly in concrete images, however, he achieves the ironic compression typical of his best work in this vein.

But his larger successes in verse are in those poems which have opposite qualities of style and structure. When the narrative becomes a substructure, when the language is reflexive and metaphor an expression of theme and action, we have Crane's verse sharing the best qualities of his fiction. Since the two genres, as we have seen, presented Crane with formal problems which he approached in different fashions, the question arises as to where Crane learned to use metaphor as a structural principle in his verse. Possibly he merely transferred to verse a technique already developed in his prose; if this is

[55] *Selected Essays,* p. 206.

so, Crane participates in the breaking-down of distinctions between prose and poetry which had been going on at least since
Baudelaire.[56] An analogous attack on these distinctions, however, is evident in the work of Whitman, who proclaimed that
"the truest and greatest *Poetry* . . . can never again, in the
English language, be express'd in arbitrary and rhyming me-
tre." [57] Perhaps it was also in Whitman that Crane observed
the use in poetry of metaphor as a primary stratagem of structure. Although apparently unaware of the French contemporaries whose poetry his own has been said to resemble, Crane
may have been writing in the context of a somewhat similar
American literary tradition in which Whitman was one of his
chief predecessors.

The question of the relation of Crane's verse to his prose
invites further scrutiny. I shall return to it again in a broader
consideration of Crane's place in such an American tradition
and of what the connection is, if there be one, between his
work and that of the symbolist movement.

5

Before we can hazard some conclusions as to Crane's role in
the history of modern verse there remain to be discussed his
relationship to two literary movements of his own day and
with another a generation later. In his time and since he has
been linked with Decadence and Symbolism, while he is still
considered a forerunner of Imagist verse.

[56] Crane, too, wrote some poems in prose. See his "Legends," *Bookman*,
III (May, 1896), 206, reprinted in the Appendix, pp. 281–82.

[57] Quoted by F. O. Matthiessen in *American Renaissance*, p. 580. See
pp. 578–96 for a discussion of Whitman's rhythms.

Decadence, said Arthur Symons, is characterized by "an intense self-consciousness. . . . an over-subtilizing refinement upon refinement, a spiritual and moral perversity . . . this representative literature of today . . . is really a new and beautiful and interesting disease." [58] Much of the argument that Crane is a Decadent proceeds from the premise that anyone who led such a life as his was given to "spiritual and moral perversity"; and it cannot be denied that much of "Intrigue" seems not dissimilar in mood from the "wicked" art of Beardsley and Conder, from the self-tormenting pathos of Dowson. But let us measure Crane against a more comprehensive definition of this movement. Holbrook Jackson offers four qualities as characteristic of the Decadence: Perversity, Artificiality, Egoism, and Curiosity, meaning by the last the Decadents, killing their desires by surfeit, "demanded of life not repetition of old but opportunities for new experiences." [59]

If Crane is thought perverse one must mean that sado-masochistic streak which made him seek "the ashes of other men's loves" and torment himself with "Ah, God—that I should suffer / Because of the way a little finger moved" (Intrigue I, III). But the perversions of Dorian Gray in literature and of his models and imitators in life were self-willed, deliberate. The Decadents, proposing an art beyond good and evil, were inverting bourgeois morality by acts of will. Crane's sexual relations were probably compulsive, anything but the adventures in sensation of a dandy afflicted with *ennui*.

The willful perversity of the Decadents was concomitant to

[58] "The Decadent Movement in Literature," reprinted from *Harper's* (November, 1893) in *Dramatis Personae*, p. 97.
[59] *The Eighteen Nineties*, pp. 62–63.

their belief in the artificiality of art. "To be natural was to be obvious, and to be obvious was to be inartistic," Jackson writes of Wilde.[60] Art creates a self-determined universe not subject to the narrow conventions of bourgeois morality. Crane, failing to observe bourgeois morality for other reasons than those of the Decadents, apparently resembles them also in that his best writing does create the illusion of a self-contained world. But it is certainly not his intention to base his art upon artifice rather than upon the truthful impressions of life itself. "I decided that the nearer a writer gets to life the greater he becomes as an artist, and most of my prose writings have been toward the goal partially described by that misunderstood and abused word, realism," Crane wrote in 1895.[61] He specifies this for his prose, and indeed we cannot call his verse "realism" in Howells' or Garland's sense of the term. But fidelity to experience is in his verse no less near to life than in his prose, although its techniques of dealing with reality are somewhat different.

As for egoism, which in Decadent art as in Decadent personality took the form of highly individualized style, this is another case of Crane's factitious resemblance to his contemporaries. His style in verse is not only individual, it is unique; but he writes this way not for effect, not to put a *persona* between himself and reality, but because his special diction is required by his commitment to complete artistic honesty. No other way of expressing his meanings *would* express his meanings.

Curiosity? The true Decadent, like Dowson, "cried for madder music and for stronger wine," seeking new sensations with

---

[60] *Ibid.*, p. 62.   [61] Stallman, *Omnibus*, p. 627.

restless energies which Jackson asserts were "efforts towards
the rehabilitation of spiritual power," a search that led many
toward Catholicism or mysticism.[62] Of this trend there is nothing in Crane, whose search for experience was certainly strong
—but he searched intensely for the *same kinds* of experience:
the love of a fallen woman, and the testing of his spirit in the
face of death. There is a world of difference between Crane's
seeming bravado—actually it was nothing of the kind—and
the romantic swashbuckling of a Richard Harding Davis; [63]
neither much resembles the explorations into bohemian ir-
responsibility, dissipation, and vice of Lord Henry and Dorian.
For a parallel to that in American writing we must look to
the masterpiece of a virile soul really lost from hope in the
malaise de la fin de siècle: Jack London's *Martin Eden*.

Yet there is that orchid trailing over the cover of *The
Black Riders*, which, the artist reports, "with its strange habits,
extraordinary forms and curious properties, seemed to me the
most appropriate floral motive, an idea in which Mr. Crane
concurred." [64] There is Peck's valid comparison of Crane to
Beardsley as a master of effect. There is "A naked woman and
a dead dwarf." Was Crane a Decadent after all? We must
conclude that he would have followed his own course had
there been no Decadence, but that he was certainly drawn
toward certain aspects of that movement. More revealing than

[62] *The Eighteen Nineties*, p. 69.

[63] See Scott C. Osborn, "The 'Rivalry-Chivalry' of Richard Harding
Davis and Stephen Crane." *American Literature*, XXVIII (March, 1956),
50–61, for an account of their relationship.

[64] Frederick C. Gordon to Copeland and Day, n.d.; Williams-Starrett
Bibliography, p. 16, reprinted in *Omnibus*, p. 609. In a letter to Garland,
Crane calls Gordon "My friend, the artist." *Omnibus*, p. 608.

anything by Crane himself is this entry in Cora's manuscript book. Although written in Crane's own hand, this is Cora's style, not his; probably she dictated it, as he dictated some of his work to her. Cora expressed herself thus:

How beautiful to see a great crowd flocking out each unit of which was thoroughly unfitted for any duties whatsoever. It makes me perpetually sorrowful to meet with people doing their duty. I find them everywhere. It is simply impossible to escape from them. A sense of duty is like some horrible disease. It destroys the tissues of the mind as certain complaints destroy the tissues of the body. The catechism has a great deal to answer for. Sometimes I like to sit at home and read good books[;] at others I must drink absinthe and hang the night hours with scarlet embroideries. I must have music and the sins that march to music— / There are moments when I desire squalor, sinister mean surroundings, dreariness, and misery— / The great unwashed mood is upon me. Then I go out from luxury. The mind has its Westend and its White Chapel[.] The thoughts sit in Park Lane sometimes but sometimes they go slumming[;] they enter narrow courts and rookeries[,] they rest in unimaginable dens—seeking contrast—and they like ruffians whom they meet there and hate the notion of Policemen keeping order. . . .[65]

This is Decadent enough, indeed. Cora's sensibility was a curious mingling of the original and the second-hand; she had by this time—in England—picked up enough clichés of the Decadence to make a paragraph of them. She is quite unlike Crane, however, in her contempt for duty.

Not only did Stephen Crane take a real Decadent, derivative though she was, to his bed, but many of his literary associa-

[65] Cora Crane's MS book, Columbia Stephen Crane Collection. Spelling corrected and punctuation supplied.

tions were with Decadents of rather a pallid sort. We must remember that this movement's hothouse aestheticism was grown from Pre-Raphaelite stems, which flowered also in other, though allied, fashions. Elbert Hubbard's Roycrofters blended William Morris with Emerson and, at least in the overwrought illustrations to the *Philistine,* with imitations of Beardsley. That Crane in England knew and entertained contributors to the *Yellow Book* is proved by the joint authorship of a farce, "The Ghost," enacted at Brede Place, Crane's baronial residence in East Sussex: contributors included Gissing, Marriott-Watson—and Henry James.[66]

The evidence as to Crane's relation to Decadence is puzzling. Apparently he felt compatible with Hubbard, with these *Yellow Book* people, and certainly with Cora. Yet he never made common cause with the most famous Decadent of all. "Wilde was a mildewed chump," Beer reports Crane as saying. "He has a disease and they all gas about him as though there was a hell and he came up out of it. . . . Mr. Yeats is the only man I have met who talks of Wilde with any sense. The others talk like a lot of little girls at a Sunday School party when a kid says a wicked word in a corner." [67] Certainly his own aesthetic was antithetical to Wilde's, yet he regarded the award by the Academy of its poetry prize to Stephen Phillips, hailed at the time as a vigorous alternative

[66] See John D. Gordan, *"The Ghost* at Brede Place," *Bulletin of the New York Public Library,* LVI (December, 1952), 591–95; and my article, "An Unwritten Life of Stephen Crane," *Columbia Library Columns,* II (February, 1953), 14–15, for a reproduction of a program autographed by most of the collaborators. The Columbia collection contains five pages of the manuscript of "The Ghost."

[67] Beer, pp. 160–61.

to Decadent verse,[68] with something less than enthusiasm calling the judgment "in the artistic sense, respectable, inexorably
respectable." [69]

What divides Crane decisively from the Decadence is his
conviction, everywhere implicit, that art, like life, is moral.
What makes him seem to resemble the Decadents is, surprisingly, a certain likeness between their original aesthetic ideal
and his own. Just as in painting Impressionism, which later led
into Cubist abstraction, was originally an attempt to penetrate the appearance of mass and line to define the essential
reality of light and color, so Decadence, which ends by ex-
alting artifice at the expense of nature, began in attempts to
render truth. Symons, in a passage which confuses several
other things, does make this clear. Finding "that the terms
Impressionism and Symbolism define correctly enough two
main branches of [the Decadent] movement," he goes on to
say,

Impressionist and Symbolist have more in common than either
supposes; both are really working on the same hypothesis, applied
in different directions. What both seek is not general truth merely,
but *la vérité vraie,* the very essence of truth—the truth of appearances to the senses, of the visible world to the eyes that see it; and
the truth of spiritual things to the spiritual vision.[70]

Decadence was not wholly unique; it shared some characteristics of the two movements with which Symons here con-

[68] For the relation of Phillips to Decadence see Jerome H. Buckley, *The
Victorian Temper,* pp. 238–40.

[69] "Concerning the English 'Academy,'" *Bookman,* VII (March, 1898),
23.

[70] *Dramatis Personae,* pp. 98–99.

fuses it—and with Realism. Crane could respect the aesthetic which sought to give the truth of the visible world to the eyes that see it. The truth of spiritual things, however, was the business not of Decadence but of Symbolism. To this truth Crane was also committed, and we must now investigate his relationship to the Symbolist movement in literature.

6

Edmund Wilson has defined symbolism as "an attempt by carefully studied means—a complicated association of ideas represented by a medley of metaphors—to communicate unique personal feelings." With this definition our readings of the most complex Crane poems seem consonant. But prior to his definition Wilson states that "the symbols of Symbolism" really were "metaphors detached from their subjects," [71] a consideration which makes our view of Crane as symbolist somewhat less assured. That Symbolist symbols are indeed detached metaphors is the burden of William York Tindall's *The Literary Symbol*. Tracing the historical evolution of symbolism, Mr. Tindall sees it as a development of the transcendental theory of correspondences, which was itself an attempt to rediscover the organic unity of the world and weld together again the chain of being which Copernicus, Galileo, and humanism had broken. But "Unlike Dante or Marvell, these transcendentalists [Caryle, Melville, Emerson] used the symbol not to express or explore the upper half of the chain but to assure themselves of its possibility. . . . However concrete their symbolic instrument, it revealed the indefinite or the

[71] *Axel's Castle*, pp. 21–22.

unknowable." What makes inevitable the indefiniteness of symbolism is the loss, in modern times, of the philosophic certainties on which the exact analogies of medieval allegory and Renaissance metaphor were based, for these "were designed to present not abstractions alone but the nature of things." [72]

Crane would seem to have reflected in his short career a similar literary progression, moving, as I have said, from the most exact of allegorical analogies toward more complex symbolic constructs. Yet the indefiniteness which resides in Crane's "Symbolist" poems is different in kind from the Hermetic mystery in Baudelaire or Yeats. It may be that Crane's poems look like Symbolist poems, seem to act like them, but are in fact something different. They could scarcely have proved identical, since Crane not only seems to have known none of the verse of his Symbolist contemporaries but was also quite unaware of the developments of aesthetic theory on which the French movement was based.

The Symbolists were rebelling against the aesthetic of positivism and naturalism, best exemplified by Taine. Applying to art principles held to be valid in the natural sciences, Taine held that the artist interprets intellectually the material of his art, and that his craft consists merely in "putting his material into communicable form." [73] The Symbolists, on the contrary, viewed art as a kind of knowledge attainable only through the simultaneous perception of form and content. "The first and most striking feature of the symbolist aesthetic

---

[72] *The Literary Symbol,* pp. 33, 35–41.

[73] A. G. Lehmann, *The Symbolist Aesthetic,* pp. 21–24; see also p. 286.

was its attempt to establish art as an autonomous branch of human activity." [74]

The refutation of positivist aesthetics by the Symbolist movement of 1885–95 had been anticipated by Baudelaire and by Laforgue. Baudelaire's insistence upon the indispensability of artistic form to artistic perception was in fact a doctrine which he had found in Poe, of whom he wrote, "Il croyait en vrai pöete qu'il était, que le but de la poésie est de même nature que son principe, et qu'elle ne doit pas avoir en vue autre chose qu'elle-même." [75] Another contribution of Baudelaire to the Symbolist aesthetic was also derived from Poe, "the notion that the composition of a poem should be as conscious and deliberate as possible, that the poet should observe himself in the process of composition." [76] Laforgue offered later poets his "theory of literary unrestraint," his belief that "only by dint of being unique, unequalled, can an artist ever attain to genius"; [77] this was taken to be an invitation to the individual talent to seek means of self-expression outside the limits which extant traditions imposed upon poetic form.

The Symbolists who were Crane's contemporaries sought philosophical justification for their new aesthetic in German transcendentalism, especially in the work of Schopenhauer. Mallarmé in particular followed the German aesthetician in

[74] *Ibid.*, p. 30.

[75] *Oevres Complètes de Charles Baudelaire, Histoires Extraordinaires par Edgar Poe*, ed. by Jacques Crepet, p. xvi.

[76] T. S. Eliot, "From Poe to Valéry," in *Literary Opinion in America*, ed. by Morton Dauwen Zabel, p. 636.

[77] Lehmann, *Symbolist Aesthetic*, pp. 48–49.

regarding art as an escape from suffering and in viewing the world of art as non-phenomenal.[78] A further influence was the vogue of Wagner, which gave impetus to earlier tendencies in the romantic century toward the dissolution of traditional formal differentiation of the arts and toward the reconstitution of a "total art." The consequent blurring of distinctions between prose and poetry and between poetry and music resulted in the loss for poetry of its former self-sufficiency. Now "the total unity of structure is conceived no longer on the plane of speech but on a higher plane altogether."[79]

It may well be asked in what particulars does Crane's position resemble that of the French school. Despite his remoteness from the influences which produced the Symbolist aesthetic, there are in fact three rather surprising resemblances to Symbolist doctrine in Crane's work. Like the Symbolists, Crane rebelled against formal versification; like them, he viewed himself as alienated from society; and both Crane and the Symbolists demonstrate in their best work the autonomy of art. These parallels deserve closer examination.

First, Crane's repudiation of extant poetic practice was certainly not based on the influence, let us say, of Wagner, nor on the examples of Baudelaire's *Petits poèmes en prose* or Rimbaud's *Une saison en enfer*. Yet the results of his rebellion are recognizable as generically similar to the work of those who followed Laforgue's invitation to be original—and developed *vers libre*. Of course, Crane's poetic situation was different from that of a Gustave Kahn or a Francis Viélé-Griffin. Writing at a time when Richard Watson Gilder was

[78] *Ibid.*, pp. 38–39, 56–60.   [79] *Ibid.*, p. 193.

widely regarded as a leading American poet, the vocation of poetry seemed to Crane to be preempted by such "a parcel of dandies and ennuyees" as Whitman had assailed twenty years earlier.[80] When Elbert Hubbard proposed a dinner to honor his contributor's "genius as a poet," Crane wrote to Nellie Crouse, "I was very properly enraged at the word 'poet' which continually reminds me of long-hair and seems to me a most detestable form of insult"; consequently Crane never called his "lines" poems.[81] When recognition came to his "lines," one form it took was an invitation to read them before the literary ladies of the Uncut Leaves Society on an evening when the guest of honor was Mrs. Frances Hodgson Burnett, whose *Little Lord Fauntleroy* Crane detested.[82] He said he "would rather die" than appear there, so excerpts from *The Black Riders* were read to Mrs. Edmund Clarence Stedman, Mrs. Richard Henry Stoddard, and their friends by John D. Barry, the editor of the *Forum*.[83] Crane, who by 1894 had already written three novels, nonetheless felt that he had to write "lines" too. But his would not be the kind of verse that such poets as Stedman, Stoddard, or Gilder wrote. Abandoning formal meter, rhyme, and stanza in his early verse—he returned to them later, with what results we shall see—Crane evolved a kind of free verse.

How did the notion of free verse come to Crane? The most likely source is obviously Whitman. And here the interesting

[80] In "Democratic Vistas," *Complete Poetry*, p. 703.
[81] *Love Letters*, ed. by Cady and Wells, pp. 25–26, 31.
[82] Beer, pp. 111–12.
[83] "They Read from Unpublished Stories," New York *Daily Tribune*, April 26, 1894, reproduced in *Love Letters*, pp. 47–48.

possibility is raised that Whitman may have been to some extent responsible for the introduction of free verse among the French Symbolists. Laforgue had published translations from *Leaves of Grass* in *La Vogue* from June 28 to August 2, 1886, following the last of these a fortnight later by the first of his own *vers libres*. Two years later Viélé-Griffin, an American by birth, published further Whitman translations, one of which, "Faces," appears to have influenced Maerterlinck's *Serres Chaudes* in 1889.[84] Yet P. Mansell Jones, who in 1913–14 interviewed ten Symbolist poets on the question of Whitman's possible influence, concludes merely that

> when the first *vers libres* were being written, the poets who knew Whitman, and they were few, were attracted mainly through the appeal made by his brusque originality to their pronounced taste for literary novelties. The "astounding" thing about Whitman was not the way his poems were composed but the man they revealed. . . . To say that certain *vers libristes* were "influenced" by Whitman's line may simply have meant that, for the observer, the French experimenters had attempted something comparable to what Whitman appeared to have done. . . . On the other hand, to admit that little demonstrable effect has been discovered where much was implied does not set a limit to inquiry.[85]

Yet we can scarcely propose conclusions more assertive as to Whitman's being responsible for Crane's free verse either. As we have already observed, what is striking about Crane's presumed debt to Whitman is that he took over so little from the greater poet. Only rarely does Crane approximate Whitman's

---

[84] P. Mansell Jones, *The Background of Modern French Poetry*, pp. 139, 143–46.

[85] *Ibid.*, pp. 149–50.

diction, and in the early poems which most resolutely repudiate conventional form he nowhere adopts Whitman's long lyrical line. We remember that those early poems, least resembling Whitman's, were actually based on prose models—the
parables of the Bible, Bierce, and Schreiner. Somehow Crane
had picked up, or thought of, the notion that the traditional
distinctions between poetry and prose need no longer apply.

There is still another possible source, however, for Crane's
rejection of formal conventions. At the time when he was writing *The Black Riders* his constant companions were a group of
pupils at the Art Student's League in New York. These young
men were studying with the first generation of American art
teachers to have brought home the doctrines of Monet, Ce-
zanne, and Seurat. Crane often slept on cots in their studios,[86]
and in several stories he drew upon the discussions of artistic
theory he overheard—and probably took part in—as well as
on the difficulties of his artist friends in earning their daily
dinners. Joseph J. Kwiat has gathered all the known evidence
as to Crane's association with these fledgling Impressionists;
his study indicates that Crane was probably influenced by impressionistic theory in his handling of mass, color, and detail in
descriptive passages in his prose, and perhaps from them he
picked up the term "impressionism" with which he sometimes
described his literary method.[87] Did Crane go on to apply to

[86] In Corwin Linson's MS memoir of Crane (in the Syracuse University
Library) there is a photograph of Crane reclining against a wall hung
with impressionistic renderings of landscapes and haystacks, doubtless the
work of Linson and his fellow-students.

[87] Joseph J. Kwiat, "Stephen Crane and Painting," *American Quarterly*,
IV (Winter, 1952), 331–38.

the problem of form in his verse the principles of freer composition his painter friends were learning at the League? His association with them seems Crane's only exposure to the discussion of aesthetic theory by a group of practising artists in any art during the period when he developed his poetic strategy. All one can conclude, probably, is that the painters' attack on representational form in the name of fidelity to the reality of color and mass may have struck a responsive note in Crane, who was inclined to reject current poetic convention anyway. The theory of impressionistic painting was most likely a corroborative, not a primary source, for Crane's free verse.

The second resemblance between Crane and the Symbolists was that his sense of isolation as the fated condition of man is to a degree paralleled by their withdrawal from society. We have examined some of the factors which contributed to Crane's isolative sensibility; if he was receptive to the literary theories of his time, it was surely the naturalistic view that seemed most consonant with what he took to be the conditions of reality. Yet it was naturalism against which the Symbolists were in revolt. Their rebellion against the naturalistic aesthetic, their denial that art is a transcription of commonplace reality and that the artist analyzes his materials as the scientist examines the slice of life on a microscopic slide, led them to assert that art is an autonomous activity, a kind of cognition different from the rationalism by which the industrial society they hated measured the validity of experience. But concomitant with their prizing of art as a self-determined kind of experience was their conviction that "The poet is, in fact a specialist in a different technique, and his art thus becomes a rite, almost an esoteric practice." [88] When Mallarmé proclaims in his sonnet to Poe that his aim is "Donner un sens plus pur aux mots de la tribu," he is defiantly announcing that the resulting intensification of language will separate him and his art from the common run of men, not serve as a means of communication between them. Although compared to Crane the Symbolists would seem to have been enviably situated in the mainstream of their long-established richer culture, one historian of their movement concludes that the voluntary isolation of these poets from their society led to the serious diminution of their resources of language and myth, and kept any from writing a major work in a large form. [89]

While Crane took for granted the naturalistic attitude which the Symbolists abhorred, he shared nonetheless their conception of art as an autonomous activity and their conviction that artistic form is the structural element in terms of which the meanings of a literary work must be given. These beliefs he leaves it to us to infer from his best-made poems and tales; nowhere does he analyze his own practices or define his poetic art at greater length than in the allusive remarks we have examined. Yet among American writers of the 1890's Crane stands almost alone in his empirical demonstrations of affinity with these Symbolist convictions. In this decade the aesthetic most widely held may be that stated by the romancer F. Marion Crawford: "The first object of the novel is to amuse and interest the reader. . . . The perfect novel must be clean and sweet." [90] Similar sentiments could be adduced for poetry

---

[88] Lehmann, *Symbolist Aesthetic*, p. 64.   [89] *Ibid.*, p. 246.
[90] *The Novel—What It Is*, pp. 11, 43–44.

on the part of the genteel versifiers whom Crane declined to imitate. Henry James would appear to be the other chief example besides Crane of an American writing in the nineties who practiced the autonomy of art. And how much more cosmopolitan than Crane's was the culture from which James drew his sustenance, how much better equipped was he to articulate his understanding of the problems of his craft.

Is it possible, despite the huge disparities in their backgrounds, to explain these three resemblances between Crane and the Symbolists? Perhaps Symbolist doctrines, far from comprising a unique aesthetic theory, are but the restatements of some characteristics inherent in all artistic experience, restatements produced by, and phrased in terms of, a particular moment in the history of French lyric poetry. A. G. Lehmann, who has scrutinized the many conflicting definitions of the symbol the Symbolists proposed, concludes that the ultimate definition under which all others are subsumed is that "the 'symbol' is the form—and, of course, the content—of a book or other piece of writing." What is more, "the symbol, under the many forms in which it appears in symbolist poetry, is . . . only empirically different from material forming the stuff of poetry before and since." [91] The Symbolists' insistence upon the essentiality of both form and content was made necessary by the simplistic aesthetic of positivism and by the formal stasis the Parnassian school tried to impose upon the lyric. These passing movements notwithstanding, the unity of content and form is in fact a necessary condition of all successful art. Cassirer, quoting Mallarmé's famous dictum that "Poetry

[91] *Symbolist Aesthetic,* pp. 313, 304.

is not written with ideas, it is written with words," remarks that it is the "images, sounds, and rhythms" of language which in "every great lyrical poem . . . coalesce into an indivisible whole . . . [a] concrete and indivisible unity." Art, he concludes, does not imitate a given reality but creates its own "objective view of things and of human life"; art is "a discovery, . . . an intensification of reality. . . . a continuous process of concretion." [92] In the presence of art we live "in a world of pure sensuous forms" in which "what we feel is . . . the dynamic quality of life itself. To give aesthetic form to our passions is to transform them into a free and active state. In the work of the artist the power of passion itself has been made into a formative power." [93] As Susanne Langer observers, " 'Artistic truth' . . . is the truth of a symbol to the forms of feeling," [94] and the forms of feeling must be evoked in the beholder by the forms of the art which elicit them. Thus "The poem as a whole is the bearer of artistic import," which resides "not [in] the literal assertion made in the words, but [in] *the way the assertion is made.*" But "artistic forms are exhaustible." [95] It is therefore continuously necessary for the artist to enlarge his technical resources in order to keep his way of making assertions true to the forms of feeling he would recreate in the beholder.

The anomaly of Crane's having practised such an aesthetic implicitly despite his preference for the naturalism abhorred by the Symbolists is explained by Cassirer's observation:

[92] Ernst Cassirer, *An Essay on Man*, pp. 183–84.   [93] *Ibid.*, p. 190.
[94] *Philosophy in a New Key*, pp. 100, 262.
[95] *Ibid.*, pp. 261, 260 (her italics), 262.

Curiously enough the great realists of the nineteenth century had
. . . a keener insight into the art process than their romantic ad-
versaries. They maintained a radical and uncompromising naturalism. But it was precisely this naturalism which led them to a more
profound conception of artistic form. Denying the "pure forms"
of the idealistic school they concentrated upon the material aspect
of things. By virtue of this sheer concentration they were able to
overcome the conventional dualism between the poetic and the
prosaic spheres. . . . The symbolism of art must be understood in
an immanent, not in a transcendent sense. . . . The real subject of
art . . . is to be sought in certain fundamental structural elements
of our sense experience itself.[96]

Hence it is that in Crane the combination of naturalistic realism with a most intense sensuous awareness and a striking
empirical command of metaphoric language could lead to
successful assertions of the forms of feeling.

7

Even an artist as original as Crane must come to the expression of his originality in the context of a literary culture. If, as
the foregoing pages suggest, it is unlikely that his individual
qualities derive from either symbolist poetics or impressionistic theories of painting, we may be better advised to examine
a context of culture nearer to Crane than these French traditions. Although his critics appear to have overlooked the possibility of his having been influenced by it, there is in fact an
important American tradition whose aesthetic assumptions
paralleled those of French symbolism. The likelihood seems
worth exploring that this native tradition may have significantly influenced Crane's use of reflexive language to define

[96] *An Essay on Man,* pp. 200–201.

and intensify reality, as well as affected his attempts to reconstitute poetic form on principles more organic than those he rejects.

Like its later French counterpart, the American symbolist movement had by mid-nineteenth century developed in protest against the restrictive view of reality and the simplistic role assigned to art in the prevailing aesthetic of the time. In "American's Coming of Age," Van Wyck Brooks suggests that the union of empirical practicality with speculative thought which characterized Puritan culture had by the middle of the eighteenth century been sundered, as the careers of Benjamin Franklin and Jonathan Edwards attest.[97] It is from each of these sundered strains—the abstract cogitations of Puritan divines and Franklin's practical morality—that nineteenth-century America inherited attitudes inimical to the free exercise of the artistic imagination. Franklin in his own literary theory adopted the Newtonian arguments supporting plainness and clarity then being espoused by the Royal Society; [98] in a letter to Hume he states that "every expression in the least obscure is a fault," [99] while elsewhere he defines more precisely the aesthetic of utilitarianism:

To be good, [a writing] ought to have a tendency to benefit the reader, by improving his virtue or his knowledge. . . . the method should be just, that is, it should proceed regularly from things known to things unknown, distinctly and without confusion.[100]

[97] Van Wyck Brooks, *Three Essays on America,* pp. 15–35.
[98] Frank Luther Mott and Chester E. Jorgenson, introduction to *Benjamin Franklin: Representative Selections,* pp. xlix–l.
[99] *The Writings of Benjamin Franklin,* ed. by Albert Henry Smyth, I, 41.
[100] *Ibid.,* I, 37.

The external view of reality Franklin professed was widely held, and this view is indeed vulnerable to the sarcasms of D. H. Lawrence: "Why the soul of man is a vast forest, and all Benjamin intended was a neat back garden. . . . Benjamin had no concern, really, with the immortal soul. He was too busy with social man." [101]

As for the other strain, "What the Puritan mind bequeathed to American writing, from the standpoint of literary method, was a special and extreme case of the modern literary situation: a conflict between the symbolic mode of perception, of which our very language is a record, and a world of sheer abstraction certified as 'real.' " [102] In a world where, as Matthiessen remarks, "every capsized dory or run-away cow" was interpreted as a "remarkable providence" manifesting the intervention of God,[103] all phenomena were taken as allegories of the Divine will. "A properly symbolic method was denied the Puritan writer by his assumptions on method in general," for the Puritans had drastically broken with the Thomistic tradition that "things have multiple meanings and that language is at one with the symbolic structure of reality." [104] It remained for Emerson to reassert that words are symbols of natural facts, that natural facts are symbols of spiritual facts, and that nature is the symbol of spirit.[105] Following Coleridge on the unity of the thought with the object of thought, Emerson maintained that through metaphor "the world converts itself

---

[101] *Studies in Classic American Literature,* pp. 21, 23.

[102] Charles Feidelson, Jr., *Symbolism and American Literature,* p. 90.

[103] *American Renaissance,* p. 243.

[104] Feidelson, *Symbolism and American Literature,* p. 84.

[105] *Complete Works,* I, 25 ff.

into that thing you name," [106] and further, that "A work of art is an abstract or epitome of the world." [107] As Matthiessen points out, "the transcendental theory of art is a theory of knowledge and religion as well." [108] This theory of art, based upon theological epistemology, directly led to a rejection of arbitrary formal conventions:

By urging his radical formalism, [Emerson] was trying to obviate the external formalism by which "poetry is degraded and made ornamental" (*Works*, V, 242). Thus he demanded a poetry which would be "the gift to men of new images and symbols, each the ensign and oracle of an age . . . poetry which tastes the world and reports of it, upbuilding the world again in the thought. . . ." (*Works*, VIII, 65).[109]

Emerson's theory, Feidelson concludes, "implies a fundamental theme of modern aesthetics—that the work of art establishes a scale of value through formal means and does not depend on any external standard." [110]

This was a theory held in common not only by Emerson and his disciples Whitman and Thoreau, but by such critics of transcendentalism as Hawthorne, Melville, and Poe as well. Was it held also by Stephen Crane?

Again the critic is severely disadvantaged by the almost total lack of proofs with which to gird his inferences about Crane. We do know that Crane had read some of Emerson— Berryman mentions Emerson, Whitman, and Poe among Crane's boyhood readings, and reports that one of his note-

[106] *Journals*, VIII, 296, quoted in Feidelson, p. 149.
[107] *Complete Works*, I, 29.   [108] *American Renaissance*, p. 31.
[109] Feidelson, *Symbolism and American Literature*, p. 310.
[110] *Ibid.*, p. 150.

books contains this sentence of Concord philosophy: "Congratulate yourselves if you have done something strange and extravagent and have broken the monotony of a decorous age." [111] Poe's influence is obvious in some of Crane's stories —"A Tale of Mere Chance" and the posthumous "The Squire's Madness"—but of the aspect of Poe to which Baudelaire responded, the analytical mind self-consciously observing its own poetic processes, there seems to be no trace in Crane. Neither is there any trace of his having read Melville or Hawthorne, yet in the development of his own craft he most nearly parallels Hawthorne's own progress, as we shall see.

Crane had the gift—it may have been second in importance only to his metaphoric mind—of absorbing all of the implications necessary to his own purpose from readings so desultory and ill-recorded as to baffle his critics by their elusiveness. Always acknowledging the limits within which his intense talents interpreted experience, we may well apply to him Henry James' praise for the hero of *The Princess Cassamassima:* here was a young man on whom nothing was lost. If the American symbolist tradition reached Crane—and I think the virtues of his best work make it plain that it had indeed—it must have been absorbed early, for *Maggie* and some of *The Black Riders* show his reliance on the symbolist assumptions of metaphor, paradox, and autonomy.

Although the symbolist views of language and art evolved from theological debate on the nature of knowledge, it is not very likely that these convictions came to Crane from his own religious background. Methodism does not possess an intellec-

---

[111] Berryman, pp. 24, 268.

tual tradition comparable to that of the Unitarians and Puritans. The breakdown of the Puritan synthesis of logic and emotion led, as we have observed, to the separate development in American culture of each of these elements. In a sphere of speculation less secular than Franklin's accommodating deism, the Unitarians who were Emerson's forerunners prized rationalism at the expense of enthusiasm. Rebelling against their pallid faith, Emerson and the whole transcendental generation returned to the fervent, mystical side of Jonathan Edwards which the intervening generation had denied.[112] But this emotionalism had already been caught up in the fervor of the evangelical movements after the Great Awakening of 1740; on the frontier, Methodism became a dominant sect,[113] and such contemporaries of Emerson as George Peck, Stephen Crane's grandfather, valued paralytic seizures and "speaking with tongues" as genuine evidences of the infusion of Divine Grace into the soul of a repentant sinner. Here was a faith of fervor outrunning even transcendentalism in its capacity for emotionalism. In its lack of an intellectual tradition, however, Methodism belongs in the opposite wing of American Protestantism from the Puritan-Unitarian-Transcendental heritage. Thus it is that the writings of Jonathan Crane and of George and Jesse Peck are concerned with the interpretation of church doctrine and practice, not with defining the nature of knowledge.[114] The distrust of imaginative literature and the animus

[112] Perry Miller, "Jonathan Edwards to Emerson," *New England Quarterly*, XIII (December, 1940), 589–617; see also Matthiessen, *American Renaissance*, p. 56.

[113] William Warren Sweet, *The Story of Religion in America*, p. 316.

[114] According to the "List of Books, Brede Place" and volumes from his library now in the Columbia Crane collection, Crane owned the follow-

against sensuous experience exhibited even by Crane's father, the most liberal and humanistic of these Methodists, makes it plain that Crane's reading of Whitman, for instance, was more a rebellion against his home training than the logical extension of anything in his own religious or intellectual tradition.

Yet, as we have seen, the didacticism of Crane's Methodist background is responsible for his early reading and for his practice of allegory. Art conceived as allegory is "an emblem of moral truth. . . . a figurative expression which under its sensuous form concealed an ethical sense," but that form has no autonomous value whatever.[115] Allegorism is the polar opposite of the symbolistic theory developed by Emerson.

It was from the limitations of this same factitious separation of meaning from artistic form in Puritan thought that the transcendental aesthetic proposed to free the artistic imagination. Yet the transcendental authors whose works proved the truth of Emerson's theories were strongly committed to the Calvinistic background of allegorism from which they were struggling to free themselves. Still another circumstance encouraged the protraction in America of allegory in a romantic

---

ing works by his forebears: by Jonathan Townley Crane, *Arts of Intoxication: the Aim and the Result* (1870), *Essay on Dancing* (1848), *Holiness the Birthright of All God's Children* (1874), *Methodism and Its Methods* (1876), and *Popular Amusements* (1869); by George Peck, *Early Methodism Within the Bounds of the Genessee Conference from 1788 to 1828* (1860), *Our Country, Its Trials and Its Triumph* (1865), *Rule of Faith* (1852), and *Wyoming: Its History, Stirring Incidents and Romantic Adventures* (1858); by Jesse Peck, *Central Idea of Christianity* (1856) and *A History of the Great Republic Considered from a Christian Standpoint* (1868).

[115] Cassirer, *An Essay on Man*, p. 177.

century: the apparent unavailability to our most gifted writers of the best European models of their own times. We think of Hawthorne and Melville (who read much more widely than did Crane), immersed in Puritan history and accounts of travel and whaling, writing as though the novel of manners had not yet been invented. Crane, too, learned his literary craft from inconsequent models; what English poet would have apprenticed himself to an Olive Schreiner or an Ambrose Bierce?

Allegory, then, is to some degree characteristic of American literature itself in the nineteenth century. Mark Van Doren is certainly right in maintaining that "Without his allegory Hawthorne would be nothing." [116] Yvor Winters, examining the Puritan culture which Hawthorne made the locus of his imagination, concludes that "In the setting which he chose, allegory was realism, the idea was life itself." [117] Yet, as Matthiessen makes clear, "both allegory and symbolism can arise from the same thinking." The difference between them, he suggests, is that symbolism "shapes new wholes; whereas allegory deals with fixities and definities that it does not basically modify." [118] Thus a typical entry in Hawthorne's notebook takes the form of an observation of the gas-pipe in a city, to which he adds the observation, "It might be made emblematical of something." [119] The problem of Hawthorne's art was to establish connections between such fixed realities and the values of which they were emblems; contrarily, starting with the spiritual values, he had to find their material tokens. But Hawthorne's allegory is not all of a piece, nor is it in his mature

[116] *Nathaniel Hawthorne*, p. 66.   [117] *In Defense of Reason*, p. 165.
[118] *American Renaissance*, pp. 248–50.
[119] Quoted in *American Renaissance*, p. 244.

work merely the mechanical attribution of emblematic meanings. If we compare the allegorical method of *The Scarlet Letter* to that of his early sketch "The Procession of Life," we can
see how, in his masterpiece, allegory transcends the crude
unitary correspondences of his first exercises in that mode.
The "A" itself is indeed allegorical, but by virtue of what Winters calls "the formula of alternative possibilities" [120] it can be
emblematic of qualities which contradict each other. This capacity of an image to contain significations in dialectic opposition produces a richness of meaning which we associate with
the symbol rather than with allegory.

In Melville, too, we see a large debt to allegory. In *Moby-
Dick* Melville creates a still larger dialectic between the unitary simplification of allegorism and the multiplicity of meaning in the symbol. (His own terminology is only confusing, for
he speaks in a letter to Mrs. Hawthorne of the "allegorical con-
struction" to which "the whole book was susceptible," and also
of "the particular subordinate allegories" within it; some of
these, as well as "the part-and-parcel allegoricalness of the
whole," [121] the modern critic would describe as "symbolic.")
Thus, to both Ahab and the mad prophet Gabriel, the white
whale is an allegorical sign—part of the irony is that their ab-
solutist interpretations of the sign contradict one another—
while for Ishmael it is a symbol whose meanings are so complex as to elude the rigid representation by which the strict
allegorist falsifies reality. [122]

[120] *In Defense of Reason,* p. 170.
[121] Quoted in *American Renaissance,* p. 250.
[122] Feidelson proposes the doubloon as the prototype of Melville's symbolism (p. 32), but it would seem that the doubloon itself is neither a

In his development from the allegorical parables in *The Black Riders* to the symbolistic use of metaphor in the later poems, Crane would seem most to resemble Hawthorne. Although there is no proof that Crane had read either Hawthorne or Melville, he shares with them as with Emily Dickinson the cultural situation described by Allen Tate. All inherit the metaphors of the book of nature which had in the past held allegorical exactitude and stated universal truths. Mr. Tate described the break-up of a theocratic community as the historical moment most favorable to literature. At such times "the world order . . . is brought down from abstraction to personal sensibility" [123]—hence in the process, symbolistic metaphor develops gradually from a persistent background of allegorism. Crane in his "symbolist" phase is never as far from his earlier allegories—nor as close to the French symbolists of his own time—as the metaphoric density of the poems might lead us to suppose. This can best be seen by reviewing quickly the stages in the evolvement of his more complex idiom.

---

symbol nor an allegory but an opportunity placed before each of the characters to interpret an arbitrary arrangement of linked images in accordance with his own view of reality. In other words, the data of experience are given, and it is the individual imagination which transforms them into constricting allegories or expanding symbols. Yet even in the case of the few images on that one small coin Melville causes us to feel that none of the characters is able to "strike through the mask" and comprehend the complex nature of reality implicit in the selected images nailed to the mast. The entire episode may be an allegory—or a symbol—of the basic problem of art.

[123] *The Man of Letters in the Modern World,* pp. 221–22.

Eight ❧ CRANE AND POETIC TRADITION

In tracing the evolution of Crane's craft let us begin with a simple allegory. Here character and action are explicit embodiments of moral qualities. Perhaps the most striking of Crane's allegorical poems is this one:

> The wayfarer,
> Perceiving the pathway to truth,
> Was struck with astonishment.
> It was thickly grown with weeds.
> "Ha," he said,
> "I see that none has passed here
> In a long time."
> Later he saw that each weed
> Was a singular knife.
> "Well," he mumbled at last,
> "Doubtless there are other roads." [WK xiii]

This allegorical cameo might well have been modeled on a medieval morality play. As in the best of Crane's poems in this vein, the language is direct and, but for the phrase "a singular knife," uncomplicated by nuance. This is a diction without association or metaphor.

At one remove from such directness are poems in which we find, instead of allegorical personages, actions whose import is

in direct correspondence to a state of feeling the poet wishes
to evoke. Here the language may be more ornate—in the fifteen lines following there are nine qualifying adjectives, ad-
verbs, and phrases—yet the narrative is still relatively straightforward.

> A youth in apparel that glittered
> Went to walk in a grim forest.
> There he met an assassin
> Attired all in garb of old days;
> He, scowling through the thickets,
> And dagger poised quivering,
> Rushed upon the youth.
> "Sir," said this latter,
> "I am enchanted, believe me,
> To die, thus,
> In this medieval fashion,
> According to the best legends;
> Ah, what joy!"
> Then took he the wound, smiling,
> And died, content.   [BR xxvii]

Mr. Stallman considers this poem "a miniature copy of *The
Red Badge of Courage*," the conflict in both being that "between *illusion and reality*." [1] Some of Henry's illusions, it is
true, are dreams of medieval glory (he thought of war as a
time of "heavy crowns and high castles" [2]) but there is surely
a difference between the panic and courage of the novel and
the satisfied nihilism of the poem. Stylistically the poem is
elaborate, dressed as it were in antique brocade. The youth's
glittering apparel is not only his clothing; his mind too is

---

[1] Stallman, *Omnibus*, p. 569 (his italics).   [2] *Ibid.*, p. 229.

dressed "In this medieval fashion." "Apparel that glittered" of course suggests armor, the function of which is to fend off poised daggers. But this youth longs for death "According to the best legends" and is purposely as defenseless as though he were naked. Although the narrative in this poem is complete in itself, the language is richer in associations than that in the simple allegories.

As Crane moves from a poetry of direct correspondences toward a less discursive, more allusive idiom, his language may take on metaphoric functions simply because the referents of the narrative are undefined, e.g.,

> On the horizon the peaks assembled;
> And as I looked
> The march of the mountains began.
> As they marched they sang,
> "Ay, we come! we come!"   [BR xxxvii]

Although much plainer in style than "A youth in apparel that glittered," this is more complex in effect. Crane leaves it to us to infer that the mountains, normally massive and immobile, represent the immitigable force in the natural universe. He does not state that their march is *toward him,* the insignificant human observer, yet we feel this to be so. Although all that is said—and that is precious little—is said in a diction sparse and plain, the tone is hugely ominous. Crane does not say, but we know, that the human protagonist stands awe-stricken, dumb and still as stone while the horizon of peaks chants as it closes in upon him—as would the growling peaked waves in the later poem, "A man adrift on a slim spar."

That poem may be taken to represent the fourth stage in

the complexity of Crane's poetic idiom. There, as we saw at the end of Chapter Three, the discursive narrative element is still further suppressed; by indirect suggestion the purposeful ambiguities and interlocking associations of the metaphoric diction reinforce the development of theme which the inferential narrative supplies.

Thus it is evident that Crane develops distinctive methods of poetic structure, as well as the several styles of diction mentioned at the beginning of the last chapter. This I take to be a refutation of Berryman's assertion that "There is no evidence in the poetry or outside it that he ever experimented in verse." [3] Indeed, it is because Crane was what later generations would call an experimental writer that the sum of his work seems as discontinuous as we have found it to be. This is true to a degree of his prose also—many readers have noted the fantasy and impressionism of *Sullivan County Sketches*, the naturalistic determinism of *Maggie* and *George's Mother*, the irony and dreamlike association of incident and metaphor in *The Red Badge*, the naturalism again in "The Open Boat" but now in combination with a superbly controlled symbolistic style, the frontier humor of "The Bride Comes to Yellow Sky," the sustained combination of tension and suppleness in "The Blue Hotel," the irony undercutting the baroque prose of *The Monster*, and the style "flexible, swift, abrupt, nervous . . . with an unexampled capacity for stasis also" which Berryman remarks as the norm for Crane's prose.[4] Although Crane's experimentalism led him to absorb many technical influences that came his way, the unifying quality which makes these

[3] Berryman, p. 274.   [4] *Ibid.*, p. 284.

stories all unmistakably his own is the sensibility they express. The authority of his style, highly individual despite all these modifications, is the guarantee of the uniqueness of that sensibility.

In verse, too, we find several varieties of excellence, unified despite variation by the authority of the style. The four stages of increasing complexity we have just noted actually merge into one another, but on the whole we can distinguish between two generic types of Crane poems, the allegories and the non-discursive symbolistic poems. The former category includes such unadorned allegorical narratives as "The wayfarer / Perceiving the pathway to truth," "There was one I met upon the road," "A man saw a ball of gold in the sky," "In heaven / Some little blades of grass," and "The trees in the garden rained flowers." There are also the parables of simple paradox—"A man said to the universe," "I saw a man pursuing the horizon," " 'It was wrong to do this,' said the angel," "A man feared that he might find an assassin," and "Forth went the candid man."

Subtler than these are the metaphorical parables capable of symbolistic extension, such as "A youth in apparel that glittered," "The patent of a lord," "On the horizon the peaks assembled," and the fable of the heart-eater in the desert.

The symbolistic poems which, by virtue of their more complex organization, the larger commitments they express, and the subtlety and resourcefulness of their language, I take to be Crane's most substantial verse, include "A man adrift on a slim spar," "Do not weep, maiden, for war is kind," and "The Blue Battalions"—these I think his three best; and also "Bottles and bottles and bottles," "The Battle Hymn," "Black riders came from the sea," "Fast rode the knight," "I explain the silvered passing of a ship at night," and the opening lines of "There exists the eternal fact of conflict." But this schematization does not accommodate such other poems worthy of mention as the impressionistic "Each small gleam was a voice," the imagistic "To the maiden / The sea was a blue meadow," or the discursive "A newspaper is a collection of half-injustices."

If we compare the intentions of Crane's most complex verse to those of the French Symbolists we can at once identify the characteristics which isolate Crane from them and which link him to the greater writers of the American Renaissance. Mr. Tindall has conveniently summarized Mallarmé's aesthetic, and it is instructive to juxtapose this to Crane's:

Without intended reference to external reality, his worlds or poems are "inclosed." Fictions or virtual realities, they exist as a piece of music does, by symmetry, interaction of parts, and what he called "reciprocal reflections" . . . as far as possible from discourse. . . . [Mallarmé] said that symbolism consisted in evoking an object little by little in order to reveal a state of mind, or, inversely, choosing an object and from it disengaging a state of mind. . . . This state, far from being a reminder of anything we have known, is a fresh creation; and this creation is the effect of analogy, not from nature's store but made by the poet. What it is an analogy for must be guessed by the reader as the poem creates his state of mind.[5]

It is evident, if the readings I have proposed of his best poems have any merit, that the means by which Crane's verse creates its intended effects resemble those of Mallarmé. But it

[5] *The Literary Symbol*, pp. 48–49.

is equally clear that despite these similarities in technique
there is a basic difference in intention. Crane's poems, autonomous though they are, are never "without intended reference
to external reality." When his verse moves "as far as possible
from discourse" it is not, as is the case with Mallarmé, to construct an autonomous private universe as an alternative to
the world of nature. "The nearer a writer gets to life the
greater he becomes as an artist" [6]—this is a constant tenet in
Crane's artistic practice. The world of his poems is made with
the allegorist's prerogative of providing an imaginary construct
to represent the real world, not, as the Symbolist would, to
substitute for it.

Crane abandons discursiveness when the truths of life which
he seeks to discover and reveal cannot be reached by means
so direct. In order to express the complexity inherent to a
faithful representation of his own sensibility, Crane felt in his
early poems that he must break with the conventions of the
genteel verse of his time. Hence the iconoclasm, the repudiation of traditional structure and ornament:

> "Think as I think," said a man,
> "Or you are abominably wicked,
> You are a toad."
>
> And after I had thought of it,
> I said, "I will, then, be a toad."   [BR xlvii]

Thus in 1893. But two or three years later Crane writes a poem
in six regular stanzas, alternating questions with replies:

[6] *Omnibus,* p. 627.

"What says the sea, little shell?" (WK II) first appeared in the *Philistine* in February, 1896. The next month the *Chap-book* printed "In the night," whose three stanzas, examined above in Chapter Three, presented a definite time scheme in consistent metrical form. By April "The Blue Battalions" had been written (see Chapter Five) with still more complicated regular stanzas incorporating internal refrains. "Do not weep, maiden, for war is kind" is perhaps Crane's most complexly organized poem, but this had been written by August, 1895. From that time on Crane was no longer in willful rebellion against such conventional techniques as stanzas and refrains, although he never did adopt rhyme or iambic meter. His best longer poems combine firm stanzaic structure with the allusiveness of controlled metaphor. This parallels the conjunction in his prose, remarked above, of metaphoric richness with the skilled organization of incident.

In these more complexly organized poems, Crane, like the French Symbolists, does demand that we guess at the significance of the states of mind or feeling which his poems little by little reveal. But whereas "a symbolist work," Mr. Tindall concludes, "has no certain meaning," [7] this we do not feel to be the case with Crane. The meaning, complex and ambiguous though it may be, is certain nonetheless. His symbols are not metaphors "detached from their subjects" but metaphors whose relation to their subjects must be inferred. They are metaphors of fixed reference, yet their use takes advantage of the ambiguous and symbolic nature of language itself. Crane

[7] *The Literary Symbol*, p. 267.

retains the certainty of the ethical significance of experience, the assurance of the spiritual significance of natural facts, which made allegory the natural expression of his early work.

2

In so far as Crane's symbols have assigned though unstated meanings they are much closer to the objective correlative described by T. S. Eliot [8] than they are to either the symbols of Symbolism or the images of Imagism. The image, as Ezra Pound defined it, "is that which presents an intellectual complex in an instant of time. . . . It is the presentation of such a 'complex' instantaneously which gives that sense of sudden liberation; that sense of freedom from time limits and space limits; that sense of sudden growth, which we experience in the presence of the greatest works of art." [9] Crane seems to resemble the Imagist poets because, like them, in many of his poems he uses direct treatment, economical diction, and organic rhythm. Yet he actually conforms to the aesthetic Pound describes in only his simplest verse. The Imagist aims at a static representation of a caught moment of experience; this, by virtue of its associations, elicits in us intellectual and emotional awareness of things outside itself. But almost all of Crane's simple "imagistic" poems are themselves in motion. They have plots as allegories have plots. Granting their governing metaphors, they force attention inward upon themselves, not outward to extrinsic associations. There are no such associations; there are only the poems.

In his more complex verse, however, Crane is more ambi-

[8] *Selected Essays,* pp. 124–25.   [9] *Literary Essays,* p. 4.

tious than the Imagist aesthetic allows. In so far as his verse resembles the work of that movement, it is in his impression-istic pieces; Imagism, after all, attempted merely to expand by association the significance of the impression. While Crane appealed to Pound, Sandburg, Edith Wyatt, and others as a forebear of the then contemporary movement, he had long since gone beyond the limitations of the Imagist aesthetic. This was a journey almost all the Imagists themselves were to make—Eliot moving toward soliloquy and drama, Stevens toward the most Symbolist symbolism in English verse, Fletcher reverting to the lush romanticism of Lanier, Mari-anne Moore developing a unique combination of moral sensi-bility and parable derived from Whitman and La Fontaine, Sandburg losing completely the economical control Imagism had imposed on his language as he literally appropriates the idiom of everyday speech for poetry.[10] Of the original Im-agists, H. D., William Carlos Williams, and Pound remained most influenced by their own programme of the Little Ren-aissance. H. D. continues with admirable integrity to chisel verbal cameos, and fails to deal successfully with themes rather than with impressions. Pound and Williams have more omnivorous ambitions, the one Ovidian, the other Whitman-esque, but in the organization of both *The Cantos* and *Pater-son* we see the limiting effectiveness of Imagist images con-

[10] I have traced Whitman's influence upon Miss Moore in some detail in a review of her collected poems in *Antioch Review*, XII (Spring, 1952), pp. 123–25. See also "Sandburg and 'The People': His Literary Populism Reappraised," *Antioch Review*, X (Summer, 1950), pp. 265–78, substantially reprinted in *Paul Bunyan, Last of the Frontier Demigods*, pp. 132–43.

nected chiefly by mood. Of the two attempted epics, *Paterson* is the more cohesive, but its flaw is another Imagist limitation: the philosophical naiveté of "no ideas but in things."

Since Crane was heralded as a forebear of the movement in which these important poets participated, why, one wonders, has his actual influence on twentieth-century verse been so slight? One reason, mentioned above, is the relative unavailability of his verse during the period when its influence might have been most felt. Neither of his books was reprinted nor, except for Stedman's collection in 1900, did any anthology contain Crane's verse until after his *Work* appeared in 1926. By then Imagism had had its heyday. But a more fundamental reason for Crane's seeming lack of influence is that despite his anticipation of some techniques later to be widely adopted, he held a conception of poetry which later poets and critics could not share.

The first tenet of Crane's view of poetry was his notion of the brevity of poetic form. This may at first seem not incongruous with Imagist compression; indeed, until quite recently twentieth-century poetry has been almost without exception based upon compact lyric techniques, whether of symbolist, imagist, or metaphysical origin. Yet at the same time modern poets have attempted to move beyond the brevity of lyric form to vehicles more ambitious: the cycles of interconnected lyrics of Yeats's Crazy Jane poems; the attempted epics of *The Waste Land, The Bridge, The Cantos, Paterson, The People, Yes;* the baroque mock-epic of *The Comedian as the Letter C;* the extended soliloquys of Senlin and *The Four Quartets;* the verse drama of Yeats, Eliot, MacLeish, Eberhart, and their younger emulators. But Crane was intransigently committed to envisaging the proper dimension of all art as brief. *War and Peace, Anna Karenina, Nana,* the books of Mark Twain, all seemed to him too long for the work they set out to do.[11] His own best fiction is either the novella or the short story. And in poetry we have seen him ruthlessly reduce to their minimal essences the works that influenced him and attempt to keep his best original compositions as tightly knit and nondiscursive as possible.

This is because Crane seeks the ultimate concentration of experience in art. His valuing of brevity may have derived from Poe's aesthetic theory, yet Crane's observance of this precept does not resemble Poe's. Crane seeks the moments of highest intensity not, like Poe, for the sake of the sensation, but because life experienced at that pitch will reveal to him the meanings which are otherwise diffused and rendered indecipherable. That intensity is the result of the collision of forces which operate upon experience, and the work, to be true to the life it represents, must contain the forces, the experience, and the intensity all together. This it can do either by presenting a dialectic or in terms of a plot. Crane's best poems use both methods; they present the bare outlines of a narrative situation in which there is a tension between two opposed forces. The tension may be expressed in terms of antithetical statements, dialogue, description, or the effect upon the observer of an action he witnesses. Crane's mind is always attuned to narrative, to the dynamic representation of man in conflict. But in his poems he seeks the most universal state-

[11] Beer, pp. 143, 147, 157.

ments possible of the themes which possess his imagination. Hence he must eliminate from the presentation all the particularities of the conflicts which might restrict his statements only to the described events. By making his human figures faceless and nameless, by pitting them against elemental forces, by describing their ambitions and their plights in simple yet overwhelming metaphors, Crane created for his poetry a symbolical form which represented a great advance in subtlety and flexibility over its allegorical beginnings.

But these considerations lead us to the second tenet of Crane's poetic credo which later writers could not share. Twentieth-century verse has recoiled not only from allegory but from narrative itself, concentrating instead upon lyric and dramatic expression. Even the attempted epics named above have been made in terms of lyric, rather than narrative or allegorical strategy (except for Stevens's *Comedian,* which in no respect resembles Crane). Crane, however, went his own way and made his own styles to do the work to which he had to put them. His diction is intrinsic to the structure of his poems; the one cannot be imitated without the other. And since the combination Crane made of allegory (explicit or implied), assigned symbols, dialectic, direct treatment, brevity, and narrative situation remains his own, his verse remains singular after almost half a century of post-Imagist emphasis on directness and economy. A style such as Crane's is the product both of his extraordinary sensibility and of his cultural situation, which was much more impoverished than that of any twentieth-century American poet of distinction.

Yet let it not be concluded that Crane's verse has been wholly without consequences in later American literature. Consider, for instance, the following poem:

MITRAILLATRICE

The mills of the gods grind slowly;
But this mill
Chatters in mechanical staccato.
Ugly short infantry of the mind,
Advancing over difficult terrain,
Make this Corona
Their mitrailleuse.

Had Crane gone to war with the A.E.F. in 1918 instead of with the Greeks in 1897 and at Guantanamo Bay in 1898, he might well have written these lines. The inexorable determinism of this poem surely suggests his attitude, as the short-phrase free verse and the very diction reproduce his style. Also characteristic of Crane is the governing metaphor equating author with soldier, to which the other images—typewriter as machine-gun and the creative process as an attack on an objective—are ancillary. The conjunction of writer with soldier happens not to appear in Crane's verse, but in his prose it is explicit. One thinks of "The Revenge of the Adolphus," "Marines Signalling Under Fire at Guantanamo," and "The Open Boat"; in each of these tales a correspondent advances over difficult terrain to interpret heroism to the civilian reader.

The author of "Mitraillatrice," we are told in the "News Notes" to the January, 1923, issue of *Poetry: A Magazine of Verse,* was "Ernest M. Hemingway, a young Chicago poet now abroad, [who] will soon issue in Paris his first book of verse." [12] The impact of Stephen Crane's work on his was tremendous, and long-lasting.

Poetic form Hemingway would shortly abandon; "Mitraillatrice" was included in *Three Stories and Ten Poems*, his first book (in 1923), but he never again wrote seriously in verse. The "News Notes" in *Poetry* also report a letter from the young Chicago poet which mentions his association in Paris with Gertrude Stein, Ford Madox Hueffer, James Joyce, Padraic Colum, William Carlos Williams, and Ezra Pound.[13] What Hemingway had learned from the poetry of Stephen Crane was immediately to be modified by his apprenticeship to these leaders of the symbolist and imagist movements, as we see in the thirteen prose poems comprising his next book, *In Our Time* (1924).[14] "In his prose, Hemingway has stuck by these principles [of Pound's "Imagist Manifesto"] as fast as any of the poets who formulated them." [15]

Hemingway's debt to Crane is important because Crane showed him how to deal in literary craft with the essential concepts on which all of his subsequent writing has been based. In Crane, some of whose best stories had been reprinted in 1921 by Vincent Starrett under the title *Men, Women and Boats*, Hemingway came upon a precedent for

[12] *Poetry*, XXI (January, 1923), 231. The poem quoted above is the first of six under the general title "Wanderings" on pp. 193–95 of the same issue.

[13] *Ibid.*, p. 230.

[14] Reprinted as the interchapters heading the stories in *In Our Time* (1925); conveniently available in *Hemingway*, ed. by Malcolm Cowley, pp. 365–491.

[15] Philip Young, *Ernest Hemingway*, p. 155.

the sharp prose and the world of fated choices and lonely suffering we find in the imagistic cameos of *In Our Time*. In Crane he found dramatized the desperate isolation of the individual, and his need for an heroic code by which to give ritualistic meaning to his sufferings. "Crane's whole dark view of existence, of men damaged and alone in a hostile, violent world, of life as one long war which we seek out in fear and controlled panic—it is all an amazing forecast of Hemingway." [16] This is an influence which Hemingway has partially acknowledged. He mentions Crane as one of the three "good writers" in America—the other two are Mark Twain and Henry James—and he states his preferences among Crane's tales: "*The Open Boat* and *The Blue Hotel*. The last one is the best." [17] In his anthology *Men at War* Hemingway reprinted *The Red Badge of Courage*, calling it "that great boy's dream of war," and adding, "It is one of the finest books in our literature and I include it entire because it is all as much of one piece as a great poem is." [18] Philip Young has noted the debt of "The Killers" to "The Blue Hotel" and of "The Short Happy Life of Francis Macomber" to *The Red Badge;* he further remarks the influence of Crane's "An Episode of War" upon Hemingway's "A Clean, Well Lighted Place." [19] One might add that parallels are probable, too, between *The Old Man and the Sea* and "The Open Boat."

The two writers favor the same subjects and settings—"war, the sea, the American west, and the men-without-women situation." But Carlos Baker underestimates the force of Crane's

[16] *Ibid.,* p. 163.   [17] *Green Hills of Africa,* p. 19.
[18] Introduction to *Men at War,* p. xvii.
[19] Young, *Ernest Hemingway,* pp. 164–68.

work on Hemingway's when he calls the latter's interest in
Crane merely "neighborly." [20] It is much more likely that Hemingway in many important respects shares Crane's sensibility.
"The parallels which exist between Hemingway and Crane as
human beings are so numerous and exact," Philip Young remarks, "that they will go a long way toward explaining why
the two men so resemble each other as prose stylists, and even
on occasion as poets." [21] The possibility of anyone's sharing
Crane's sensibility may seem remote when we consider the
extremely specialized conditions which shaped his mind and
art. Yet, by a coincidence perhaps unparalleled in literary history, Hemingway, whose view of reality is essentially the same
as Crane's, shares with him also a religious mother, a father
early dead, rebellion against gentility, journalistic training,
journeys to wars in Cuba and Greece.

It was eventually in warfare, sought out and embraced, that each
man found a fascinating formalization of violence, and his essential
metaphor for life. . . . Chiefly they were compelled to learn what
it had to teach them about themselves, and to test themselves
against it, to make of danger a kind of mystic ceremony, or rite, or
crucible. The results were identical.[22]

It is obvious that Crane's impact has been chiefly felt
through his prose. But the literary beginnings of his most famous disciple remind us that Crane's poetry has been effective
too. The purposeful confusion in Crane's work of poetic and
prosaic elements in fact allows us to see his prose as an extension of his poetry. When fiction writers as masterful as Crane

[20] *Hemingway: The Writer as Artist,* pp. 181–82.
[21] *Ernest Hemingway,* pp. 162 ff.   [22] *Ibid.,* p. 162.

or Hemingway feel they have to write in verse, the fact alone is suggestive of significance. In Crane's case the poems were necessary explorations of theological, ethical, and psychic conflicts which he apparently could not deal with in his prose. These themes are not only more abstract than those of his tales; they are also more personal, more introspective. The poems deal with ultimate confrontations, the individual alone against huge and inscrutable elementals. Those are themes for which fiction, demanding some sort of human community as requisite for plot, cannot treat as well as verse.

In Crane's fiction, at the moment of most unbearable danger when the individual is most alone with fear and insufficiency, there is still the possibility of his finding the comradeship that redeems man from ultimate isolation. This may be the brotherhood of suffering, as in "The Open Boat"; or the comradeship of courage, as in *The Red Badge* and "The Price of the Harness." [23] It may also be the brotherhood of fear, as in "The Five White Mice"; the New York Kid (manifestly Stephen Crane himself), menaced by a knife-wielding Mexican, pulls his revolver and discovers in astonishment that his adversary fears *him:* "There had been an equality of emotion—an equality!" [24]

None of these emotions of equality is available to the Crane surrogates in the poetry. To the New York Kid we may compare "A youth in apparel that glittered," who, far from opposing his assassin's dagger, is outrageously in love with death. His smiling nihilism is the only answer to the immitigable

[23] *Work,* IX, 37.　　　　　[24] *Ibid.,* XII, 174.

hostility of the universe in a poetic world so isolated that there is no possibility of brotherhood. Therefore, as we noticed in comparing Crane to Whitman, death in Crane's poems does not provide the metaphoric significance of grasping life at its most proximate and poignant center. It is instead a metaphor of his isolation.

Does Crane's theme of love, then, give his art the power of relating the self to the universe otherwise than inexorably in conflict? Crane abjures the theme in his serious fiction; his world is a world without women, save as women appear to the mind of a child, in *The Monster* and *Whilomville Stories*. (Maggie is so passively the pawn of fate that she seems a child herself, even to her lover Pete.) In only one of the best war stories is love so much as mentioned, and the circumstance is so curiously exceptional as to invite remark. In "Death and the Child" the identification of correspondent with soldier, remarked above, is sundered by contrasting Peza, the panicky Greek correspondent whose mind is a porridge of patriotic slogans, with a young officer "above [whose] high military collar . . . appeared a profile stern, quiet, and confident, respecting fate, fearing only opinion." [25] Of Peza—not of the lieutenant—it is said as the battle begins that

He remembered the pageants of carnage that had marched through the dreams of his childhood. Love he knew; that he had confronted alone, isolated, wondering, an individual, an atom taking the hand of a titanic principle.[26]

This juxtaposition of love with carnage parallels that made in the poems. But it is the coward, not the disciplined military

[25] *Ibid.*, p. 244.   [26] *Ibid.*, p. 246.

man, who makes the association here. Crane's war tales are mainly concerned with defining the conditions of courage—and courage is the most sublime "equality of emotion." The self-mastery of the soldier, however, may not protect him from the panic that love, "confronted alone, isolated," inspires. The artist who would imagine the lover as an atom in the grasp of a titanic principle will not find fiction, a social art, a fitting vehicle for expressing his attitude toward love. In Crane's verse the lover is always isolated and the act of love is imagined as fearfully as any death in battle.

What we conclude then, is that in fiction Crane deals with ways of escaping from isolation, of freeing himself from the dominion of death. He learns that even the emotion of fear, which he thought oppressed him alone, is known to all men; courage is a bond of communion; self-sacrifice is his unifying principle. But in his verse he submits to death's dominion in an imaginative world where even love is a dying, not sacrificially but in total isolation. The governing metaphor of almost all of his verse is his absolute aloneness.

3

A final comparison of Crane's treatment of the same theme in verse and in prose should make clear the unique authority which his relentless exploration of the isolated soul bestows upon his work. One of Crane's best poems and his most powerful story render imaginatively the same experience. But how different are the metaphors and the emotions of which they are the tangible forms in "The Open Boat" and "A man adrift on a slim spar."

The first contrast between poem and tale, obviously, is that the correspondent in "The Open Boat" is not alone. Three companions share his predicament. Nor is their plight so dire as that of the "lost hand" clinging to the spar. Where he is from the outset doomed to perish in the destructive element, they have at least an open boat, and hope, between them and the sea. There is in the poem a dialectic of opposition between the grim reality and the possibility of God's merciful intercession, but this tension is proposed ironically only to emphasize the failure of God to intercede for man. The first images of the man afloat are followed by a widening of vista—"Oceans may be turned to a spray"—but in the final third of the poem there is the ineluctable closing of all possibilities save extinction as "tented waves" contract to "A horizon smaller than a doomed assassin's cap." When in the tale the castaways swim desperately for shore, the correspondent, helpless in the current's grip, thinks, "Perhaps an individual must consider his own death to be the final phenomenon of nature." [27] The triumph of death is the obliteration of the individual.

In the story the direction of narrative and symbolic action is similarly downward to a nadir of hopelessness, the confrontation of seemingly certain death—but it then moves upward again to a new truth, as we shall see. The symbolic center of the story, the turning point, comes at the beginning of the sixth chapter, yet the gravest danger awaits the very end ten pages later, when we are no longer so obsessed by the fear of it. Then death, with malicious irony, claims the strongest and most generous man, the oiler who by his endurance and sea-

[27] *Ibid.*, p. 59.

manship proved best deserving of life. Yet from the outset of the tale the four men experience not only the isolation imposed by fear of death but also a "comradeship, that the correspondent . . . who had been taught to be cynical of men, knew even at the time was the best experience of his life." The tension between the aloneness of fear and this "subtle brotherhood of men" [28] governs the development of the key metaphors in the tale. The relation of man to nature provides an important cluster of these.

The chief image here is of course water, as in the poem. Associated with it in the story are other images drawn from the ocean scene—gulls, sharks, seaweed—and contrasting images of land and domesticity. Water is not only implacably menacing; it is also the source of life. When "the four waifs rode impudently in their little boat . . . with an assurance of impending rescue. . . . Everybody took a drink of water." [29] Water's ambiguous connotations lend further irony to the image at the outset: "Many a man ought to have a bathtub larger than the boat which here rode upon the sea." In the domestic bath, water serves man; but a craft which is a tub among waves "most wrongfully and barbarously abrupt and tall" offers "problem[s] in small-boat navigation." [30] When the waves pour into this tub "There was cold sea-water swashing to and fro in the boat, and he lay in it"; had the boat capsized "he would have tumbled comfortably out upon the ocean as if he felt sure that it was a great soft mattress." Again, "As soon as the correspondent touched the cold comfortable sea-water in the bottom of the boat . . . he was deep in

[28] *Ibid.*, p. 36.   [29] *Ibid.*, p. 39.   [30] *Ibid.*, p. 29.

sleep." [31] This boat may be a bed as well as a coffin, the ocean a womb as well as a tomb. The metaphors multiply the contrasting possibilities of death or life. Survival is a real possibility here, not merely a rhetorical contrast as in "A man adrift."

Their predicament imposes almost complete immobility on the men in the boat. Contrasted to them are creatures who live in the destructive element. When gulls approach we feel their homey adaptability to the sea on which they "sat, near patches of brown seaweed . . . like carpets on a line." These gulls are like "a covey of prairie chickens a thousand miles inland." When one jumped in the air "chicken-fashion" and tried to alight on the captain's head, he "wished to knock it away . . . but he did not dare do it, because anything resembling an emphatic gesture would have capsized his freighted boat; and so, with his open hand, the captain gently and carefully waved the gull away." [32] A man whose powers of movement and self-assertion are thus inhibited has but a precarious grasp on life, indeed. Barnyard images recur to emphasize the dire immobility of the men: "It is easier to steal eggs from under a hen than it was to change seats in the dinghy." A few pages later "Fate. . . . is an old hen who does not know her intention." [33] But immobility—the threat of death—can characterize also the land where rescue awaits them; "There is a certain immovable quality to the shore . . ." [34] Indeed, it is when he reaches land that the oiler is killed.

A further irony of their predicament is that observers on shore completely misconstrue their relation to the sea, twice

[31] *Ibid.*, pp. 43, 54.   [32] *Ibid.*, pp. 33–34.   [33] *Ibid.*, pp. 34, 41.
[34] *Ibid.*, p. 58.

taking them for a fishing party. Far from hunting fish, they are themselves the hunted. "The correspondent saw an enormous fin speed like a shadow through the water, hurling the crystalline spray and leaving the long glowing trail." This fin appears when the others are dozing, "and the correspondent thought that he was the one man afloat on all the oceans. . . . He looked at the babes of the sea. They certainly were asleep. So, being bereft of sympathy, he leaned a little way to one side and swore softly into the sea." In this moment the story comes closest to the absolute aloneness of "A man adrift on a slim spar." But in the tale the sense of ultimate isolation proves to be an illusion; the correspondent later speaks to the captain:

"Did you see that shark playing around?"
"Yes, I saw him. He was a big fellow, all right."
"Wish I had known you were awake."

When the captain and correspondent "slept once more the dead sleep[,] Neither knew they had bequeathed to the cook the company of another shark, or perhaps the same shark." [35]

It is directly after the first view of the shark, before the correspondent learns another shares his fear, that a second parallel to Crane's verse appears in the story. The view of fate proposed in the poem, "A man said to the universe, / 'Sir, I exist.'" is elaborated in the passage at the nadir of the tale: "When it occurs to a man that nature does not regard him as important, and that she would not maim the universe by disposing of him. . . . A high cold star on a winter's night is the word he feels that she says to him." [36] But in "The Open Boat" this view is not the end of human wisdom. One might

[35] *Ibid.*, pp. 50, 53–54.   [36] *Ibid.*, p. 51.

continue for some pages to elucidate the interlocked meanings, mutually reinforcing, of such other associated images as seeing, light, dark; boat, bronco, bicycle, omnibus; height, towers, waves. Such a complete explication would be necessary adequately to indicate the "meaning" of the story, so intrinsic is that meaning to its formal statement.

One other element of that formal statement must be remarked, however. That is the recurrence not only of metaphoric parallels and contrasts, but of actual refrains. Such phrases as "The oiler rowed," "The correspondent rowed," and "Funny they don't see us" recur in the same manner as the refrain in poetic form. A more intricate refrain, thrice repeated, is an invocation in which the rhetorical language ironically suggests the helpless impotence of the correspondent who uses it to voice his despair: "If I am going to be drowned—if I am going to be drowned—if I am going to be drowned, why, in the name of the seven mad gods who rule the sea, was I allowed to come thus far and contemplate sand and trees? . . . ." [37] In its third occurrence, just after he sees the shark and thinks himself "the one man afloat on all the oceans," it leads directly into the passage "When it occurs to a man that nature does not regard him as important. . . ." This is the psychological bottom of the story, the immanence of unmerciful death.

Everything that has led us in the tale to this final presentation of the individual's absolute isolation resembles the formal means of Crane's best poetry, which he developed there to deal with exactly this same there. In "A man adrift" we have

[37] *Ibid.*, pp. 41, 47, 51.

similarly the reiterated refrain ("God is cold"), parallel development of linked metaphors, and the tensions produced by a dialectic of opposite possibilities in the interpolated central section beginning "The seas are in the hollow of the Hand." But where death dominates the poem, and the cosmic isolation of its victim deprives the poet of a metaphoric range comparable to that in the tale, death's victory in "The Open Boat" is only partial. Three men survive to enjoy "the welcome of the land to the men from the sea," rituals of proffered blankets, coffee-pots, and flasks, "remedies sacred to [the] minds" of their rescuers, the first of whom had "a halo . . . about his head, and he shone like a saint." For the oiler, however, "the land's welcome . . . could only be the different and sinister hospitality of the grave." The obligation of the survivors is not over:

When it came night, the white waves paced to and fro in the moonlight, and the wind brought the sound of the great sea's voice to the men on shore, and they felt they could then be interpreters.[38]

At the beginning of the story the correspondent had "watched the waves and wondered why he was there." [39] He was there to become an interpreter of "the snarling of the crests." [40] In the poem, we saw at the conclusion of Chapter Three, a dispassionate observer similarly interprets to us the "growl after growl of crest" as the coldness of God. The correspondent, too, learns of "the serenity of nature amid the struggles of the individual," and recognizes nature as neither cruel, beneficent, treacherous, nor wise, but "indifferent, flatly indifferent." [41] Here, however, the coldness of the universe is attributed not

[38] *Ibid.,* p. 61.　　[39] *Ibid.,* p. 30.　　[40] *Ibid.,* p. 31.　　[41] *Ibid.,* p. 56.

to God, but to nature. The experience of "subtle brotherhood," unavailable to the man adrift on the spar, makes room in the cosmos for mercy and gives meaning to death beyond what it seemed to the individual in his isolation—"the final phenomenon of nature." [42] A last irony in the tale makes this final significance not yet evident to the correspondent: he views the vacationer who rushes down the Florida beach to "save" him as haloed and saintlike. But he does not think in such terms to tell us that "In the shallows, face downward, lay the oiler," [43] their real savior by the grace of whose sacrifice the three others may live. The truth of the correspondent's interpretation lies not in his last impressions but in the manner in which he recreates the entire experience in the reader's imagination. And the techniques Crane uses for this purpose, I suggest, are essentially the techniques of poetry. "The Open Boat" is his greatest poem. We may take license for so considering it from Crane's own repudiation of the formal distinctions between prose and verse, as well as from his incorporation into the tale of formal elements apparently of poetic derivation.

Although Crane's poems are restricted in range, they have the unexampled authority which the work of an original artist who explores the furthest reaches of the human spirit, in whatever direction, rightfully commands.

Only Poe and Hemingway have neared Crane's lonely outpost from which in his verse he views, and makes us feel, the reality of a universe where force is law, where love is doom, where God is cold, where man's lot is fated misery, where hope is narrowed to the possibility of courage, and the

[42] *Ibid.*, p. 59. [43] *Ibid.*, p. 61.

reward of courage is self-sacrifice. None has surpassed him in the imaginative expression of this sensibility of isolation. Emerson, with his openness to life, could scarcely have had such an artist in mind when he defined "The Poet," yet we do no violence to either man in applying to Crane these words:

He is isolated among his contemporaries by truth and by his art, but with this consolation in his pursuits, that they will draw all men sooner or later. For all men live by truth and stand in need of expression. In love, in art . . . We study to utter our painful secret. The man is only half himself, the other half is his expression.[44]

What Crane's poems express is partly his private doom. But the sensibility of isolation is a bitter gift which Stephen Crane did not hold alone. In lesser degree than was true of him, it is also a characteristic of his country and his culture. Crane takes his authority to be an interpreter from the very extremity of his commitment so widely shared. In these poems which explore the menaced condition of man in isolation, Crane developed new techniques and made available to poetic expression a further reach of imaginative experience than had any American writer before him. His best poems impose aesthetic form on the stark vision that haunted his imagination. They free us to participate in that vision and to contemplate with deepened understanding a part of ourselves.

[44] Emerson, *Complete Works,* III, 5.

Appendix 5 *FURTHER UNCOLLECTED POEMS OF STEPHEN CRANE*

LEGENDS

I   A man builded a bugle for the storms to blow.
    The focussed winds hurled him afar.
    He said that the instrument was a failure.

II When the suicide arrived at the sky, the people
        asked him: "Why?"
    He replied: "Because no one admired me."

III A man said: "Thou tree!" The tree answered with
        the same scorn:
    "Thou man! Thou art greater than I only in thy
        possibilities."

IV A warrior stood upon a peak and defied the stars. A little
    magpie, happening there, desired the soldier's plume, and
    so plucked it.

v   The wind that waves the blossoms sang, sang, sang from
     age to age. The flowers were made curious by this joy.
     "Oh, wind," they said, "why sing you at your labour,
     while we, pink beneficiaries, sing not, but idle, idle, idle
     from age to age?"

First published in the *Bookman*, III (May, 1896), 206, these
verses were reprinted in a private edition of 45 copies "for the
friends of Vincent Starrett and Ames W. Williams" in 1942 (Ysleta,
Texas). According to the colophon of this edition, "These lines
were intended for publication in *The Black Riders.*" (Colophon reproduced in Starrett and Williams, *Stephen Crane: A Bibliography,*
no. 46, p. 72.)

A "LOST POEM"

Little birds of the night,
Aye, they have much to tell
Perching there in rows
Blinking at me with their serious eyes,
Recounting of flowers they have seen and loved,
Of meadows and groves of the distance
And pale sands at the foot of the sea,
And breezes that fly in the leaves.
They are vast in experience,
These little birds that come in the night.

A Lost Poem by Stephen Crane: "Of this first printing / One
hundred copies have been issued / for the friends of / HARVEY
TAYLOR / HARVARD PRESS / New York." Starrett and Williams, *Bibliography,* no. 45, p. 72.

UNPUBLISHED POEMS

A grey and boiling street
Alive with rickety noise.
Suddenly, a hearse,
Trailed by black carriages
Takes a deliberate way
Through this chasm of commerce;
And children look eagerly
To find the misery behind the shades,
Hired men, impatient, drive with a longing
To reach quickly the grave-side, the end of solemnity.
Yes, let us have it over.
Drive, man, drive.
Flog your sleek-hided beasts,
Gallop-gallop-gallop.
Let us finish it quickly.

Typescript in Stephen Crane Collection, Columbia University.

Ah, haggard purse, why ope thy mouth
Like a greedy urchin
I have naught wherewith to feed thee.
Thy wan cheeks have ne'er been puffed
Thou knowest not the fill of pride
Why then gape at me
In fashion of a wronged one
Thou do smilest wanly
And reproach me with thine empty stomach
Thou knowest I'd sell my steps to the grave
If twere but honestie
Ha, leer not so,

Name me no names of wrongs committed with thee
No ghost can lay hands on thee and me
We've been too thin to do sin
What, liar? When thou wast filled of gold, didst I riot
And give thee no time to eat?
No, thou brown devil, thou art stuffed now with lies as
  with wealth
The one gone to let in the other.

Manuscript in the Stephen Crane Collection, Syracuse University Library.

My cross!

Your cross?
The real cross
Is made of pounds,
Dollars or francs.
Here I bear my palms for the silly nails
To teach the lack
—The great pain of lack—
Of coin.

Typescript in Stephen Crane Collection, Columbia University.

.   .   .

intermingled,
There came in wild revelling strains,
Black words, stinging.
That murder flowers
The horror of profane
speculation

Manuscript fragment in Stephen Crane Collection, Columbia University.

S BIBLIOGRAPHY

HOLOGRAPHS, TYPESCRIPTS, PROOF SHEETS, AND OTHER PRIMARY SOURCES

Unless otherwise noted, the following items are from the Stephen Crane Collection, Department of Special Collections, Columbia University Libraries.

UNPUBLISHED WRITINGS OF STEPHEN CRANE
Poems

Ah, haggard purse, why ope thy mouth. Holograph; in Stephen Crane Collection, Syracuse University Library.

The Battle Hymn. Typescript; with duplicate copy.

Bottles and bottles and bottles. Typescript.

A god came to a man. Holograph and typescript.

A grey and boiling street. Typescript.

If you would seek a friend among men. Holograph and typescript.

Intermingled / There came in wild revelling strains. Holograph; fragment.

A lad and a maid at the curve in a stream. Holograph and typescript.

My cross. Typescript; two copies.

Oh, rare old wine ye brewed for me. Holograph; second copy in Cora Crane's hand.

On the brown trail. Holograph; second copy in Cora Crane's hand.

One came from the skies. Holograph.

The Patent of a lord. Typescript.

A row of thick pillars. Typescript.

A soldier, young in years. Holograph; on first page of MS prose article, "Gratitude of a Nation to its Soldiers."

Tell me not in joyful numbers. Holograph.

There exists the eternal fact of conflict. Holograph.

There is a grey thing that lives in the tree tops. Holograph and typescript.

Prose

"City of Mexico." Holograph; three untitled press articles.

"Gratitude of a Nation to its Soldiers." Holograph; article intended for publication in the New York *Press* on Decoration Day, 1894.

List of Crane's poems. Holograph.

List of magazine acceptances of Crane's poems. Holograph.

PUBLISHED WRITINGS OF STEPHEN CRANE

Poems

Chant you loud of punishments. Holograph and typescript (*Collected Poems,* p. 131).

The chatter of a death demon in a tree top. Typescript (WK xix).

Do not weep, maiden, for war is kind. Typescript (WK i).

Forth went the candid man. Holograph (WK ix).

I explain the silvered path of a ship at night. Holograph and typescript (WK vi).

I have heard the sunset song of birches. Proof sheet (WK vii).

The impact of a dollar on the heart. Signed Typescript (WK xx).

In the night. Typescript and proof sheet with corrections in Crane's hand (WK xviii).

Intrigue. Incomplete typescript.

A little ink, more or less. Typescript; a holograph, lacking first six lines, is in the Syracuse University Library (WK iv).

A man adrift on a slim spar. Signed holograph; second copy in Cora Crane's hand (*Collected Poems,* pp. 129–30).

A naked woman and a dead dwarf. Signed holograph; second copy in Cora Crane's hand (*Collected Poems,* p. 132).

On the desert. Corrected proof sheet from *Philistine* (WK xi).

Once a man clambering to the housetops. Holograph (WK xv).

The successful man has thrust himself. Holograph signed and dated December 5, 1897, and typescript (WK xvii).

There was a man with tongue of wood. Holograph (WK xvi).

There was one I met upon the road. Holograph (BR xxxiii).

The trees in the garden rained flowers. Typescript (WK xxvi).

What says the sea, little shell? Signed holograph, titled "The Shell and the Pines," in the Berg Collection of the New York Public Library (WK ii).

When a people reach the top of a hill. Holograph ("The Blue Battalions"; WK xxvii).

You tell me this is God. Proof sheet from *Philistine* (WK x).

Prose

"The Squire's Madness." Holograph; begun by Stephen Crane, finished by Cora Crane. Also a clipping from *Crampton's Magazine,* XVI (October, 1900), 93–99, annotated in Cora Crane's hand, in Stephen Crane's red scrapbook.

LETTERS

Stephen Crane to C. E. S. [Cora Stewart] Undated, letter 54.

Stephen Crane to C. E. S. November 4, 1896, letter 55.

Stephen Crane to Elbert Hubbard. Undated, written on MS of "A little ink, more or less" (WK iv); in Syracuse University Library.

Stephen Crane to Edmund Clarence Stedman. September 4, 1899; in the collection of the Historical Society of Pennsylvania.

William H. Crane to Cora Crane. August 14, 1899, letter 114.

William H. Crane to Cora Crane. April 21, 1900, letter 120.

Mary Holder to Cora Crane. July 29, 1897, letter 133.

William Dean Howells to Stephen Crane. Eight letters dated from March 26, 1893, to July 30, 1896, letters 200–207.

Sir Norman Stewart to Cora Crane. March 7, 1901, letter 137.

Sir Norman Stewart to Cora Crane. October 17, 1901, letter 138.

Ames W. Williams to Daniel G. Hoffman. Letters of July 17 and November 29, 1955.

OTHER PRIMARY SOURCES

Linson, Corwin Knapp. "Stephen Crane, A Personal Memoir." Typescript in the Syracuse University Library.

List of Books, Brede Place. In Cora Crane's hand.

Manuscript book. Cora Crane's (red covers).

Notebook. Cora Crane's (paper covers).

Scrapbooks (2). Stephen Crane's; clippings of his prose (red covers).

Scrapbook. Stephen Crane's; clippings of British reviews, chiefly of his own works, containing also reviews of Walt Whitman's *The Wound Dresser* (blue covers).

OTHER PUBLISHED WRITINGS OF STEPHEN CRANE

"Adventures of a Novelist," New York *Journal,* September 26, 1896. An unpaged clipping is in the Columbia University collection.

"Ancient Capital of Montezuma," Philadelphia *Press,* July 21, 1895, p. 2.

The Black Riders and Other Lines. Boston, 1895.

The Collected Poems of Stephen Crane. Ed. by Wilson Follett. New York, 1930.

"Concerning the English 'Academy,'" *Bookman,* VII (March, 1898), 22–24.

"Great Bugs in Onondaga," New York *Tribune,* June 1, 1891, p. 1.

"Legends," *Bookman,* III (May, 1896), 206.

Lines by Stephen Crane. Printed in 100 copies for the friends of Melvin H. Schoberlin. Baltimore, 1947. ("Love comes like a tall swift ship at night.")

A Lost Poem by Stephen Crane. Printed in 100 copies for the friends of Harvey Taylor. New York, n.d. [1932] ("Little birds of the night.")

Men, Women, and Boats. Ed. by Vincent Starrett. New York, 1921.

"Nebraska's Bitter Fight for Life," Philadelphia *Press,* February 24, 1895, Part III, p. 25.

The Red Badge of Courage and Other Stories. Ed. by Daniel G. Hoffman. New York, 1957.

Stephen Crane: An Omnibus. Ed. by Robert Wooster Stallman. New York, 1952.

Stephen Crane's Love Letters to Nellie Crouse. Ed. by Edwin H. Cady and Lester G. Wells. Syracuse, 1954.

"Stephen Crane's New Jersey Ghosts: Two Newly-Recovered Sketches," ed. by Daniel G. Hoffman, *Proceedings of the New*

Jersey Historical Society, LXXI (October, 1953), 239–53.
("Ghosts on the Jersey Coast," New York *Press,* November 11,
1894, Part IV, p. 2; and "The Ghostly Sphinx of Metedeconk,"
ibid., January 13, 1895, Part v, p. 1.)
The Sullivan County Sketches of Stephen Crane. Ed. with an in-
troduction by Melvin B. Schoberlin. Syracuse, 1949.
War is Kind. New York, 1899.
"Wheels," *Philistine,* VIII (December, 1898), front cover.
The Work of Stephen Crane. Ed. by Wilson Follett. 12 vols. New
York, 1925–27.

BOOKS AND ARTICLES

Adams, Henry. The Life of George Cabot Lodge. Boston and New
York, 1911.
────── The Selected Letters of Henry Adams. Ed. with an in-
troduction by Newton Arvin. New York, 1951.
Ahnebrink, Lars. The Beginnings of Naturalism in American Fic-
tion. Upsala and Cambridge, Mass., 1950.
Arms, George, and Joseph M. Kuntz. Poetry Explication: A Check-
list of Interpretation since 1925 of British and American Poems
Past and Present. Denver and New York, 1950.
Auden, W. H., "The Anglo-American Difference: Two Views of
Poetry," *Anchor Review,* I (1955), 205–19.
Baker, Carlos. Hemingway: The Writer as Artist. Princeton, 1952.
Barry, John D., "A Note on Stephen Crane," *Bookman,* XIII (April,
1901), 148.
Baudelaire, Charles. Oeuvres Complètes de Charles Baudelaire,
Histoires Extraordinaires par Edgar Poe. Ed. by Jacques Crepet.
Paris, 1932.
Baum, Joan H. Stephen Crane (1871–1900): An Exhibition of His
Writings Held in the Columbia University Libraries, September
17–November 30, 1956. New York, 1956.
Beer, Thomas. Stephen Crane. New York, 1923.
Berryman, John. Stephen Crane. New York, 1950.
Bierce, Ambrose. The Collected Writings of Ambrose Bierce. Ed.
by Clifton Fadiman. New York, 1946.
Bogan, Louise. Achievement in American Poetry, 1900–1950.
Chicago, 1951.

Bosquet, Alain. Anthologie de la Poèsie Américaine des Origines à Nos Jours. Paris, 1956.

Brooks, Van Wyck. Three Essays on America. New York, 1934.

Buckley, Jerome H. The Victorian Temper. Cambridge, Mass., 1951.

Cassirer, Ernst. An Essay on Man. Garden City, N.Y., 1956.

Chase, Richard. Walt Whitman Reconsidered. New York, 1955.

Crane, Jonathan Townley. Christian Duty in Regard to American Slavery. A Sermon preached in the Trinity Methodist Episcopal Church, Jersey City, on Sabbath morning, December 11, 1859. Jersey City, N.J., 1860.

—————— Holiness the Birthright of All God's Children. New York and Cincinnati, 1874.

—————— Methodism and Its Methods. New York and Cincinnati, 1875.

Crawford, F. Marion. The Novel—What It Is. New York, 1893.

Cunliffe, Marcus, "Stephen Crane and the American Background of Maggie," *American Quarterly*, VII (Spring, 1955), 31–44.

Davis, Robert H., "Introduction to *Tales of Two Wars,* in *The Work of Stephen Crane.* New York, 1925. Vol. II.

Dickason, David H., "Stephen Crane and *The Philistine,*" *American Literature*, XV (November, 1943), 279–87.

Dickinson, Emily. Poems. Ed. by T. W. Higginson and Mabel Loomis Todd. Boston, 1890.

Dictionary of American Biography. Ed. by Allen Johnson *et al.* 20 vols. New York, 1928–.

Eliot, T. S., "From Poe to Valery," in *Literary Opinion in America,* ed. by Morton D. Zabel (New York, 1951), pp. 626–38.

—————— Selected Essays. New York, 1950.

Emerson, Ralph Waldo. The Complete Works of Ralph Waldo Emerson. Ed. by Edward Waldo Emerson. 12 vols. Boston, 1903.

Fadiman, Clifton, "Ambrose Bierce, Portrait of a Misanthrope," in *The Collected Writings of Ambrose Bierce.* New York, 1946.

Fatout, Paul. Ambrose Bierce, The Devil's Lexicographer. Norman, Okla., 1951.

Feidelson, Charles, Jr. Symbolism and American Literature. Chicago, 1953.

Franklin, Benjamin. Representative Selections. Ed. by Frank Luther Mott and Chester E. Jorgenson. New York, 1936.

———— The Writings of Benjamin Franklin. Ed. by Albert Henry Smyth. 10 vols. New York, 1905.

Freud, Sigmund. Collected Papers. Ed. by Ernest Jones. 3d ed. London, 1946. Vol. IV.

Gaer, Joseph, ed. Ambrose Gwinnett Bierce: Bibliography and Biographical Data. ("California Literary Research Monograph," No. 4, n.d.)

Garland, Hamlin. Roadside Meetings. New York, 1930.

———— "Stephen Crane, A Soldier of Fortune," *Book-Lover,* II (Autumn, 1900), 6–7.

———— "Stephen Crane as I Knew Him," *Yale Review,* N.S. III (April, 1914), 494–506.

Gibson, William M., ed. Stephen Crane: Selected Prose and Poetry. New York, 1950.

Gillis, Everett A., "A Glance at Stephen Crane's Poetry," *Prairie Schooner,* XXVIII (Spring, 1954), 73–79.

Goldberg, Helen W., "Techniques and Attitudes in the Fiction of Stephen Crane," unpublished Master's Thesis, Columbia University, 1953.

Gordan, John D., "*The Ghost* at Brede Place," *Bulletin of the New York Public Library,* LVI (December, 1952), 591–95.

Gregory, Horace, "Stephen Crane's Poems," *New Republic,* LXIII (June 25, 1930), 159–60.

Gregory, Horace, and Marya Zaturenska. A History of American Poetry, 1900–1940. New York, 1946.

Hemingway, Ernest. Hemingway. Ed. by Malcolm Cowley. New York, 1944.

———— Green Hills of Africa. Garden City, N.Y., 1954.

Hemingway, Ernest, ed. Men at War. New York, 1942.

Hemingway, Ernest M., "Wanderings," *Poetry,* XXI (January, 1923), 193–95.

Henley, William Ernest. Lyra Heroica. New York, 1891.

Hoffman, Daniel G., "Miss Moore," *Antioch Review,* XII (Spring, 1952), 123–25.

———— Paul Bunyan, Last of the Frontier Demigods. Philadelphia, 1952.

Hoffman, Daniel G., "Sandburg and 'The People': His Literary Populism Reappraised," *Antioch Review,* X (Summer, 1950), 265–78.

———— "An Unwritten Life of Stephen Crane," *Columbia Library Columns,* II (February, 1953), 12–16.

Holder, Charles Frederick. The Holders of Holderness. Pasadena, n.d. [1902].

Hopkins, Gerard Manley. Poems of Gerard Manley Hopkins. Ed. by Robert Bridges and W. H. Gardner. 3d ed. New York and London, 1948.

Jackson, Holbrook. The Eighteen Nineties. Harmondsworth-Middlesex, 1950.

Jones, P. Mansell. The Background of Modern French Poetry. Cambridge, 1951.

Kazin, A'lfred. On Native Grounds. New York, 1942.

Knight, Grant C. The Critical Period in American Literature. Chapel Hill, 1951.

Kwiat, Joseph J., "Stephen Crane and Painting," *American Quarterly,* IV (Winter, 1952), 331–38.

Langer, Susanne K. Philosophy in a New Key: A Study in the Symbolism of Reason, Rite, and Art. Cambridge, Mass., 1942.

Lawrence, D. H. Studies in Classic American Literature. Garden City, N.Y., 1953.

Lehmann, A. G. The Symbolist Aesthetic in France, 1885–1895. Oxford, 1950.

Lowell, Amy. Introduction to *The Black Riders and Other Lines,* in *The Work of Stephen Crane,* ed. by Wilson Follett. New York, 1926. Vol. VI.

Lucky, Robert E., "Apreciación del Poeta Stephen Crane," *Revista iberoamericana,* V (October, 1942), 317–43.

Lüdeke, Henry, "Stephen Cranes Gedichte," *Anglia,* LXII (1938), 410–22.

McClintock, John, and James Strong. Cyclopaedia of Biblical, Theological, and Ecclesiastical Literature. New York, 1877. *Supplement,* New York, 1887.

Matthiessen, F. O. American Renaissance. New York, 1941.

Melville, Herman. Moby-Dick or, The Whale. Ed. by Luther S. Mansfield and Howard P. Vincent. New York, 1952.

Miller, Perry, "Jonathan Edwards to Emerson," *New England Quarterly*, XIII (December, 1940), 589–617.

M[onroe], H[arriet], "Stephen Crane," *Poetry*, XIV (June, 1919), 148–52.

Moody, William Vaughn. The Poems and Plays of William Vaughn Moody. Ed. by J. M. Manly. 2 vols. Boston and New York, 1912.

O'Donnell, Thomas F., "An Analysis of the Poetry of Stephen Crane," unpublished Master's Thesis, Syracuse University, 1947.

Osborn, Scott C., "The 'Rivalry-Chivalry' of Richard Harding Davis and Stephen Crane," American Literature, XXVIII (March, 1956), 50–61.

Peck, George. The Life and Times of Rev. George Peck, D.D., Written by Himself. New York and Cincinnati, 1874.

Peck, J. K. Luther Peck and His Five Sons. New York and Cincinnati, 1897.

Peck, Jesse T. What Must I Do to Be Saved? New York, 1858.

Pound, Ezra, "A Few Don'ts by an Imagiste," *Poetry*, I (March, 1913), 200–206.

———— The Literary Essays of Ezra Pound. New York, 1954.

Pratt, Lyndon Upson, "The Formal Education of Stephen Crane," American Literature, X (January, 1930), 460–71.

Richie, Donald, "Stephen Crane," *The Study of Current English* (Tokyo), X (October, 1955), 33–41.

Riggs, Thomas, Jr., "Prometheus 1900," *American Literature*, XXII (January, 1951), 399–423.

Schreiner, Olive. Dreams. Boston, 1891.

Spiller, Robert E., *et al.* Literary History of the United States. 3 vols. New York, 1948.

Stedman, Edmund Clarence. An American Anthology, 1787–1900. Boston and New York, 1900.

Stolper, B. J. R. Stephen Crane: A List of His Writings and Articles about Him. (Public Library of Newark, for The Stephen Crane Association.) Newark, N.J. 1930.

Sweet, W. W. The Story of Religion in America. New York and London, 1939.

Symons, Arthur. Dramatis Personae. Indianapolis, 1923.

Tate, Allen. The Man of Letters in the Modern World. New York, 1955.

Tindall, William York. The Literary Symbol. New York, 1955.

Tocqueville, Alexis de. Democracy in America. The Henry Reeves text, ed. with an introduction by Phillips Bradley. 2 vols. New York, 1945.

Trent, William Peterfield, et al. The Cambridge History of American Literature. 3 vols. New York, 1912.

Trilling, Lionel. The Liberal Imagination. New York, 1950.

Van Doren, Carl, "Stephen Crane," American Mercury, I (January, 1924), 11–14.

Van Doren, Mark. Nathaniel Hawthorne. New York, 1949.

Van Doren, Mark, ed. The Portable Walt Whitman. New York, 1945.

Wells, H. G., "Stephen Crane from an English Standpoint," in The Shock of Recognition, ed. by Edmund Wilson. New York, 1955.

West, Herbert Faulkner. A Stephen Crane Collection. Hanover, N.H., 1948.

Whitman, Walt. Complete Poetry and Selected Prose and Letters. Ed. by Emory Holloway. London, 1938.

Williams, Ames W., and Vincent Starrett. Stephen Crane, A Bibliography. Glendale, Calif., 1948.

Wilson, Edmund. Axel's Castle. New York, 1931.

——— The Shores of Light. New York, 1952.

Wilson, Edmund, ed. The Shock of Recognition. New York, 1955.

Winters, Yvor. In Defense of Reason. New York, 1947.

Wyatt, Edith, "Stephen Crane," New Republic, IV (September 11, 1915), 148–50.

Yeats, William Butler. Introduction to Oxford Book of Modern Verse, 1892–1935. New York, 1936.

Young, Philip. Ernest Hemingway. New York, 1952.

ANONYMOUS ARTICLES, CLIPPINGS, AND REVIEWS

ANONYMOUS ARTICLES

1894. "First Memorial Day," New York Press, May 27, Part v, p. 2.

1894. "Veterans in Line," New York Press, May 27, Part v, p. 2.

1894. "Day of Heroes Dead," New York Press, May 30, p. 2.

1894. "Dead on the Field of Honor" (editorial), New York Press, May 30, p. 4.

1894. "Veterans Ranks Thinner by a Year," New York *Press,* May 31, pp. 1–2.
1896. "Lyrics of the Day," *Literary Digest,* XI (February 29), 520.
1896. "Chronicle and Comment," *Bookman,* III (March), 1.
1923. "News Notes," *Poetry,* XXI (January), 230–31.

CLIPPINGS IN COLUMBIA UNIVERSITY COLLECTION

1896. Herbert P. Williams, "Mr. Crane as a Literary Artist," New York *Illustrated American,* July 18, p. 126.
1896. Untitled, unpaged clipping from New York *Press,* July 25. Bierce attacks Crane.
1896. Vance Thompson, "American Literature Discussed," New York *Commercial Advertiser,* August 7, unpaged.
1896. "Poetry of the Month," New Orleans *Times-Democrat,* October 11, unpaged.
1896. Untitled, unpaged clipping from Cincinnati *Commercial Tribune,* October 18.
1898. Untitled, unpaged clipping from London *Daily Chronicle,* March 7. Review of Walt Whitman's *The Wound Dresser;* in Stephen Crane's blue scrapbook.
1898. "Books and Bookmen," *Manchester Guardian,* May 26, unpaged. Review of Walt Whitman's *The Wound Dresser;* in Stephen Crane's blue scrapbook.
    Untitled, unpaged, and undated clipping from Atlanta *Constitution.* Refers to Bierce and Crane.

REVIEWS OF *The Black Riders*

1895. Harry Thurston Peck, "Some Recent Volumes of Verse," *Bookman,* I (May), 255.
1895. "Literary Notes," New York *Daily Tribune,* July 9, p. 24.
1895. "Recent Poetry," *Nation,* LXI (October 24), 296.
1896. "Six Books of Verse," *Atlantic Monthly,* LXXVII (February), 267–72.
1896. Minnie Kidd, Atlanta *Sunny South,* July 18; untitled, unpaged clipping in Columbia University collection.
1897. "Recent Verse," *Athenaeum,* No. 3626 (April 24), p. 540.

REVIEW OF *War Is Kind*

1899. "Recent Poetry," *Nation,* LXIX (November 16), 378.

℥ INDEX OF FIRST LINES

∫ INDEX OF NAMES AND TITLES